OVER THE MOON, BRIAN

Football writer Alex Leith is co-author of *The Virgin Book of Football Records*, *Ryan Giggs: Football Genius* and *It Was Magic*.

OVER THE MOON, BRIAN
THE LANGUAGE OF FOOTBALL

Alex Leith

BOXTREE

First published in 1998 by Boxtree, an imprint of Macmillan Publishers Ltd,
25 Eccleston Place, London, SW1W 9NF and Basingstoke

Associated companies throughout the world

ISBN 0 7522 2488 3

9 8 7 6 5 4 3 2 1

A CIP catalogue record for this book is available from the British Library

Typeset by SX Composing DTP Rayleigh, Essex
Printed by Mackays of Chatham PLC, Chatham, Kent

To Lil,
who would have been so happy

Contents

Acknowledgements

There's only one:

George Leith, my father, for his invaluable research; Kenneth Wolstenholme, Martin Tyler, Simon Keller, David Elleray, Jim Phelan, Pete Nash, Alan Oliver, and Karen Buchanan for agreeing to be interviewed, Jim Drewett for running our sportswriting company Deadline Features (0171 278 5353) single-handedly in my absence and Francesca for putting up with me whilst I wrote the thing on our kitchen table; Clive Batty for proof-reading the first draught one wintry Sunday; Matthew Hirtes for occasionally fruitful trips to the British Library; David Barber from the FA for being as charming and helpful as ever; Mary Pachnos, my agent, who introduced me to Jenny Olivier, my editor, who joins this list for showing Platini-like creativity with my deadline. Oh, and my brother William for inspiring me to take up writing, and my mother Mavis for having me in the first place.

Introduction

The poor old ball has to put up with a lot these days. It can be banana'd, bent, chipped, curled, hit, shot, smashed, tapped, thumped, thwacked, volleyed or weighted. You can have it driven, piled, crashed, looped, back-heeled, corkscrewed, tucked, notched, sidefooted, trapped, wellied, hoofed, scrambled, held up, cleared, rammed or crossed. I've seen balls forced over the line, struck, cut back, tapped in, hooked, blasted and touched behind. I've read about them being laid off, lofted, passed, blazed over, dragged wide, buried, threaded, drilled, slid home, netted, charged down, stabbed, passed, nudged, knocked, deflected and fired. You can sweep it to safety, crack it, control it, dip it, hammer it, slip it, slice it or scrape it home. I've seen the ball Hoddled, Nat Lofthoused into the net and Wimbledoned up front. It's like the Eskimos and their snow – the language used to describe foot meeting ball has become so rich, the term kicked is rarely used any more. When players 'kick' something they kick each other, themselves (metaphorically speaking) and, on rare but notable occasions, the opposition's fans.

The language of football has got a very bad image. People just think of thick footballers giving post-match interviews. What a lot they're missing. The sport has a vibrant and ever-changing idiom. It has its own grammar and vocabulary, its own set of imagery, its own set of definitions, its own poetry and literature. It has many dialects – the language used on the pitch by players is entirely different from the language used in the stands by fans which is completely unlike that used by the commentators in their gantries, which is different again from that used by the journalists who write about it. This book is a mazy dribble through the nuances of the language used to describe the most talked about subject in the country, an end to end account of the language of football.

Part One
Football Clichés

- 1 -
Maybe That's Why They Call It Hackney Marshes

The referee blew the final whistle and I turned, as you do, to leave the pitch. A member of the pitchside reporter scrum came running towards me. 'Oh shit,' I thought. She poked a microphone in my face. A cameraman arrived behind her. 'How do you feel?' she asked. I was seconds away from making my television début.

Don't get me wrong, I'm not very good at football. I play centre back for Clissold Park Rovers in the Thames League Third Division; it's about as far down the football hierarchy as you can go. We weren't at Wembley Stadium or Old Trafford, we were on windy Hackney Marshes. The events that had led to a media pack being there were odd and complex and I'll explain them to you later.

My immediate worry was the fact that I'd been asked a question, and had to answer it. My lungs were burning, my legs were aching, most of the blood that usually helped my mind do its thinking was still churning round my tired muscles. I found myself completely bereft of irony. I paused rather too long. The woman jabbed her mike again. I had to say something.

'I'm gutted.'

My television career had just begun and I'd already made a fool of myself. I'd used one of the worst football clichés in a very long book.

It wasn't too late to save myself. One word sufficed...one word that would have told the whole of the audience at home that I was up with the game. I could have simply added the word 'Brian' to my sentence to show that I was beating footballers, not joining them. That I was making an ironic statement about clichés, and not just using the first one that sprang to my mind. Unfortunately this didn't happen.

'To go from 2-0 up to 2-2 is just lackadaisical,' I continued. 'And to let one in in the last minute...' I was banging own goals in left right and centre. Still, it could have been worse.

Until recently I was unaware of the origin of the word cliché, so I looked it up in the *Oxford English Dictionary*. It was originally a French word used to describe a metal stereotype made from a wood-engraving, used to print extra copies. The word is onomatopoeic, recalling the sound of the matrix hitting the molten metal. So a cliché has come to mean something of value which has been devalued by being imitated many times.

It is undoubtedly true that football is full of clichés. So many words are spoken and written about the game by so many people that it's bound to be. But what most of the critics of the language of the game ignore is the value of the original images, the beauty of the original engraving. It's a bit like the word cliché, actually, in itself a poetic image which has lost its original meaning.

When I said 'I'm gutted' I was echoing the stock response of a disappointed footballer. When you hear the statement you groan, because you have heard it so many times before. But if you think about it, it's a wonderful image. It means 'I'm so disappointed I feel like I have been disembowelled'. If I had said 'I feel gutted, like a fish' the metaphor would have turned into a simile and my meaning would have been clearer. What has happened is that we have lost sight of the original meaning of the image because it has become so overused.

I could have said, in an equally hackneyed manner, 'I'm choked' which too would have been greeted with disdain. Again, though, the image is a strong one – 'I am so disappointed it is difficult for the words to come out.'

If, on the other hand, Clissold Park Rovers had scored a third goal in the last minute and we'd won the game I could have said 'I'm chuffed' which would have literally (again with the help of my *OED*) meant, 'my cheeks are swelled out' and therefore 'I'm very happy'. Again, a football cliché, again an interesting image.

Now I'm not saying that all footballers are poets or linguistic historians who are aware of the origins of what they say. What I am saying is that if we ignore the fact that much of football's language has become stereotyped and look at its original meaning, we find ourselves in an extremely rich linguistic territory which crosses class divides, incorporates dialect words from many sources and which is always expanding. It's widely assumed that the language of football is *all* hackneyed. It's not, because, like all languages, it's always changing. It only takes a second to make an image, Brian, and when it's been copied ad nauseam, it only takes a second to make another one.

One of football's most enduring clichés has been the subject of much debate as to its origins. It's the forerunner to 'I'm gutted' or 'I'm choked' and is attributed to former Liverpool captain Phil Thompson, who, in interview after defeat in the League Cup final of 1978 said he was as 'sick as a parrot'. David Pickering, author of the intriguing bog read *Cassell's Soccer Companion*, has come up with some particularly queer theories as to the origins of the term. He traces the expression back to the 17th century when the playwright Aphra Behn wrote 'melancholy as a sick parrot'. He also notes that poet Robert Southey wrote 'sick as peeate' in an 1834 dialect poem, to suggest that a heavy sense of oppression would feel like having some peat in your stomach. Other equally unlikely theories allude to the disease psittacosis (which can be passed from parrots to humans), the fact that French pierrots were traditionally melancholy and the fact that exotic bird smugglers are known to drug their cargo with tequila. The *OED* mentions parrot-tongue being a condition common in typhus-sufferers whereby your tongue shrivels up. It's unlikely, however, that Thompson was familiar with any of these references and thus far more likely that he was simply referring to the *Monty Python* 'Dead Parrot' sketch.

Around the same time another expression became popular with footballers in post-match interviews to express joy after a victory. I haven't been able to pin down which footballer first said 'over the moon', but the image was being used quite regularly before it became a stock-in-trade expression of delight. In 1968 on the eve of Manchester City's European Cup campaign, manager Malcolm Allison said his players were going to 'take football to the moon' (sadly their lunar adventure got no further than Turkey as they got knocked out in the first round by Fenerbahce). In 1972 Sir Alf Ramsey, after an England victory, said he 'felt like he could jump over the moon'. The expression was commonly used, in fact, in the mid 19th century to express delight. It probably derives from the old nursery rhyme which had the dish running away with the spoon and, of course, the cow jumping over the moon (which could, in turn, refer to the way that cows behave strangely when they have grazed in pastures full of magic mushrooms).

Whoever is responsible for bringing the expression into the language of football, they should be praised, rather than ridiculed, just as Phil Thompson should be given a medal for introducing the parrot expression. The big defender wasn't, after all, responsible for the fact that the expression became a cliché, any more than Shakespeare is to blame for the overused expression 'more sinned against than sinning'.

Shakespeare didn't have a microphone stuck in his face after he'd just exhausted himself writing the final couple of scenes of *King Lear*, either. And if, in such circumstances, he had been asked a question as banal as 'how do you feel, having just completed what may well come to be considered to be the greatest tragedy of all time', he may well have been hard-pressed to come up with an eloquent and witty off-pat reply. And what if he'd been asked to demonstrate his keepie-uppie skills?

The fact is that a lot of football's more persisting clichés, at least those that come from the footballers themselves, are uttered by tired men in need of a bath more than an interview, whose brains aren't at that point in top working order after a huge bout of physical exertion. What's more, they are not being asked interesting questions designed to make them think. There has been as little thought gone into them as usually goes into the answers. Let's look at some examples.

Cliché: Gutted, choked, sick as a parrot.
Question: How do you feel after losing the most important match of your life?
(Does the interviewer expect the loser to take a philosophical view of the world and work out that there are far more tragic things happening at this very moment in war-torn Africa?)
Cliche: 'The ball just come to me and I stuck it in the net.'

Question: Can you describe your goal to me?
(The interviewer is forgetting that, unlike himself, the footballer didn't have an overall view of the game, that maybe, after running into position, the first he saw of the ball was it coming towards him.)
Cliché: 'The ball just didn't run for us.'
Question: Do you feel the result was fair?
(The interviewer is perfectly aware of the fact that if the player gives in to his natural urges and slags off the referee for denying three clear penalties he will probably get into trouble with the FA.)

Back in the 1970s and 1980s, before the sort of mass coverage football gets nowadays, most footballers had very little chance to express what they felt to the public, and when they were asked to they weren't used to doing so, and appeared inarticulate. People who wished to parody the 'typical thick footballer' would mimic the post-match interview syndrome, often using the over the moon/sick as a parrot expressions to prove their point. Football was at a low ebb and it was fashionable to view it as an oikish sport for oiks.

Nobody thought of the poor knackered men unused to the microphone. And nobody, either, picked up much on the point that many of the more abiding and lameheaded football clichés didn't come from the footballers themselves but from those paid to commentate and write about it. But more on that later.

Another form of football cliché is the truism. A truism, according to the *Oxford English Dictionary*, is 'a self-evident truth...a statement so obviously true as not to require discussion'. Men have been playing association football for over 130 years, and some fundamental aspects of the game haven't changed in all that time. Thus important aspects of football are as true today as they were in 1864. The only difference is that now people have been talking about them for five generations.

The first person who came up with the expression 'it's a game of two halves' was saying something quite valid. If his team, let's say back in 1896, for argument's sake, had played a stinking first half and a fan of the opposing team was taking the mickey out of him about it, it would be quite a pertinent thing to say, suggesting that halftime might revitalise his boys, and so help them stuff the opposition in the second period. The fact is that the situation has arisen so many times, and the sentence has been said so many times, that it's regarded as a cliché.

Most truisms are thus observations about the game in general. 'It only takes a second to score a goal' (attributed to Brian Clough but surely said in some form or other beforehand) is another classic, although, strictly speaking, it is an *un*truism. It only takes a second to kick the ball in the net, but surely the 'goal' includes the build-up beforehand. Another classic is 'you can't score a goal if you haven't got the ball', which is attributed to Bill Shankly (and which doesn't, of course, allow for own goals). Like most truisms there is a hidden wiseness to this statement. It's a subtle way of saying 'win possession, for fuck's sake'. Similarly 'it's a game of ninety minutes' might not seem worth pointing out, unless of course you want to point out that an early goal doesn't necessarily mean a victory for the scorers.

One of my favourites is 'the cup's a great leveller', which is another doesn't-quite-ring truism. I wonder if anyone said it before Bon Accord played Arbroath in the 1885 Scottish Cup. (Arbroath won 36-0, as you may well know, in Britain's biggest first-class victory).

The problem with truisms is that sometimes they need to be said to make a point. Footballers, ever more used to the press, ever more articulate, are well aware of this, which is why they have developed various formulas for trying to get out of the trap of sounding hackneyed. Adding 'Brian' on the end of a cliché is one of these methods, hence the title of this book. 'Brian' refers to commentator Brian Moore, and the word is used as a suffix to make sure that the listener is aware that the speaker is imitating a 'thick' 1970s footballer who is being interviewed by the commentator. Garry Nelson, an articulate footballer if ever there was one, and author of two books on football, uses the technique twice in his 'diary of a journeyman footballer' *Left Foot Forward*. 'It's a game of two halves' he writes, then adds, to avoid the awful own-goal of using such a hackneyed phrase, 'Brian'. He uses the technique again later in the book. 'Let's look on the bright side, Brian,' he writes, even though 'look on the bright side' has nothing to do with football. Perhaps in time others will follow his lead, and adding 'Brian' to the end of a sentence will enter the general vernacular as a way of excusing yourself the use of a cliché.

Another method, and one currently favoured by footballers in interviews, is saying 'I know it's a cliché, but...' before saying a truism, or adding after one '...if you'll excuse the cliché'. This habit isn't merely a trait of footballers. Football writers, too, sometimes feel they have to excuse their statement of the bleedin' obvious. The *Guardian*'s Martin Thorpe uses this method, for example, when he writes on 4 September 1997 'clichés are clichés because they are repeated so often; they are repeated so often because they tend to contain a truth. Confidence makes a difference and Ripley can provide personal evidence.' Blackburn winger Stuart Ripley had just been recalled to the England squad, by the way, after a four-year absence.

In an interview in 1973 the former Liverpool manager the late Bill Shankly said, 'Some people think football is a matter of life and death. I don't like that attitude. I can assure them it is much more serious than that.' The quote, which has commonly been misquoted as the more concise 'football isn't a matter of life and death, it's more important than that' has become one of the most overused clichés in the game.

Of course when Shankly said it it wasn't a cliché, it was original and witty, like many of the other things he said. It only became a cliché when the press started using it ad nauseam, which has largely happened in the last five years or so since the boom in football literature. There should be a fine on any journalist who uses it so it can retain some of its dignity, and be dusted off in the future to surprise people again in years to come.

Other witty or intelligent quotations by players have gone the same way. When Tommy Docherty stated, 'I've had more clubs than Jack Nicklaus,' little did he know that the phrase would become a stock-in-trade device for lazy journalists and TV broadcasters to inject a bit of 'humour' into their work when describing *any* manager with a string of clubs to his name. When George Graham said that the League was 'a marathon, not a sprint' after an early-season defeat, he wouldn't have realised that he'd be so oft quoted in the future as to make his words sound stale just four years later. Again, who is more culpable for the cliché: the originator of the phrase or the media that repeat it?

The truth about clichés is that they are far more likely to come from certain elements of the media than from the players themselves. Certain images have become so common that they can be churned out without the commentator, or journalist, even thinking about them. Sometimes they become so stock-in-trade as to lose their original meaning completely, especially when one image comes tumbling after another it is unconnected to.

Let's consider this phrase from the *Sun*: 'Armstrong, razor-sharp when plundering his 63rd-minute winner.'

'Razor-sharp' is a wonderful image to imply that Armstrong was alert to the opportunity of scoring. Consider the sharpness of a razor blade. How quickly it can slice. But did you think of this when you were reading the sentence? I suggest not. Because strikers are razor-sharp all the time in media coverage the image is tired and blunt, like a too-many-times-used Bic shaver.

And Armstrong 'plundered' the goal. Troops plunder villages they have just taken. The word carries an emotive weight – the plunderer is violating other people's personal property. It's a forceful type of theft, therefore Armstrong's team (Tottenham) didn't deserve the goal. Did the writer, though, think of this military image in his head when he wrote the sentence? I think he didn't – or at least not consciously.

Even, however, if the journalist has bought his imagery in Marks and Spencer rather than designed it himself, at least he's chosen well. You get the sense, in a short space of time, that Armstrong was quick, and that he scored a goal which led to a victory that his team didn't deserve.

Here's another cliché-filled sentence from the same edition of the *Sun* that doesn't work so well: 'Bryan Robson slammed his Boro flops after Fabrizio Ravanelli silenced the boo-boys with a last-gasp winner.'

The word 'to slam' literally means to push something with force; we usually slam doors shut when we are angry. In newspaper footballese, however, you lose sight of that meaning and it takes on the sense of 'criticise'. A 'flop' means a failure. Stolen from the theatre, this onomatopoeic image means something soft-landing dully, with a thud. 'Silencing the boo-boys' is a concise way of saying 'making the critics change their minds'. Its conciseness is its downfall – the image has been overused and lost its original impact. Finally (and aptly so) 'a last-gasp winner' means a goal late in the game; again it's a great image – the idea is that the crowd are still gasping about the goal when the final whistle goes. There is no time for any more gasps in the game. Again the image has been weakened through overuse.

And what does this hastily-put-together collection of clichés really mean, anyway? Not a lot, when you look at it. That the manager (Robson) had criticised his team, who were failures, after one of them (Ravanelli) had scored a late goal which had won the match and stopped the fans from complaining. Contradictory, or what? A case of a journalist who can't see the truth for the clichés. I wasn't at the press conference, I admit, but I'll bet, moreover, that Robson's 'slamming' of his team was little more than guarded criticism dressed up in the report to make it seem more interesting.

After the 0-0 draw that England achieved in Italy in 1997 to get to the World Cup finals in France in 1998 the *Guardian*'s David Lacey wrote a paragraph in which, he later explained in his defence, he tried to liken England's tactics to the defensive squares that Wellington used to good effect during the Napoleonic Wars. 'Led by Captain Ince and Sergeant Major Adams, with Lance-Bombardier Batty producing another performance worthy of a mention in dispatches, England coolly and effectively blocked Italy's avenues of approach, sabotaged their lines of connection and silenced their guns.'

Lacey's images, if you analyse them, were pretty accurate. The trouble was that he was, and he should have realised it, writing in clichés. Ever since football has been written about, writers have been using martial images to describe it. The sport draws its stock imagery from all sorts of fields, but more than anywhere else from the battlefield.

The young *gun*, a great *capture* from Portsmouth, could be *called up* into the *squad* for the vital relegation *battle*, for example. He might *charge* down the *flank* and be about to *shoot* but be *halted* by an *over-the-top challenge*. The *defender* might get his *marching orders*, and with their *opponents' forces* thus depleted the team might go on the *rampage*, going in front thanks to a *blockbuster ricocheting* into the net after a goalmouth *melée*.

If you think my made-up version a little exaggerated consider this caption from the *Sun* in 1996: 'Robbie Fowler dances with delight after hitting the target during an eight-minute Liverpool salvo which blew the Premiership title race right open.'

Military imagery is no new thing in football journalism. Early football reports, back in the 1870s, often referred to the goal as the 'enemy citadel' and the goalkeeper as a 'sentinel', for example. And in many ways football *is* a metaphor for war – young men from one community taking on young men from another in a struggle for territory, and all that.

The result is a magnitude of martial clichés and expressions in the language of football. It's almost impossible to talk about the game without using military analogies. Here are a few examples.

To attack and to defend. That's what the game's all about really. It's a war of ninety minutes. I'd rest my case, if I didn't have more examples to give you. Even the term *midfield* is taken from military jargon.

Victory, defeat, to win or to lose. The terms for the result of the game are culled straight from the language of war.

To annihilate, massacre, rout or sink. When one team scores a large number of goals against the other, the result is viewed in martial terms.

To battle. A midfielder can battle for the ball, a forthcoming match can be referred to as a battle, and matches are sometimes even remembered as if they'd been an episode of war (England v Italy 1934 is known as the Battle of Highbury after violent challenges left the Italian centre half Monti with a broken toe and the England captain Hapgood with a broken nose).

Troops. 'Howard Kendall had time to reorganise his troops' (the *Sun*).

A shot, a volley, a blockbuster, a howitzer. A player in possession is like a man with a loaded gun, the goal is his target.

Football clichés aren't just culled from military jargon, however. They come from all over the place. If football isn't war, it's theatre. The drama unfolds on the pitch. Certain players are seen as being a class act, and they often run the show. The Charity Shield is the season's curtain-raiser; a league match between the same teams that are to contest a Cup Final is a dress rehearsal. Halftime is sometimes referred to as the interval; top players are stars and so on.

Music also plays a part. A bad striker couldn't hit a cow's arse with a banjo. If he can't decide when to retire he's had more comebacks than Status Quo or Gary Glitter. The game is never over till the fat lady sings.

Money, as we well know, plays a big part in the game. A quick striker can turn on a sixpence (though most people under twenty-five won't have ever seen a sixpence; maybe this one, in time, will change to turn on a 5p piece). If the striker's cost his team a lot of money he might be weighed down by his price tag. If he's sharp he might cash in on the goalkeeper's mistake. But he won't get many goals if the opposition shuts up shop.

Food gets a look in, too. A glorious goal is a peach, or a peach of a goal, a curling shot around a defensive wall is a banana shot and a match which gets steadily worse for a team has gone pear-shaped. A player who is caught between two opponents is sandwiched. A player can save his team's bacon with a last-gasp winner. If your team loses badly, they are given a roasting or a stuffing. A midfielder feeds his forwards.

Motoring lends football some more of its clichés. A particularly long-standing one is a team that is firing on all cylinders, which could also be said to be putting its foot down. A team that takes a two-goal lead is often said to be in the driving seat. But if they then go 3-2 down they may find that the wheels have come off.

Football is often linked to criminal activity. If you think the quote 'He was instantly robbed by Strachan' comes from the '80s you'd be right and you'd be wrong. It comes from the 1880s, and is the first instance the *OED* has found for this particular use of the verb. (It's amazing to think that Gordon Strachan was playing back in the 19th century – must be something to do with that seaweed and banana diet of his.) Otherwise a winger can steal a yard from a defender and a team can sneak a goal through the back door. If it's not the crime, it's the punishment. A lucky escape for a team enables them to get out of jail. But if they're put on the rack for the whole game they might end up being thrashed.

Football also borrows many of its clichés from other sports. Quite a new term that has come into the game is a forward's 'strike rate' meaning the number of goals he scores per game played. The term is borrowed from rowing, meaning the number of strokes an oarsman makes in a given time. Horse racing gives exciting football matches grandstand finishes; boxing a team that 'lacks punch up front'; fencing lends the verb 'to parry' as in what the goalie does when he doesn't catch the ball; golf chips in with a drive.

We can thank cricket for the term 'outfield' players and 'cricket scores' (though the highest football scores very rarely reach the lowest cricket scores, however badly the Bon Accord defence or the Durham batsmen conspire to play). Missing a sitter refers to a sitting duck, and comes from rifle-shooting – the term 'target', often used to describe the goal, is from archery. Level pegging, on the other hand, refers to the scoring mechanisms of various games such as stoolball or *pétanque*, where the scores are marked on the wall with pegs.

It is give and take, however. Football lends imagery to our language as well as borrowing it, as we'll see in chapter three.

- 2 -
The Boy Done Good – The Grammar and Vocabulary of Footballers

Part of the reason for people's misapprehension that most footballers are thick is that the language footballers use amongst themselves is slightly different from that used by the commentators of the sport. Many football clichés are just gobbets of footballspeak.

Graham Taylor will always be remembered for one quote, his 'do I not like that' uttered during England's 2-0 defeat in Rotterdam in 1993 which virtually put paid to their chances of getting to the 1994 World Cup finals. Strictly speaking the phrase isn't grammatically incorrect; just odd. Taylor is turning a statement into a question form as a rhetorical device. Unfortunately it backfired on him because it sounded daft – something he acknowledged later in an advert for BT when he played on the fact with the sentence 'do I not like orange'. Taylor was following in a fine tradition of footballspeak which dictates that players should, if they want to be accepted amongst their peers, speak what is in effect a slightly different dialect from the rest of us.

The most celebrated example is the difference in the past form of the verb 'to be' where the form 'were' disappears in favour of 'was'. This manifests itself most commonly in the phrase 'we was robbed' (sometimes written we wuz robbed), but can also be used in other sentences:

'we was slaughtered', for example.

The phrase was first uttered, according to *FourFourTwo* magazine, after a boxing match in 1927 when Jack Dempsey, after a dodgy decision against him, moaned, 'I was robbed of the championship.' In 1932 a manager of another unlucky boxer grabbed the mike, and, making the pronoun plural to include himself as well as his charge, but forgetting to change the verb, yelled, 'We was robbed.' The most famous excuse in the sporting dictionary was born – and incorrect grammar became fashionable in sport.

When footballers talk footie they have a grammar of their own which does not obey all the common laws. One trait is to use the past participle instead of the past simple – the 'gone' part of the verb instead of the 'went'. Since the past simple and the past participle of regular verbs is the same (to score, he *scored*, he has *scored*, for example) this only comes into play when the verb is irregular. Here are a few examples:

'The boy done his marker.'
'The referee never seen that foul.'
'The third goal really sunk us.'

This may have its origins in Southern English dialects, but in footballspeak it translates itself right across the board. Professional football teams, after all, mix together people from all over the country, and increasingly in Britain, all over the world.

Scotsman Andy Gray tells the story of how he found himself in problems when he first started working for Sky while he was still coaching at Aston Villa. 'I'd be talking in the mike after the game and every time I used a verb the producer would be correcting me in my earphones. So I'd say something like "he run past his marker" and I'd hear "ran" in my ear. It happened every time.'

The habit got a lot of airing in the 1986 World Cup when Mick Channon was on the ITV panel. One viewer irked by the grammatically-challenged nature of one of football's finest strikers wrote into the *Guardian* with this suggestion for the declension of the verb 'to do great' in footballspeak:

I done great
he done great
we done great
they done great
the boy Lineker done great

Channon, by the way, pronounced Lineker 'Lin Acre' throughout the tournament and got increasingly on the nerves of Brian Clough who took his revenge in the following exchange.

Channon: 'The Germans done it...the French done it...'
Clough: 'Even educated bees done it.'

Another grammatrical quirk of the football world is the use of the present perfect in narrative description. For some reason players dislike the present and past tenses, usually used for this purpose. This special tense usage usually comes about when players are describing action they are watching at the same time on a video recording. For example, 'Mooro's played a long ball out of defence, I've run along with it a few yards, then I've just hit it.' Or, 'I've seen Carlos making a run towards the box, I've laid the ball into his path, and he's thumped it past the keeper.'

Strangely, considering footballers' love of the past participle, they don't like using it in the passive form. Thus you're more likely to hear 'we got beat 3-0' rather than the more correct 'beaten'. This doesn't, however, apply to all verbs. 'We got done' would be used, correctly, for example, instead of 'we got did'.

As well as messing around with verbs, footballers are averse to adverbs, as the *Guardian* letter-writer pointed out. This practice has entered into clichédom with the phrase 'the boy done good' instead of 'the boy did well'. The cliché is turned on its head in the 1996 collection of footballing misdemeanours *The Lad Done Bad* and also inspired the 1980s fanzine title *The Boy Done Brilliant*. If the football adverbs 'good' and 'bad' don't suffice after such constructions as 'we played...' they can be replaced by their hyperbolic cousins 'great', 'fantastic', 'marvellous' or, on the other hand, 'terrible', 'awful' and 'rubbish'. This kind of (un)grammatical nuance isn't a recent phenomenon; as early as 1972 Alf Ramsey (*Sir* Alf Ramsey) is quoted as saying, 'I thought the England team played magnificent.' (This betrayed Alf's Essex roots, and happened despite his taking elocution lessons in an attempt to recreate himself as a 'toff' manager.)

However much we can pick holes in the language of footballers, we have to accept that even if it's different from BBC English, the fact that it's *consistently* different means that it isn't a case of footballers making mistakes as foreigners would, but a case of them speaking their own brand of English, having been in close contact with it all their adult lives. Calling a footballer thick because he doesn't speak proper English to a football reporter is rather like calling a Catalan thick for not speaking proper Spanish to a fellow Catalan.

Professional footballers talk about football in a different way from the people who are paid to describe it, and this comes out in the way some former pro players talk about the game when they are colour commentating alongside the professional commentator on the TV or radio. This isn't particular to football; every trade has a slang for its own terminology. It's just that football's trade slang is given much more airing than any other profession's because more people are interested in football than in any other trade. Like city trading, prison and military slang, it's particularly rich because it's spoken by a group of men who spend a lot of time together and whose lives fluctuate from periods of extreme boredom to periods of intense drama.

Ron Atkinson is one of the most famous colour commentators and a most articulate speaker of football's trade slang; thus he's credited for inventing many 'clichés' he has, by his own admission, merely picked up from the training ground.

You might, for example, hear that a player has hit the ball with his 'left peg'. The expression of course, derives from 'peg-leg' or wooden leg, although in footballspeak peg means foot rather than leg. You rarely hear 'right peg' because most footballers are right-footed so their left one is more likely to be clumsy. Nobody does anything brilliant with their left peg, otherwise they would be two-footed, footballerspeak for ambidextrous.

Here's a short list of some of the language that footballers use and the equivalent in BBC English.

The back stick – the far post
Penno – penalty
Lino – linesman
Stiffs – reserves
Afters – a post-foul fight
Handbags – a near fight
The gaffer – the manager
The channels – the wings
The nine – the opposing number nine
Early doors – early on in the game
The deck – the ground
Hans Krankl (1980's Austrian striker) – ankle
Humpty – a strong kick
In the mixer – in the penalty area
Nuts/megs (depending on whether you're from the North or the South) – nutmeg, or a ball passed between the gap between your legs. (It's thought that the term 'nuts' referred to the testicles of the player through whose legs the ball has been passed and nutmeg is just a development from this.)

All of these terms might be classed as clichés, mainly because they've caught the public's attention and entered football's general vernacular. Two are particularly popular. The first is 'early doors', a lovely expression used in sentences like 'you've got to keep tight at the back early doors', meaning the defenders have to be particularly vigilant early on in the game; this expression very possibly comes from the theatre where you could once get cheap tickets if you arrived 'early doors' (ie, several hours before the performance). The second is 'handbags' (or its fuller form 'handbags at ten paces'), which implies that the two players who are shaping up to fight are merely 'women' and won't go through with it (football's sexism, not mine).

- 3 -
Spitting for England – Football in the General Vernacular

It's not just one-way traffic (another driving cliché, by the way, overused in football), football lends as well as borrows its imagery. But if you look back at sporting language used in the general vernacular you'll find that the sport has been sorely under-represented given its massive appeal. Cricket terminology has been used for years; a politician might bowl a googly, for example, which could hit his opponent for six. Racing has been running neck and neck with our top summer sport; any race between the two would go right to the wire. Even boxing has given us the expression 'below the belt', the adjective 'knockout' and, more recently, Chris Patten's 'double whammy'.

It's obvious to see why, too; these sports have traditionally been the favourites of the middle- and upper-classes, and the language-makers of the world – authors, politicians, journalists or any people who are regularly quoted – have traditionally been middle- and upper-class too. I know you might quibble with that definition of boxing, until you remember that it used to be widely practised in public schools and the rules were formalised by the Marquis of Queensberry.

Some football terminology has slipped through the net in the past, though, and come into general use. (A fishing net, that, by the way, rather than a football one). Did you know, for example, that 'back to square one' probably originates from football radio reports back in the 1930s?

The first few years that the BBC did live broadcasts from football matches on the radio a picture of a pitch divided into squares was printed in the *Radio Times*. The main commentator would describe the action and a second man in the background would interject when the ball moved into another area of the pitch. Thus:

Commentator: 'And Arsenal's Jack pushes the ball upfield.'
Square Man: 'Square 3.'
Commentator: '...and passes it wide to Hapgood.'
Square Man: 'Square 4.'

'Square One' was the centre circle, hence the expression. I use 'probably'; this particular etymological theory has been questioned recently. The *OED* suggests that the phrase might well have originated from snakes and ladders. Good story, though.

Other early instances of football language to be used in general speech can be questioned, too. For example, in 1911 Rupert Brooke describes a friend of his saying. 'Are you ready to kick off?' 'I gathered it merely meant was he ready to go out to San Lorenzo?' writes Brooke. It's certain that the friend was using a sporting allusion – the fact is that we can't tell if he was alluding to the round or oval ball version of the game. Whatever the case the expression – however new it was to the poet back then – has now become general currency to the extent that it is common in business to say that a meeting kicks off at three o'clock.

All this quibbling about pre-war etymology doesn't really matter – for centuries people have been kicked around 'like a football' or 'used as a political football', and it's likely that people have been likened to the leather sphere as long as the leather sphere has been kicked around. An early, and highly colourful, 15th-century poem by Thomas Hoccleve, 'A Description Of His Ugly Lady', ends with the four lines:

Hir mouth is nothing scant with lippes gray
Hir chin unnethe [scarcely] may be seen at al
Hir comely body shape as a footbal
And she singeth full like a papejay [parrot]

(A parrot! Maybe Phil Thompson had been genning up on his medieval poetry in the late 1970s.)

If it isn't the ball itself, it's the player. Shakespeare, for example, in his greatest tragedy, *King Lear*, uses the image of a footballer as an insult. The scene comes when Lear's stock is so low that even the courtier Oswald is pushing him around, much to the annoyance of Lear's loyal (and disguised) servant, Kent.

> *Lear: Do you bandy looks with me, you rascal? (striking him).*
> *Oswald: I'll not be strucken, my lord!*
> *Kent: Nor tripped neither, you base football player (tripping up his heels).*

Other expressions, which almost certainly predate the splitting of the two football codes in 1864, include 'moving the goalposts' and 'a level playing field', but again they have probably remained in literary currency through their relevance to rugby as much as football.

As association football's appeal has broadened, however, its terminology has entered more and more into the language. Now in this post-Taylor, post-Sky, post-Hornby, post-hooligan, post-modern, post-Postman Pat football-is-a-valid-dinner-party-topic world you'll find more and more footie expressions bandied about in different contexts.

Oddly Margaret Thatcher, who at one point looked like she was going to practically destroy the game in the country by introducing identity cards in an ill-informed attempt to bestow law and order in troubled times, perhaps kicked the whole thing off with the use of a football allusion in a crowd-pleasing speech back in 1986. 'If we can sell Newcastle Brown to Japan,' she bellowed, 'if Bob Geldof can have us running round Hyde Park, and if Wimbledon can make it to the First Division, then surely there is no achievement beyond our reach.'

Even earlier, in 1985 *The Times* had seen fit to use a football pitch as a unit of measurement, 'The concentration of debris into an area scarcely bigger than a football ground showed that the missile had crashed', an example followed by the *Financial Times* a year later, 'The development will have a dealing floor the size of Wembley football pitch'.

Now we have a plethora of expressions which are being used more and more. As football's stock rises the value of football imagery increases. You can boot an idea into touch, a meeting can move into injury time, a dodgy business or political ploy can be deemed offside, and if it's particularly dodgy, be considered a professional foul. Any miscreant might be given the yellow card, especially if he's just scored an own goal. If the case goes to court a hung jury means the whole thing will go to penalties. Pretty soon any custodial sentence will see the poor guy having an early bath.

Football has become so fashionable that some language which had already passed into the general vernacular and from there into football usage is now starting to take on purely a football meaning. A marked man, for example, brings the idea of an attacker with a defender at his shoulder. If you sell someone a dummy, the image of a football player leaving the ball when it looks like he's about to kick it comes to mind. The expression originally came from a dumb or fake hand in cards and became used for anything counterfeit.

'In a different league' or 'in a league of their own' are football expressions which have long been used, but are originally attributable to the American version of the game. However, top companies are now referred to as being a 'Premiership' outfit, and lesser ones are seen as being 'Second Division'. But really that should have been First Division since 1992, but imagery is imagery and 'a new First Division outfit' seems a little long-winded to bother with. To avoid the problem I've heard second-raters (in other fields than football) being described as 'strictly Endsleigh League' or 'a bit of a Nationwider'. This makes you question the wisdom of these companies in endorsing products (or football leagues, to be exact) which *are* unequivocably second-rate.

One football expression which was hilarious when it first came about, but dulled in tone as it became a cliché is the 'for England' quip, as in 'he could spit/shit/drink/smoke for England'. This expression, by the way, became general currency *after* the Graham Taylor era, and means that somebody is good at something, rather than stunningly, Carlton Palmerishly mediocre at something. The late Michael Hutchence said of his lover Paula Yates that she could 'flirt for England'. When *England* magazine briefly surfaced in 1995, I was proud to say that I was 'writing for England'. It was true, after all.

That's this chapter over bar the shouting then (an expression, by the way, which has been used in football since Victorian times). Or over bar one last point. If you think that football imagery has left its studmarks all over the English language, spare a thought for the Italians. In Italy a roadsweeper is as likely to appreciate the art of the composer Puccini as a politician is Paolo Maldini's. And both are likely to appreciate both. Their society has long been virtually classless (in the cultural sense) and football allusions have long been a fundamental part of their language. To the extent that, when I was sent to Rome in 1994 to report on the general election, I attended a political speech by a businessman who was about to set up a new party, and in an attempt to make the party more votable he thought up a name which would capture the imagination of the people. The politician was Silvio Berlusconi and the name, nicked straight from the football terraces, was Forza Italia. They stormed into power, the equivalent of us being governed by a party called Engerland Engerland Engerland.

Part Two

Definitions

- 4 -
Football, Soccer, Footie or Camp – The Name of the Game

The language of football is so rich that it provides two perfectly acceptable titles for the game itself, football and soccer, as well as the colloquial (and ever-more-common) 'footie'. England being England the discrepancy is rooted in class division.

When the game was still in its pre-teething stage in the mid 19th century (when the crossbar was a thing on a penny-farthing bicycle) football was a generic term for a number of different, usually extremely violent leather-ball games which had been played all over the country for centuries but which were being refined in the public schools.

Each school had a different form of the game; some allowed handling, others didn't. Some allowed 'hacking' (kicking your opponents in the shins) or the ball to be passed or thrown forward, others didn't. Problems started arising when the schools (and the old boys of schools) started playing each other at these games and had to agree each time to abide by one set of rules or to make a compromise (some games were played for one half according to one school's laws and in the second according to another).

It became apparent that it was necessary to form a uniform set of rules for everybody; after various proposals Charles Alcock chaired the first meeting of what he called the Football Association to do just that. The FA agreed on a basic set of principles and called their new game

'Association Football' to distinguish it from Rugby Football. At the time there was a trait for public schoolboys (and ex public schoolboys) to shorten words and add 'er' on to the end to form a new word. Thus breakfast becomes 'brekker', etc. The trait went so far that in 1903 D Coke satirised it by referring to 'the receptacle of torn up letters' as a wagger-pagger-bagger. Rugby, of course, became rugger, by which it is still known in certain circles (ie, amongst rugger buggers).

There is a story (which may well be apocryphal, but who cares?) that a certain Charles Wreford Brown was asked one day at college whether he fancied a game of rugger. 'No thanks, I'd rather play asoccer,' he said, shortening the word 'association'. The term caught on and became the popular nickname for the sport amongst public schoolboys, losing its initial 'a' by the wayside. Wreford Brown went on to become Chairman of the FA.

The game, however, soon became a hit with the working-classes, especially in the North, and pretty soon the days of amateur gentlemen players were over, as 'professors' or professionals started becoming more common. The hoity-toity term 'soccer' started going out of fashion. 'Football' was much more earthy and to the point, especially as rugby was still a largely upper-class sport, and therefore didn't come into most fans' or players' lives.

'Soccer' has lived on in the public schools, however, and also in countries where 'football' describes another (related) sport. Saying 'football' to an American can be as confusing as asking him for a fag. To Australians and many Irishmen it means a violent game played by large men who can jump very high.

Most footie fans in Britain still hate the word soccer. It smacks of colonials trying to poke their nose into our business. But the term is making something of a comeback – thanks to the Internet. If you do a search for 'football' related items half the stuff you get is junk about Dan Marino, the 49ers or the NFL. 'Soccer' gets you the sort of round-ball trivia you're after.

Sitting at your computer console is still, however, a long way away from taking your boots down to Hackney Marshes on a Sunday morning or taking the bus to Boothferry Park on a Saturday afternoon – and it looks like 'football' will maintain its dominance in this country for the foreseeable future. The game is all about striking the ball with your foot, after all. And most other countries who play the game have translated the term either semi-phonetically or directly. In France, *on joue au fut*. In Spain and Spanish-speaking South America, *se juega al futbol*. In Germany, *Spielt Man Fussball* and in Portugal and Brazil, *voce joga futebol*. The Italians simplify matters even further. No messing around in the boot. They call the beautiful game plain old '*calcio*' which simply means 'kick'.

Call it what you like, football has passed through many stages to get where it is now, and every stage has contributed to the grammar and vocabulary that form its language.

We like to think that we taught the game to the world – but the truth is that it was most probably the other way round. The first game of football historians have discovered was the Chinese game *tsu-chu*, which means kick-ball. The Greeks played a form of football – which they called *episkyros*. When I was first researching the etymology of the word I linked it to a legendary highway robber who used to make his victims wash his feet on a rock and then kick them into the sea. Unfortunately this was a red herring – the word derives from *skyros* – or line. The Greek poet Homer talks of the soldiers besieging Troy playing *episkyros* around the city walls.

The Romans had a game which they called *harpastum*, which derives from the Greek *αrpaston*, a ball. Both Julius and Augustus Caesar were keen players – rumour has it that Julius, having just invaded England, entered the town now called Brentford kicking an Ancient Briton's head before him. Some mosaics showing the sports around the time of young Julius's education suggests that the balls were made of leather panels and inflated. The Romans had special buildings for the practice of indoor ball games.

This habit was taken up by many Europeans in the middle ages, who became so fond of playing ball games they built big all-weather high-ceilinged arenas for the practice, known as ball-houses. Soon the buildings became used for all sorts of entertainment such as singing and dancing; hence the words ballad, ballet and ball. So now you know.

The first English-Latin dictionary, written by Galfredus Grammaticus in 1440, shows that medieval Latin, which was very different from classical Latin, called the game of football '*pedipilo*' (pedi = foot, pilo = ball), although the English word for the game was camp (from the medieval German *kemp*, meaning campaign or struggle, as in *Mein Kampf*). However, the dictionary describes the Latin word pedilusor (literally foot-player) as '*camper* – player at foote-balle' so it appears that even in the early days there was a discrepancy in what to call the game.

Camp, which was heavily influenced by the Norse game 'battle ball' was a dangerous game in which players were often severely wounded and sometimes killed. Playing camp was said to be good for the meadow, or *pightel*; a 15th-century poem reads:

In meadow or pasture, to grow the more fine
Let campers be camping in any of thine

And although it was also considered to be manly and salutory, the extremes of violence to which the games led caused them to be outlawed by Edward III in 1389, who gave the excuse that the game interfered with his soldiers' archery practice. However, the game continued and even flourished, much to the chagrin of the upper-classes who considered it violent and ungodly.

In 1583 Puritan pamphleteer Philip Stubbes wrote in his tirade against evil customs of the time *The Anatomy of Abuses*, 'Some spend the Saboath Day in foot-ball playing and other such deuilish pastimes', and just after the turn of the 17th century James I tried to ban the game, declaring, 'From this Court I debarre all rough and violent exercises, as the foot-ball, meeter for lameing than making able the users thereof.' Around this time the first recorded mention of goalscoring is made. In 1600 the playwright John Day writes in his play *The Blind Beggar of Bethnal Green,* 'I am Tom Stroud of Hurling, I'll play a gole at camp-ball.'

Football continued to be a hugely violent game. In 1722, the *OED* records the first usage of the Scottish word 'fouty' with the example 'He beat out another fouty bastard's brains.' In an 1825 history of Northumberland a match is described which took place between the Scots and Northumberland border reevers, which might well constitute the first-ever international. Since the 14th century clans from North and South of the border had been involved in bloody clan feuds that involved the raiding of villages and the stealing of sheep. By 1790 the situation had calmed down enough for the feud to be decided on the football field. The names of the participants are interesting: the Scots included such families as the Armstrongs, the Eliots and the Maxwells; the Northumberland reevers were almost entirely composed of four clans: the Robsons, the Milburns, the Charltons and the Dodds. All these names have produced descendants who have more recently been involved in the game. The history gives an early example of a match report. 'A memorable match at the football took place near Kealder Castle, about the year 1790. A vast concourse of people assembled from Liddesdale on the Scotch side of the border and from the pastoral vale of North Tynedale. 20 were chosen by the people of each of these districts to play five games [games here means goals]. The contest was carried out with inconceivable eagerness until the end of the fourth game, each party having won twice; but the North Tyne boys got the fifth and were declared victors. Some of the players were so completely exhausted as to be unable to walk home; and a few who died soon afterwards dated the commencement of the illness from that day.'

Border areas produced, it seemed, the bloodiest games. In March 1887 the *Oswestry Observer* pointed out, 'It seems that eighty years ago the population, rich and poor, male and female, of opposing parishes, turned out on Christmas Day and indulged in the game of "Football" with such vigour that it became little short of a serious fight.' By now the term camp-ball or camp had largely been abandoned, or used to describe a different game, played with a cricket-sized ball, in Essex, Suffolk and Norfolk. Elsewhere 'football' was taking hold.

Football was becoming such a popular game in the country that many towns would have a game to celebrate national holidays. The game usually took place between one parish and another and the object was for one set of townspeople to get the ball to a landmark in the other set's parish. One well-documented game took place in Derby between the parishes of All Saints and St Peters. The two 'goals' were the gates of a nursery ground and the wheel of a watermill. A 19th-century description of the game talks about the object of the game being 'to goal the ball'. The narrator, defending the game against critics, points out that 'life is rarely lost' but by all accounts it was rather violent, with hundreds of people taking part. The term 'a local derby' has incidentally usually been assumed to derive from the Epsom Derby and to have arrived at its modern meaning of a match between two local teams via the meaning of 'an important sporting occasion'. Perhaps the etymologists have got it wrong.

Similar games to Derby's Shrove Tuesday football match were played at Workington, at Chester-Le-Street (between the 'up-streeters' and the 'down-streeters'), at Kirkwall (between the 'up-the-gates' and the 'down-the-gates') and at Asbourne, where the game is still played between the 'uppards' and the 'downards'.

In the mid 19th century the public schools started encouraging their boys to play versions of football, which was considered to be manly and healthy. However, they started imposing laws on the games which restricted the numbers playing and the violence allowed. Which brings us back to the beginning of this chapter.

- 5 -
The Language of Tactics – From WM to the Christmas Tree

The way football is played has changed immensely since those Victorian times, and so has the much of the language we use to describe the game. An important part of that language is how we talk about the formations of players on the pitch.

The classical English formation was one which lasted for seven decades and wasn't described in numbers, but in letters. It was called the WM formation and might nowadays be known as 3-2-5. It's worth taking a close look at the different players used in this formation because a lot of the terms we still use derive from this era. Imagining the goalkeeper at the top of the diagram, here's the 'W'.

Right Back   Left Back
                    Centre half
        Right half   Left half

And here's the 'M':

        Inside Right   Inside Left
Right Winger   Centre Forward   Left Winger

Helping the goalkeeper defend the goal were two defenders, the full backs. In front of the full backs were the halves, who would nowadays be called midfielders. There was the left half, the centre half and the right half, collectively known as the half backs. The left and right halves were also known as wing halves. After the 1920s, because of a change in the offside law which made it easier to score, the centre half moved back into the defence, but he still kept his name. To accommodate for this move the wing halves moved slightly infield so between the two of them they controlled the midfield.

The attack consisted of five forwards. The man in the middle was called then as he is called now, the centre forward. Either side of him were the inside forwards, the inside left and the inside right. Either side of them were the wingers (left and right). Many people imagine that the game in early times was a series of forward-heavy charges, but if you look at the formation closely there is a five-man defence balancing a five-man attack, which explains the fact that scores were similar to today's.

Apart from a few tactical nuances the same positions were used from the 1880s to the 1960s, so anybody over the age of forty is prone to still use the same terminology to apply to what they see on the pitch today.

Nowadays we are used to talking about tactical formations by using three sets of numbers, the first describing the defence, the second the midfield and the third the attack. So when we say 4-4-2 we mean that there are four defenders, four midfielders and two attackers. The players actually stick to this rigid format only before kick offs, and during the game the formation mixes up, especially the midfield whose job it is both to defend and to attack. The goalkeeper is never mentioned in these tactical formations – it's assumed that he will stay in goal behind the defence. Perhaps this is why the Rotor Volgograd players didn't pick up Manchester United keeper Peter Schmeichel when he scored a last-minute equaliser against them in the UEFA Cup in 1995.

The standard British formation after 'WM' was called 4-3-3 or even 4-2-4 which employed two attackers playing wide on the pitch. The invention of 4-3-3 is credited to Sir Alf Ramsey whose England side, nicknamed 'the Wingless Wonders' won the World Cup in 1966 using that formation. At the time (and even after the final) Ramsey was criticised for using negative tactics. Michael Parkinson wrote in his book *Football Daft* (published in 1968), 'I think Alf should go a long way – Australia perhaps', and summed up England's performance in the 1966 final as 'a classic example of how to win cups and lose friends'. Ramsey simply argued that there simply weren't any good wide forwards around. Here's that 1966 side in the formation in which they started the match:

Cohen	Charlton (J)	Moore	Wilson
Ball	Stiles		Peters
Hunt	Charlton (B)		Hurst

Around the same time the Italians started using a system known as *catenaccio*. It is a word that is bandied about by football experts but rarely explained (or, as the satirical football magazine *When Saturday Comes* suggests, 'a word used by Brian Glanville to demonstrate his knowledge of world football'). It literally means 'bad chain' which is usually mistranslated as 'doorbolt', and is a defensive system of football designed in Italy in the 1960s. '*Catena*' means chain, the suffix '*accio*' adds a negative intonation to the word. The idea is that the opposing attack is chained up by the defence.

The precursor to *catenaccio* was called *le verrou* (which means doorbolt in French), a system used by Swiss manager Karl Rappan in the 1930s to staunch the flow of goals into his team's net. The first man to win trophies with the system was Helenio Herrera, the Argentine manager of the highly successful Inter Milan side of the 1960s. Herrera employed a four-man defence whom he instructed to man-mark the opposing attackers. Behind the defence (ie, between them and the goal) he positioned a player named Armando Picchi, whose job it was to clear the ball if it ever went through the defence or tackle any player who had dribbled past their man. It was an extremely effective formation – Inter Milan won the European Cup in 1964 and 1965 and got to the final in 1967, only to lose to Celtic, who had devised a system of their own to beat it.

The typical gameplan for a team which used *catenaccio* was to go a goal in front and then defend for the rest of the match. Their attacking options were increased by allowing one of their full backs to attack, knowing he was covered by the free man at the back, or '*libero*'.

The successor to 4-3-3 which was introduced in the 1970s by the likes of Jack Charlton and called 4-4-2, was considered at the time to be very negative as it brought an attacking player back into midfield. However, it was highly effective – Charlton's Middlesbrough won the Second Division title by a record fifteen points in 1973-74 – well before the three points for a win ruling. Other managers started to see the tactic's success and realise its validity. Aston Villa's manager Vic Crowe wrote in his programme notes at the end of that season 'Charlton's brigade were accused of being ultra-defensive because they played 4-4-2 and in truth they were committed to not giving anything away. But I can't see anything wrong in that.'

4-4-2 is considered nowadays to be the classical British formation, though more and more teams are changing to the 5-3-2 system (sometimes called 3-5-2), in which two of the wide defenders are given more licence to attack, leaving three central defenders as insurance against the counter attack.

4-5-1 (sometimes written as 4-4-1-1) is another popular formation, especially when teams are playing away and would be happy to avoid defeat. In this formation there is a lone forward, sometimes aided by a man 'in the hole' or between the midfield and the attack. This formation was popular with Terry Venables in the run up to Euro 96, and became known as the Christmas Tree formation because of the triangular shape the players made when they were lined up in formation. Here's a typical Venables Christmas tree team, which he used in the friendly against Colombia in September 1995. Shearer's isolation up front led him to a barren spell of twelve international games without a goal, which was much noted in the press.

Neville (G) Howey Adams Le Saux
McManaman Gascoigne Redknapp Barmby Wise
Shearer

Such rigid systems definable by numbers were eschewed in the 1970s by certain teams, especially the Dutch national team which got to the World Cup finals of 1974 and 1978, which played a brand of football known as 'total football' in which (in its purest form) every outfield player was given licence to play everywhere on the pitch (as long as he was aware of the need to cover occasionally for his team-mates). This was a perfect antidote to the negative tactics that preceded it, influenced by the success of *catenaccio*.

- 6 -
Left Back in the Changing Room – The Language of Positions

The Goalkeeper

There is no mention in the rules of a specialised goalkeeper who can handle the ball until 1871; before that the player nearest the goal did as best he could to keep the ball out.

The goalkeeper has had many titles: in the 1870s he was known as the basekeeper, net-minder or the sentinel. Journalists, paid by the word and apt to over-egg the pudding, referred to him as the guardian of the posts and even 'the wearer of the goalkeeper's gloves'!

In 1876 Charles Alcock, in his annual of football, wrote, 'One player should be stationed in the very centre of the goal in order to save it in case the outer lines of defence have been passed by the enemy, the extreme width of the space rendering such a course in most instances absolutely necessary. The man selected to occupy this post should be an adept at catching, cool, and not prove to be flurriable', though Alcock later advises, 'when contending against weak opponents it is politic to bring the goal-keeper (I mean by this the player stationed between the sticks) up to the front.' Did you hear that, Peter Schmeichel?

Nevertheless, a 1917 edition of the *Sportsman* warns olden-day keepers about the dangers of coming out of their box. It advised them, 'The last but one resort is the dash out with intent to rob the opposing attacker, for the step leaves the space between the posts in the same state as the cupboard of the late Mother Hubbard.'

In more modern times the goalkeeper has been shortened to goalie, which has largely gone out of fashion now, and 'keeper, which hasn't (although it's now deemed unnecessary to put the inverted comma in front of the k). In the 1990 World Cup the Colombian keeper Rene Higuita played as a last defender when Colombia were in possession, taking the ball way out of his box and passing it around like an outfield player. He was dubbed the 'sweeper-keeper'; in the second round he was robbed of the ball by Cameroon attacker Roger Milla, who scored with a grin on his face as wide as a drug baron's line of coke, and the revolution was over.

The Full Back

In the early days of the game there were eight forwards and two 'behinds'. Pretty soon full backs got sick of this unflattering moniker, though, and started to call themselves by their modern name. In 1876 Charles Alcock writes, 'A back player ought essentially to be a good kick, a fast player, destitute of every vestige of "funk" and quick of action.'

We can see what sort of role the defender had from a certain R Hughes's Malvern College end-of-season report from 1884. 'A first-rate back; cool and plucky; sticks well to the ball, and never goes in for gallery kicking.' His team-mate JH Boxwell was said to have 'a sublime disregard for his shins'.

In the 1920s the full back was joined by a centre half in the defence, but from then on his role was pretty much the same until the mid 1960s when Argentine manager Helenio Herrera invented the *catenaccio* system, which gave his left back, Giacinto Facchetti, the licence to roam around in midfield and attack. As no one had been designated to mark Facchetti the tactic was highly effective – he scored up to ten goals a season from open play.

Facchetti influenced the use of the 'overlapping fullback' in the 1970s and 1980s whose job it was to hug the touchline and overtake the midfielder with the ball to provide an extra attacking option. Celtic used the tactic to great effect to beat Inter Milan in the 1967 European Cup final with full backs Jim Craig and Tommy Gemmel. More recently Liverpool's Alan Kennedy was a perfect example of the position – he scored the winning goal in the 1981 European Cup final.

In the 1990s it became fashionable for teams to employ a wing back, essentially a full back who operated in a more midfield position but still had to come back and defend when necessary. All the running makes it a demanding role – or as Arsenal wing back Lee Dixon put it when I interviewed him on the subject, 'It's knackering.'

The Centre Half, or Centre Back

Until the mid 1920s the centre half was in effect a central midfielder, otherwise known as a pivot. Then Newcastle full back Bill McCracken and his defensive partner Frank Hudspeth devised the offside trap which meant that opposing teams were caught offside up to thirty times a game. The FA changed the rules to make it harder to be offside, which led to a spate of goals by the likes of Dixie Dean (sixty in season 1927-28).

To counter the advantage given to the attack, after a 7-0 defeat at Newcastle, Arsenal manager Herbert Chapman moved his centre half back into the middle of the defence – Arsenal won their next match 4-0, and went on to become the most successful side of the era. In 1934 *The Times* wrote 'the defensive pivot is essentially a "stopper" – a destructive player, if you like', and the term 'stopper' has since been an alternative name for the centre half.

As football became more defensive in the 1960s a second centre half was added to most formations, and nowadays there are sometimes three, when the wing-back system is used. Centre halves are also known as centre backs or central defenders.

The Sweeper, or Libero

The sweeper, called the *verrouller* by its inventor Karl Rappan in the 1930s, then the *libero* by the man who first used it with great success in the 1960s, Hellenio Herrera, was at first a completely defensive player, but later on became an attacking option, too.

The *OED* suggests that the term 'sweeper' was first used by *The Times* in 1964; '[Bobby] Moore played a giant part in his role as "sweeper" of the rear.' The image is a little out-dated now as the sweeper is expected to do more than merely 'sweep' behind the defence. Moore, and to a greater extent German sweeper Franz Beckenbauer changed the role in the 1960s and 1970s by using their freedom to come out of defence into the midfield and sometimes even attack to create chances as well as stop them.

The Midfield

The midfield is the place where the ball spends most of its time, so the role of midfielder is a very exacting one. In 1917 the *Sportsman* declared, in a rather sexist manner, 'Your half back and a woman are alike in this respect – their work is never done.' The midfielder has defensive as well as attacking responsibilities, though over the years the linear system of the three halves has changed a good deal, with a number of specialised roles developing.

The anchor man

The anchor man is a largely defensive midfielder whose job it is to stay in front of the defence and halt attacks, winning possession and delivering the ball safely to another midfielder. The best example of the role in recent years is the German Dieter Eilts, who earned the nickname 'the Destroyer' in Euro 96 for his effective negative tactics.

The playmaker

The playmaker is what the centre half used to be, an attacking pivot through whom most of the team's attacks are filtered. In fact he was referred to as 'the pivot' or, if he was short, 'the pygmy pivot'. His role is to read the runs of other midfielders and attackers and find them with 'intelligent' passes. He is also sometimes referred to as the 'midfield general'.

The midfield dynamo

Called 'the lawnmower' in Germany (because he covers most of the pitch) and often referred to as a 'box-to-box midfielder', it's the dynamo's job to make himself available to receive the ball all the time and to defend as well as attack.

The wide midfielder

An essential ingredient in the 4-4-2 system, the wide midfielder is essentially a winger with a lot more to do besides attacking down the touchline. His duties are defensive as well and he is responsible for much of the (left or right) half of the pitch he is playing on.

The player 'in the hole'

A cross between a midfielder and an attacker, the player in the hole has to link the forward (or occasionally forwards) in front of him with the midfield, and also run into goalscoring positions himself.

The Winger

In the early days of football the winger was also called 'the side', as in left side and right side, or the left or right 'front'. The term 'wing' soon started to take over, as wing play became hugely important around the turn of the century. In 1898 a certain J Goodall, in his *Association Football* refers to 'the wing game, ie, two positions playing together leaving the centre forward waiting for something to turn up'. Goodall had been the centre forward of the 'Old Invincibles' Preston North End. What the centre forward was waiting for was a cross or a centre, but it wasn't always called that. Malvern College's left side of 1884 was told in his report that he should 'learn to middle better'.

The winger stayed an integral part of the game until Alf Ramsey started tinkering with the game as manager of Ipswich Town in the late 1950s and early 1960s. Ramsey took the Suffolk side from the (very old) Third Division to the League Championship in 1962 by replacing their left winger with an extra wide midfielder, Jimmy Leadbetter, who played in a deeper position from where he had time to deliver diagonal passes into the box. Since then the winger has made various comebacks, and is often referred to as the 'traditional' or 'orthodox' winger.

The Centre Forward

Originally called the 'centre front', the centre forward is traditionally the focal point of a team's attacks. In the late 1960s and 1970s, when tactics started changing around and two men instead of one shared the responsibility of scoring, the centre forward also started becoming known as the 'striker'. Another term that came in during the 1970s was the 'target man', first noted by the *OED* in 1975 in *The Times* (which had first called the role the target player a year earlier). The target man's role was to collect long passes from defence and, more often than not, lay them off to another player.

- 7 -
A Duff Bottle of Hirondelle – The Language of Numbers

Around the time of the 1974 World Cup, in which the teams who were competing sent out squads of twenty-two players, each with a number (from 1-22) on his back, a series of ads came out for the wine company Hirondelle. The premise for the campaign was that Hirondelle was a wine you could trust. The ads had a series of pictures of events that would never, that *could* never happen. One of them showed a player with the number 23 on his back. At the bottom of the ad ran the punch-line. It read 'It's about as likely as a duff bottle of Hirondelle.' Twenty years on, the number 23 was a common sight on the playing fields of the Premiership, which had introduced a system whereby every team gave each of its squad members a different number. Some teams used over thirty players in a single season. Hirondelle had long gone bust.

There's a famous picture of the 1933 FA Cup final between Everton and Manchester City in which you can see Dixie Dean flying headfirst into the goal with the ball marginally in front of him. The goalkeeper, who has sensibly got out of the way, has got 22 on his back. This was the first game in English football to use numbering on the back of players' shirts; Everton wore 1-11, Manchester City sported 12-22. It was a success – but it took until 1938 before the Football League voted in favour of numbered shirts, though for the sake of economy each team was required to wear the numbers 1-11.

In those days of fixed positions which position the numbering represented was quite clear. The goalkeeper wore number 1, the full backs, right and left, numbers 2 and 3. The three half backs or 'halves' wore, from right to left, the numbers 4, 5 and 6 (although by that time the number 5 had moved back into defence). The right winger wore 7, the inside right 8, the centre forward 9, the inside left 10 and the left winger 11.

But as tactics changed, and different teams started playing different formations, things became more complicated and you were no longer necessarily able to tell what position a player played in from his number.

To make matters more complex the method of giving squad numbers in the Premiership (with the names of players above the number) hasn't been taken up in the lower divisions in England, who keep on using the traditional method of numbering, mainly because it's much cheaper to maintain.

No. 1 has always represented the goalkeeper. This has enabled the Arsenal fans to chant at their keeper David Seaman 'England's number one', which has a beautiful double-meaning: he is the number one in the country and he wears the number 1 shirt. However, each Premiership team has two, and sometimes three, goalkeepers in their first-team squad. Traditionally the second goalkeeper, wanting to avoid the number 12 shirt and its substitute connotations, has either been given the number 13 or the number 14 shirt. 13, of course, is meant to carry bad luck and is sometimes avoided entirely by a team.

Numbers 2 and 3 still represent the full backs (right and left in that order) even if, in some systems, these players have become more like midfielders than pure defenders. Some teams, however, prefer using attacking players as wing backs (Kevin Keegan sometimes put traditional wingers like David Ginola and Keith Gillespie in the role) so the position isn't as clearcut to the fan, who has now to look to see where the player was playing to work out his position, rather than referring to the number on his back.

Number 4, originally the left half, is a floating number which can be used in any defensive or midfield position. Because it's a lower number it has often come to represent the defensive midfielder, or anchorman. One of the most famous number 4s in the country is Nobby

Stiles who wore that shirt in the 1966 World Cup final. Teams that use three central defenders often give the number 4 to one of them.

Numbers 5 and 6, traditionally given to the centre and left halves, have become more defensive in their connotation and are usually sported by the two centre backs in a 4-4-2 formation. 6, because of its former midfield connotations, has more of an air of seniority – if a team has a sweeper he is usually given the number 6 shirt.

The number 7 is traditionally given to the right winger, and if such a player still exists he will probably be allotted this shirt. However, it has become another 'floating' number, used sometimes in central midfield, and sometimes even in attack – Kevin Keegan used to sport number 7. The number 7 gives the idea of the playing being nippy and fast.

Number 8, too, can mean a number of things nowadays, but because it used to belong to an inside forward it now tends to be given to an attacking midfielder. It is Paul Gascoigne's favoured shirt and was also worn at Newcastle by Peter Beardsley who played 'in the hole'. Sometimes the centre forward's strike partner wears number 8.

Number 9 is and has always been the number given to the centre forward. It's a very powerful number and usually gives its wearer a good deal of responsibility. More likely than not he is expected to score more goals than anybody else in the team. Two anecdotes confirm the importance of the number 9 shirt. The first is about Don Revie, who wore number 9 for Manchester City in 1954. Revie played as a 'deep-lying' centre forward, a tactic which had been used to great effect by Hidegkuti of Hungary. The English defences simply didn't know how to cope. Because he was wearing number 9, and was therefore a centre forward, they would push their centre half up to mark him. That would leave a gaping great gap in the defence, which City exploited. In effect he was an attacking midfielder but the numbers on players' backs were in those days so representative of where they were supposed to play that players couldn't cope with any change.

The other story is more recent. Before Alan Shearer would agree to his £15 million move from Blackburn to Newcastle in August 1996 he made two conditions to Kevin Keegan. The first was that he took the team's penalties. The second was that he wore the number 9 shirt. Keegan agreed, but only after he had sorted the matter out with Les

Ferdinand, who was used to having 9 on his back. Ferdinand wasn't happy, but said it would be OK if he wore the number '99' (which represented, no doubt, double 9 rather than one short of a hundred). Unfortunately, the Premiership didn't sanction such an outrageous proposal, which would have pushed the shifting-numbers game way further than it had already got. So Ferdinand had to settle for 10.

Number 10 isn't, however, such a bad one to have to settle for. It can either represent the midfield playmaker (such as Michel Platini or Glenn Hoddle) or the centre forward's strike partner. It's rather like the number 8, but with long hair and its socks rolled down. The most famous number 10 of all is the player who has made it the most prestigous shirt of all for would-be creative players, Pele.

Traditionally number 11 is the number given to the left winger – Ryan Giggs is proud to wear the shirt which was most famously on the back of his illustrious Manchester United predecessor George Best. However, since the demise of the winger in the 1970s and 1980s, 11 has become another 'floating' midfield number, usually given to the left-sided man in a 4-4-2 system.

The substitute's number was always 12, and thus is largely avoided by players in squads. The substitute, however, as well as being the guy who can't quite get in the team, is a romantic figure who can save the game when things are going wrong. The most famous number 12 is David Fairclough, who often warmed the Liverpool bench in the late 1970s. He was given the nickname 'supersub'.

In the 1970s Johan Cruyff was rarely a substitute, but when he was asked by Ajax manager Rinus Michels in 1970 to choose a number to wear for the whole season, he decided on 14. His reasoning was clear: all the other attacking numbers brought to mind the world's great players (Charlton, 9; Pelé 10 etc) and Cruyff wanted a number of his own. Hitherto entirely unglamourous, the number 14 took on a new meaning, and every kid wanted it on his back.

Part Three

Names

- 8 -
The Clissold Park Pelés

For about four years I've been playing in a whoever-wants-to-play kickaround in Clissold Park in North London. I'll not tell you the time and the day or it'll get even more crowded than it already is. It used to be the absolute highlight of my week, but it started to go to pieces after a year or so because it ceased to be just a group of friends having a laugh and everyone started arguing about whether it was a goal or whether it had gone over the imaginary bar. (Goals are represented by a pile of jumpers and bags.) So we were pleased when one of the players, Clive, announced in the pub afterwards that he was arranging an eleven-a-side match and did anyone want to play. There would be real nets, and everything.

We started thinking about a name for our team – the one that sprang to mind immediately was Clissold Park Rangers. It was a little joke because it sounded a bit like Queens Park Rangers. A very little joke. We played our first match miles away in Hayes in Middlesex and won 3-2. We started playing quite regularly and pretty soon there was talk of joining a league. When we actually found one we had to officialise what we were called and get team shirts.

We had a meeting in the pub to work out what we should be called and what sort of shirts we should get. There were five of us. Everybody had their say – I suggested we should all wear Brazil shirts with the number 10 on the back, and call ourselves the Clissold Pelés. I knew just where to buy the shirts, they cost £20 each. It was a joke. We'd be crap, but we'd all be wearing the Pelé strip. Ho ho ho.

There was a lot of discussion and argument; Clive in particular was against the idea. But in the end I got a majority vote and got my way. Or so I thought. Clive had become the manager and had to organise getting the shirts and signing our name on the London FA affiliation form. I hadn't realised, but he'd privately decided with Des, his best friend and our striker, that we couldn't wear the Brazil shirts because the sleeves were short and their arms would get cold in the winter months. With the shirts went the name. Clive had a deadline to sign the form and without my knowledge we became known as Clissold Park Rovers.

There was an angry confrontation in the pub when I found this out. But it was too late. After a while I asked him why, in any case, he had chosen Rovers instead of Rangers. At least there was a semblance of post-modern irony in the name Clissold Park Rangers. 'Oh, were we meant to be called Rangers?' he said. He hadn't realised.

So there we are. We are the only team in our league without a comedy name. We are like a blast from the past. The other teams are called things like Strollers, Old Utopians, Jokers, Golden Boots, Red Menace, Nepalese Academicals, Perfidious Albion and Daz Automatic. Daz aren't sponsored by the washing powder company, they just play in white shirts. That was *their* joke.

It's become par for the course for Sunday League teams to have silly names. *FC* magazine, the FA-affiliated mag for people who play football, did a little survey recently and came across some of the better ones. The most common humorous technique used was choosing a foreign team name and mixing it with something English to create a bathetic effect. Thus we have Real Ale Madrid and their counterparts Imaginary Madrid. Or Borussia Munchenflapjack, PSV Hangover or JCB Eindhoven. Not to forget A3 Milan, Atletico Neasden or Bayern Banana. The women's team Old Fallopians play on the old names of Victorian times – unfortunately the women's FA have insisted that they are officially known as Camberwell WFC. Other names are just plain daft – a Bournemouth team are called Amanda de Cadanet just so their players can claim to have scored with her. And who knows the reasons behind Bacon Sandwich FC, Slippy Fingers FC and Where's Rupert FC? My personal favourite is a Durham team called Norfolk Enchance. Clue: try saying it in a Geordie accent.

Some strange names do have a reason. The Crouch End Vampires, for example, play their football overlooking a cemetery. The Windy Millers play at the Windmill Social Club and are sponsored by a company called Mildon. Lobster FC, who used to enjoy the services of centre back Mike Lyons, are sponsored by the Lobster pub. You can now see why Clissold Park Rovers seems a bit staid.

Strangely enough there was a similar levity employed in the team-naming process back in Victorian times, although the names the pioneers of the game gave their teams were a shade more dashing.

A quick look through the *FA Annual* for 1871 shows the Hampstead Heathens, the Harrow Chequers, the Gitanos and the Kilburn No Names to be amongst the registered clubs. The most successful team of the early years of association football, originally called Forest from their home in Epping, lost their ground and started calling themselves the Wanderers. The team won five out of the first seven FA Cup finals.

With all this talk nowadays about football being hijacked by the middle-classes it's easy to forget that the original game, or at least in its original eleven-a-side organised form, was very much an upper-middle-class game, whose players were predominantly former public school-boys. Some of the early names of the clubs reflect this. Old Etonians got to the FA Cup final in 1874 and 1875 – other teams from public schools to perform in the competition include Old Brightonians, Old Carthusians, Old Harrovians, Old Westminsters, Old Wykehamists and Old Ham Athletic (only joking). The competition in those days was rather haphazard – in the first edition, for example, a draw led to both teams getting through to the next round, which was all very well until the semi finals when the competition's first replay was arranged to avoid three teams playing out the final. Many of the teams which entered in the early days weren't around very long – but long enough to enter their idiosyncratic names into the record books, which are much the richer for their existence. Here's to the Swifts, the Mosquitoes, the Pilgrims, the Crusaders, Esher Leopold, Dreadnought, Grey Friars, the Druids, Brigg Britannia and the Panthers.

Pretty soon the organised form of the game started becoming increasingly popular amongst the working-classes and a new breed of team started playing, and forming a new breed of name. The first industrial Northeners to make their mark were Darwen, who took Old Etonians to two replays in the semi final of 1879 and signalled a new force in football. Darwen is simply the name of the town.

- 9 -

United We Stand – The Need for Suffixes

The first team of Northeners to win the FA Cup was Blackburn Olympic, whose team included three weavers, one spinner, one cotton worker, an iron worker, a dentist's assistant, a picture framer, a plumber and two probable professional footballers. They beat the Old Etonians in the 1883 final, and the age of gentlemen's amateur football was dead. The game was thriving in the North – Olympic were the third team from the same city to set up and one of four to play in the FA Cup that decade. There were so many teams forming that it became necessary, when a team was named after the town it was from, to apply a suffix to the name of the club to distinguish it from its local rivals. Thus Blackburn Rovers started first, closely followed by Blackburn Park Road, Blackburn Olympic and the short-lived Blackburn Law. When Liverpool began in 1892 (as a split-off team from Everton FC) they were aware that two other teams had already affiliated themselves with the FA – Liverpool Stanley and Liverpool Ramblers (who still exist as a cricket team).

To avoid the problem some teams (such as Everton) named themselves after the area of the town that they came from. But this could cause problems in days when teams moved ground frequently, looking for their ideal home. Newton Heath, for example, was the early name for a highly successful railway team from Manchester who played their way into the Football League in 1892. However, when the team moved in 1893 from their North Road ground in Newton Heath to Bank Street in Clayton, a good walk away, they didn't change their name, which led to a number of fans, and, according to legend, opposing teams, arriving in the wrong place at the right time for matches. Clearly something had to be done, and at a meeting in 1902 the 'Heathens' decided to change their name to avoid the confusion (and to reflect their national status). Manchester Central was rejected for sounding too like a railway station, Manchester Celtic was rejected for sounding too Irish. Manchester United was settled upon, to reflect on the fact that the club was uniting the old concern of Newton Heath with a group of businessmen who had invested £2,000 in the club to save it from bankruptcy. Nowadays if somebody talks about 'United' on the television or in the press, their audience will automatically assume they mean the Manchester version.

Of the ninety-two 1997-98 Football League clubs United is easily the most common suffix, however, with Cambridge, Carlisle, Colchester, Hartlepool, Leeds, Manchester, Newcastle, Oxford, Peterborough, Rotherham, Scunthorpe, Southend, Torquay and West Ham making a total of fifteen (depleted from sixteen after Hereford's sad demise). The first team thought to have adopted the suffix was the Barnes team Hanover United, who formed in 1873 and played in the FA Cup for nine seasons from 1879-87, without ever going past the third round. The reason for them adopting the name appears to be unknown, though most other early clubs who did so used the term to represent a merger between two clubs; Newcastle United, for example, was so named after the merger of the two rival teams Newcastle East End and Newcastle West End in 1892 (East End had just beaten West End 3-0 at home in the FA Cup and enough was enough).

But Uniteds aren't always born from unification. When the Hobbins brothers decided to enter their team into the Eltham and District Under 15 league in 1964 they decided to give it the name Welling United simply because it made the team sound rather grand. It was a prescient move. United became the best team in the area and gradually moved up through the leagues – eight promotions later they reached the heady heights of the Vauxhall Conference.

The next common suffix in English pro football (after the split between the Football League and the Premiership there's no other term for it) is City. Lincoln City were the first club to adopt the suffix in 1883 – most other teams either formed with it in their name after the turn of the century (Cardiff, Hull, Exeter) or adopted it in a name change. Manchester City were known as Ardwick until 1894, Leicester were Leicester Fosse until 1919, while Birmingham was Small Heath and then just plain Birmingham until 1945. Swansea and Chester didn't adopt the term 'City' until as late as 1970 and 1983 respectively. 'City' is very much a term used by small cities wanting to assert themselves, or by a large city's second club trying to flex their muscles a bit.

Town comes next with nine entries, and is a much more traditional moniker than the grander sounding 'City'. Macclesfield Town, as I write the newest entrants into the Football League, have been using the name since the 1850s (albeit until 1874 as a rugby-rules club), Ipswich, Luton, Northampton, Shrewsbury and Swindon were all formed as 'Town' in the 1880s, and Grimsby, who adopted the name in 1878, had previously been called 'Grimsby Pelham' for just one year. Only Mansfield Town, formed in 1910, adopted the name this century, although they were the last in a succession of teams using the same name.

Teams which in their early history had no permanent home often gave themselves a suffix which fitted their fate. Rovers is the most common existing name, with four clubs in pro football. Perhaps no team deserves the title more than Bristol Rovers. Originally (and gloriously) named the Purdown Poachers, then, when they got a set of black shirts, the Black Arabs, Rovers had five different grounds between 1883 and 1894, when they finally settled at Eastville Football and Athletic Ground, and changed their name to Eastville Rovers. There they stayed (although they had two more name changes, eventually settling for Bristol Rovers) until 1986 when they moved again, right out of the city, to Twerton Park in Bath. Blackburn Rovers, who were soon to become the first dominant professional team in the country, called themselves Rovers because they didn't have a ground when they formed in November 1875. They didn't find a place to call home until mid 1876, when they claimed the aptly and wonderfully named Oozehead. They moved to their current home Ewood Park in 1890, but in the intervening years moved twice, to Alexandra Meadows and Leamington Street.

Other suffixes which suggest such vagabond spirit are Wanderers, Rangers, Strollers and Ramblers (though no Football League teams retain the last two). It's likely that Wolverhampton Wanderers got their name in a merger between St Lukes (a football team) and Blakenhall Wanderers (a cricket team). Wycombe, on the other hand, fully merited their Wanderer status. Legend has it that when the team first started in the 1880s they used to play on pitches on common ground known as the Rye, which was so popular that they had to put up their goals as the clocks struck midnight on Friday to book their place for Saturday morning.

Arsenal are the only team with the word 'arse' in their title. There, that's woken you up a bit. Arsenal *aren't* one of the twenty-five League clubs who, for varying reasons, have never had or no longer have a suffix in their name. Arsenal in itself is a suffix. The club was originally called Dial Square after one of the workshops in the Royal Arsenal. As they got more successful, workers from the whole factory joined in, and they became known as Royal Arsenal. Two of their members had played for Nottingham Forest, from where they scrounged a set of red shirts and became known as 'the Woolwich Reds'. On turning professional in 1891 they changed their name to Woolwich Arsenal. Eventually, though, they were moved to their current site ten miles away in Highbury. The 'Woolwich' prefix was no longer particularly relevant, so since 1913 they have been known as Arsenal (or, to their supporters, *The* Arsenal, or simply, as a term of endearment, the Arse). I bet not many Gooners know, by the way, that originally the word 'arsenal' derives from the Arabic *dar-sinaa* which literally means 'house of art'. Arsène Wenger would be pleased.

Most clubs with just one word in their name have shortened it or changed it at some point in their history. Everton were originally the St Domingo Church Sunday School Football Club, which would have caused James Alexander Gordon a problem or two. Southampton dropped the rather girlie 'St Mary's' tag after five years (but retained the Saints part of it in their nickname). Wimbledon were known as the Wimbledon Old Centrals until 1905, until the majority of their players were no longer old boys of the local school. But Barnet's story is the most complicated. Barnet were formed as plain old Barnet in 1888 but were disbanded in 1901 after an FA enquiry and were amalgamated with local rivals Barnet Avenue. Meanwhile, a dental works' team called Alston FC started calling itself Barnet Alston. When this team decided to merge with Barnet Avenue, they decided to call the new hybrid Barnet and Alston (as if to say that the 'Barnet' bit came from the Avenue club, rather than the Alston one). After seven years with this compromise name the club became plain old Barnet again in 1919.

Other teams have just given themselves one-word titles to lord it over their neighbours. In 1892 Everton decided to leave their stadium at Anfield for pastures new after a quarrel with their wealthy landlord, John Houlding. Houlding decided to form another club, and tried to use the name Everton. When the FA wouldn't sanction this he decided to call the team after the whole city and not just the local area and Liverpool FC were formed. Chelsea were created in a similar way. In 1904 Gus Mears formed a plan to create a football stadium on the property he owned at Stamford Bridge, and proposed the site to Fulham FC when it looked like they were moving from Craven Cottage. When Fulham chairman Henry Norris refused to move, however, Mears formed a new club which he tried to enter in the Southern League. He was refused admission there but allowed into the Second Division of the Football League. He bought players, such as the talented goalkeeper 'Fatty' Foulke, to fill the team, which he called Chelsea. As the borough of Chelsea and Kensington had just been granted the designation 'Royal Borough' by Edward VII the new concern immediately seemed much grander than their cross-Thames rivals.

If modern Sunday League team names reflect a what-the-hell *fin de siècle* lack of seriousness the majority of the teams that we support, formed around the turn of the century, have got names that were invented in the oh-so-serious Victorian age. The two English teams which have ended up with the strange suffix 'Albion', Brighton and West Bromwich, reflect the age more than others. Many Victorians were hopeless romantics and the word 'Albion' is a legendary name for the British Isles (probably deriving from the Latin for cliff, *albus*, or the etymologically linked Celtic word for mountain, *alp*). There is no reason why these clubs, rather than others, should have ended up with this tag, apart from the whims of fashion. Brighton, by the way, were going to be called Brighton and Hove United until local rivals Hove United lodged a complaint with the FA.

Most of England's more exotically named clubs are those who have an original suffix. Nottingham Forest, for example, who were originally called Forest Football Club, because they played at the Forest Racecourse (and had nothing to do with the original Forest FC from Epping who by that time had changed their name to the Wanderers and are now Luton Town).

Sheffield Wednesday, who have spawned a thousand Sunday League football team names (two I have played against include Old Street Tuesday and Brockwell Thursday) were so named as early as 1817, though they were then a cricket club, because they met on Wednesday half holidays. When their fans chant 'The Wednesday' they might not realise that this was the club's official title until 1929 when their city name was added. Early references to the club usually call them 'Sheffield's the Wednesday'.

Until I looked it up I was convinced that Leyton Orient were so called because they were based in East London. Not so. It is because many of their players originally worked on the Orient Steam Navigation shipping line in the area; they changed their name from Eagle FC in 1888. Other mysterious names I knew nothing about until I looked them up are Tottenham Hotspur, Crewe Alexandra, Aston Villa and Plymouth Argyle. Hotspur FC used to play their football on Tottenham Marshes – the Hotspur family, glamorised by Shakepeare's Harry Hotspur in the *Henry IV Part I*, used to own large areas of land in Tottenham. The club added the area prefix in 1885.

Crewe Alexandra, it has recently been revealed by club historians, were not named because the team used to meet in a local pub called the Alexandra, as was previously assumed. Nobody can find any trace of any such pub. It's more likely that they were named after the Danish Princess Alexandra, who was married to Edward (later VII). Aston Villa were culled from members of the Villa Cross Wesleyan Chapel in 1875 and they played their first games in Aston Hall's old deer park – hence the name. Plymouth Argyle were originally Argyle Athletic, a cricket and athletics club formed in a house in Argyle Avenue.

- 10 - Manchester Umbro – Changing Your Name

In Victorian times teams seemed to find it difficult to decide exactly what to call themselves: nowadays clubs' identities seem to be much more stable. Occasionally teams like Orient think they need a change of image and tweak their moniker; in 1987 they added Leyton to their name to try to appeal more to the local community. In 1983 Chester added the suffix 'City' to their name, presumably to try to make themselves seem like a bigger club. But it seems on face value unlikely that many clubs are likely to follow suit. What if Manchester United suddenly decided to rename themselves? Imagine the uproar. Yet such a scenario might not be too far away. With the game prostituting itself more and more to money, how long will it be before English League clubs start changing their names to incorporate a company? The fans have bowed, in the end, to all the changes that have come so far. They won't stop being interested in the game if this happens.

First it was competitions that started renaming themselves, next came the grounds. How long will it be before clubs follow suit? Are we likely to see Manchester Umbro? Newcastle Brown Ale? Tottenham Hewlett Packard? It's happened to a certain extent in other countries. It's happened, for hell's sake, in Wales, where Inter Cardiff changed into Inter Cabletel AFC in 1996. It's happened in Israel, where Maccabi Tel Aviv have become Maccabi Visa Tel Aviv. And it's happened, most sadly, in Poland, where that proud old club, six times winners of the Polish National Championship, Legia Warsaw became Legia Daweoo.

Birmingham City could be the first to go. Their commercial director

Karren Brady has publicly stated that she would be prepared to change Birmingham's name if they got the right sponsor – and presumably found the right price.

Money hasn't always been the reason for clubs changing their name. Politics, of one sort or another, can often play a part. Sometimes a team's name is not deemed politically correct and a change is forced. The main reason for this is when totalitarian regimes feel that a club name doesn't fit in with their policy. This particularly happened in Fascist times – the nationalistic nature of the many Fascist regimes deemed that foreign words should be eliminated from the language. When Franco came to Spain he felt that all the clubs which had English in their name should be changed. Thus Athletic Madrid and Athletic Bilbao, both teams formed by British ex-pats, were changed to the Spanish *Atletico*. When El Generalissimo died in 1975 Bilbao, fiercely Basque and decentralist, changed their name back. Atletico Madrid remain Atletico Madrid.

Mussolini did the same thing to the English-named clubs in Italy: AC Milan became AC Milano in 1939 – the 'o' was dropped again in 1945. As early as 1930 Genoa became Genova 1893 – again they changed back after the Fascist era. Inter Milan's full title, Internazionale di Milano, was particularly offensive: Mussolini deemed it far too similar to a certain Socialist federation of workers and their song and forced the club to change their name to Ambrosiana-Inter to reflect the patron saint of Milan, St Ambrogio.

It's not only totalitarian regimes that force name changes in football clubs. Political correctness doesn't have to be dictated from the government. Bristol club Clifton FC were until recently called the Clifton All-Whites because of the colour of their strip. Despite the fact that they included a number of black players in their team this name was deemed racist and they were made to change it by their local FA. Another example of political influence on a name change came in the 1980s when anything nameable became named after Nelson Mandela, imprisoned in South Africa for his political beliefs. Surely it was going a bit far, though, calling a Sunday League team Mandela United? No worries. The players quickly shortened it to Man United.

The silliest name change of all was made by Bournemouth.

Desperate for a lift after relegation to the fourth division the club decided in 1971 to follow the example of companies like A1 vans and Aardvark minicabs: they changed their name to AFC Bournemouth so they could head alphabetical lists of clubs. Statisticians and editors, however, paid no heed and they still find themselves listed between Bolton and Bradford City.

- 11 -
Stadiums of Shite – Naming Your Ground

So you've got a new stadium – what are you going to call it? Sunderland, who finally moved from Roker Park at the end of 1996-97, cheekily gave their brand new 42,000-capacity home the name 'Stadium of Light' after the magnificent Estadio da Luz in Lisbon, home to mighty Benfica – it's the first time that I've ever heard of one stadium name deriving from another. Nearby Newcastle fans weren't going to let the Mackems get away with that sort of behaviour – and immediately nicknamed their neighbours' home the 'Stadium of Shite'.

At least Sunderland didn't go the same way as Middlesbrough down the road and have their new stadium partially named after a sponsor. The place the fans know as the Riverside Stadium is officially called the Cellnet Riverside Stadium. Most journalists have stopped using the Cellnet bit of the name, too; and after a lack of communication on the pitch saw moneybags Boro being relegated to the First Division in 1997, the mobile phone people must be having second thoughts about their investment.

Middlesbrough weren't the first club to let Mammon pick their stadium name – that dubious honour fell to Scarborough who in 1988 renamed their Seamer Road ground the McCain Stadium after chairman Geoffrey Richmond (owner of the Ronson shaving company) sold the naming rights of the ground to the oven chip and frozen pizza company. Imagine the ignominy! Having your field of dreams named after a frozen pizza!

The next club to follow suit were Huddersfield, who in 1994 named their new state-of-the-art stadium the Alfred McAlpine Stadium – though show me an Alfred McAlpine dwelling that looks anywhere as nice as Huddersfield's ground and I'll go and live in it.

As early as 1910, however, Cardiff City let commercial considerations dictate their choice of name for their ground. Cardiff were all set to move to a new ground provisionally named Sloper Park until one of their backers abruptly pulled out. Lord Ninian Crichton Stuart saved the day with some dosh and Sloper Park became Ninian Park. In the same year Bournemouth named their ground Dean Court after the gravel pit it was built on owned by local businessman Cooper Dean.

There's more stadium building going on nowadays than there has been since the days of Archibald Leitch at the turn of the century. After a hundred or so years many of those old Victorian jobs are past their sell-by date, and clubs are building homes further away from the city centre where there's better parking and the land is cheaper. But, when you move from a ground whose name holds an enormous amount of emotive value, what the hell do you call the new place?

Derby County, who played their last game at the wonderfully named Baseball Ground in May 1997, decided to put instant emotive value in their new stadium name and call it Pride Park. There weren't many heads held high at the League inauguration of the new ground, however, when the match was abandoned after floodlight failure (which led to a number of jokes along the Stadium of Light-Stadium of Darkness vein). The Lions of Millwall, who moved from the dark forebidding Den to a new stadium a couple of miles away, perhaps made the right sort of choice when they opted for a compromise and called their cantilever-roofed box 'the New Den'.

Other clubs who are looking to move might, before they name their new stadium, look at the criteria that have been used in the past for naming grounds. One way of doing it was to refer to a local landmark. When I used, as a kid, to walk down Goldstone Lane to get into Brighton's Goldstone Ground, I never questioned the origins of the name. It derives from a stone once used by druids which lay in the farmland that was originally the site of the ground. The farmer got bored with all the tourists coming to have a look at it, so he buried it in 1834. In 1900 it was dug up and placed adjacent to the ground in Hove Park.

Southampton's picturesquely named ground, the Dell, was named after the beauty spot it was built on, which included a pond that was turned into an underground river when they decided to make the place into a football ground. Similarly Gay Meadow was originally a popular meeting spot in Shrewsbury. Another picturesque stadium name, the Hawthorns, home to West Bromwich Albion, derives from the fact that their ground, built in 1900, was on an area of ground once known as Hawthorn Estate, because it had been lined by two hawthorn bushes. Club secretary Frank Heaven discovered the map and decided this would be a good name for the club.

Chelsea's Stamford Bridge was named after a bridge which went over the now defunct Chelsea Railway near the main entrance of the ground (and not after the second most famous battle in 1066). Just over the Thames, Craven Cottage was a local landmark and a fashionable leisure spot for the well-heeled, built in 1780 and once owned by the writer Edward Bulwer-Lytton who is (probably incorrectly) said to have written his novel *The Last Days of Pompeii* in the premises, a fact that has been commented upon by a number of unimaginative hacks. In 1888 the cottage was destroyed by fire and the site left to rot until 1894 when Fulham moved in. The remains of the cottage, if there are any, are under the Main Stand. When the ground was constructed a new cottage was built which still forms the cornerstone of the ground.

There is a stadium in the Premiership (at least as I write) named Boleyn Stadium after Boleyn House that stood next to the stadium until the 1950s. West Ham fans, perhaps, didn't want their ground named after a headless queen and refer to the place as Upton Park, after the local train station and area.

Arsenal Stadium in Avenell Road, Highbury, is, in a similar way, also known as Highbury Stadium. The fans, after all, needed the team, which moved to the area from ten miles away in Plumstead in 1913, to have some sort of local relevance. Although, oddly, as well as the name of the area being used to name the club's stadium, the name of the club is increasingly being used to define the area. This started in November 1932 when wily Gunners' manager Herbert Chapman encouraged London Underground to change the name of the local tube station, Gillespie Road, to Arsenal. Nowadays estate agents and local residents alike are starting to refer to the area around the ground as Arsenal Village. It sounds a lot better than Finsbury Park.

One of the most intriguingly named (and pronounced) grounds in the country is Wolverhampton Wanderers' stadium Molineux. The story of its naming goes back some way. In 1750 local ironmaster Benjamin Molineux built himself a grand mansion he called Molineux House, which was sold to an OE McGregor in 1860. McGregor turned the grounds of the house into a pleasure garden, with boating lake, fountains, croquet lawns and a skating rink. But he realised that a spectator sports ground would bring in more revenue so in 1880 he changed the name of the house to the Molineux Hotel and built a small track and grandstand around it. The Northampton Brewery took over the grounds and in 1899 entered negotiations with Wolverhampton Wanderers who played their first match there as early as that September. For some reason the name of the original owner was never dropped, although pronunciation of the name by the club's supporters has changed a bit since its French origins. How would you pronounce it if you hadn't been aware of it since you can remember?

Considering the pre- and post-match activities of a large proportion of active football fans perhaps the most relevant way to name a football ground is after the local boozer. Tottenham's White Hart Lane, for example, was built on land which the brewery originally intended to use for housing. The landlord of the White Hart Inn, however, thought that it would be better for trade to have a football ground on the doorstep. He was right. Similarly Brentford's Griffin Park on the other side of London was named after the Griffin Pub – the brewers Fuller, Smith and Turner owned the orchard on which it was built. And, best of all, just before the turn of the century Millwall used to play their games at a ground called the Back of the Lord Nelson.

- 12 -
Seagulls and Eagles – Club Nicknames

I wasn't actually at the match, but I remember the bitter rivalry between the teams. As a kid I hated Crystal Palace. My friends put a ban on the name of the club being used; we had to say Norwood instead. There was an intense period of rivalry between Brighton and Palace in the late 1970s and throughout the 1980s. The only reason it died down in the 1990s was the change in relative stature of the clubs. Brighton dropped to the bottom of the Football League; Palace regularly yo-yoed between the First and the Premiership. Palace had been nicknamed 'the Eagles' for some time. Brighton were officially called 'the Dolphins', although the name wasn't popular with the fans. As if to taunt us for our stupid one, the Palace fans used to chant their nickname, prolonging the first syllable to make 'Eeeeeeeeea-gles'. The 'gles' bit went up and down in pitch. It sounded great. During one match in 1975-76 (when the teams were locked in a bitter FA Cup first-round marathon the like of which you don't see any more thanks to penalty shoot-outs) the Palace fans shouted their name ad nauseam, until the Brighton fans came up with a riposte. 'Seeeeeea-gulls' they chanted, and the club had a new nickname, which they were very quick to make official and adopt into a new club badge. 'Dolphins' was shoved in the football-nicknames wastebasket, where it seemed to belong. Although why we should have preferred a smelly, noisy, dirty scavenger bird to an intelligent sea mammal, God only knows.

The Seagulls and the Eagles are two of many species of animal represented in the footballing nickname world. Torquay are known as the Gulls for their seaside location. West Bromwich Albion are known as the Throstles because the landlady of the pub they used to meet in kept a song-thrush. Huddersfield are known as the Terriers as they are from Yorkshire, like the dog. Derby are the Rams because a local regiment kept one as their mascot. Leicester are the Foxes because the area used to be well known for its fox-hunting. In Italy in the 1930s and 1940s it was fashionable for clubs to be named after animals, a habit which didn't catch on. In some cases it's not that surprising: Napoli were for a time nicknamed '*Il Ciuccio*', a colloquial word meaning 'the donkey'.

Other teams are given animal names because of the colour of their strip. Thus Newcastle and Notts County are the Magpies, Norwich are the Canaries, Cardiff the Bluebirds and Bristol City, Charlton and Swindon the Robins. Some colour combinations throw up different animals for different teams. Yellow and black gives us the Bees (Barnet), the Hornets (Watford), the Wasps (Alloa) and the Tigers (Hull City).

Some clubs haven't had the imagination of making the lateral jump from colour to animal and are rather boringly simply referred to by colour. Thus Liverpool are known as the Reds. They're not the only team to show such a distinct lack of imagination; Carlisle, Birmingham and Chelsea are officially the Blues, Blackburn couldn't think of anything other than the Blue and Whites, Dundee are the Dark Blues and Coventry and Forfar are known as the Sky Blues. Some clubs are no more imaginative, but at least wear less common colours to make their nicknames seem less mundane. Burnley are known as the Clarets; nearby Blackpool glory in the nickname the Tangerines.

This trend is widely adopted in Italy, where the clubs often don't have an official nickname, but are referred to by their colours by fans and media alike. Thus Milan are known as the '*rossoneri*' (literally the red-blacks), Inter are the '*nerazzuri*' (black-blues) and Juventus the '*bianconeri*' (white-blacks). Sampdoria, who wear strikingly original blue shirts with a white, black and red stripe round the chest are known as the '*blucerchiati*' (circled blues). As I'm sure you have learnt, the Italians are simply known as '*Gli Azzurri*'; azzurro means mid-blue in Italian. (Light blue, if you're interested, is '*celeste*', and dark blue simply '*blu*'; if you weren't interested it's too late now.)

Some teams don't even bother using a colour, but merely shorten their own name. Couldn't Middlesbrough have come up with something better than 'Boro'? They share equal first prize for unoriginality with the Dale, the Dee, the Dons, the 'Gers, the Gills, the Well, the Os, the Rs, the Us and Pool. I'll leave you to work those out.

Some clubs glory in nicknames that are derived from their real name, which fortuitously mean something different. The nickname 'the Hammers' mightn't reflect the sort of beautiful football played at Upton Park until the arrival of Iain Dowie, but it certainly sounds good, and has given West Ham their emblem. The same applies to Wolves, although nowadays the Molineux club doesn't seem to be that big or bad any more. Spare a thought, in this category, for Shrewsbury, who have become nicknamed the Shrews. Not an animal that strikes fear into the hearts of opponents, and one that is easily tamed, to boot, as many a headline writer has noticed.

Local dialect provides the reason behind some of the other nicknames. 'Tyke' is Yorkshire for a fellow, so Barnsley become the Tykes. Livingston, who used to be called Meadowbank Thistle, are nicknamed the Wee Jags; jag is a local word for thistle. Heart of Midlothian, or Hearts for short, are also known as the Jammies. This comes from Scottish rhyming slang; jammie stands for jam tart.

Some of the more interesting nicknames in British football come from local architectural oddities. Chesterfield are known as the Spireites due to the crooked spire on its parish church, the 14th-century St Mary and All Saints. York are the Minstermen after the glorious 13th-century cathedral in the town. Lincoln are known as the Imps because of the large number of gargoyles which feature in the town's medieval architecture. Montrose are known as the Gable Endies because of the large number of houses with gables in the town: this is a general Scottish nickname for the townspeople as well as just a nickname for the football team. Norwood, I mean, Crystal Palace, as well as being the Eagles, are known as the Glaziers because of the large amount of glass needed in the old exhibition hall. And Arbroath are the Red Lichties because of the light cast by the famous Bell Rock lighthouse.

If it's not a local landmark it's local industry. What do you think they used to traditionally make in Luton, home of the Hatters? The Blades from Sheffield, the Chairboys from Wycombe, the Mariners from Grimsby, the Merry Millers from Rotherham, the Railwaymen from

Crewe, the Saddlers from Walsall and the Shrimpers from Southend all fall into the same category, as do, in a way, the Pirates of Bristol Rovers (who haven't been re-nicknamed the Landlubbers since their enforced move to Bath). No team was ever referred to as the UB40s or the Dolies, by the way, after the ravages of Thatcherism. And if you start looking for a munitions factory in Islington you're going to be a long time; Arsenal became the Gunners when they were based in Woolwich.

Some clubs derive their nickname because of other traits of the local inhabitants. Darlington are the Quakers after the large Society of Friends in the community. Exeter are known as the Grecians because of the large Greek community in the area (rather than the big number of retired oldsters who dye their hair). Rather more imaginatively, to step outside the UK a moment, the Hungarian team MTK-VM are known as *Libasok* or the Goose Eaters thanks to the large Jewish community in Budapest, where they are based (goosemeat, as I'm sure you've worked out, was an alternative to pork).

The most interesting nicknames, and I've saved them for last, are the ones which don't fall into typical categories. As well as 'the Throstles' for example, West Brom became known as 'the Baggies' because of the voluminous shorts they wore in the days of Brylcreemed hair and big ears. Peterborough are 'the Posh' because back in 1934 the team looked swank when they sported a brand new strip in a game against Gainsborough Trinity. Everton suffer from the nickname 'the Toffees' because the club was formed in a hotel which sat outside 'Ye Ancient Everton Toffee House'. Bury have been the Shakers ever since 1891, when the club chairman said he expected them to shake up the opposition. Bolton Wanderers are known as the Trotters because their team was well known back in the mists of time for its practical jokes; a trotter is an old word for a Jeremy Beadle.

- 13 - Come on You Yids – Supporters' Nicknames

In certain cases teams' supporters get given a nickname: often a derogatory one. In the 1980s Tottenham became known, especially by Arsenal, their rivals from just down the Victoria Line, as the Yids, because of the large Jewish quarter in the area. (Actually the biggest Hassidic Jewish area in London is in Stamford Hill, which is nearer to Highbury than White Hart Lane, but who's quibbling?) To their credit the Spurs fans turned this round, like a wise child in the playground, by saying 'see if I care' and calling *themselves* the Yids, or the Yiddoes. Now both teams simply refer to one another as 'the Scum' which has been taken on by other sets of rival fans, like Ipswich and Norwich.

A similar phenomenon occurred in Aberdeen where during a televised game against Celtic at Pittodrie in 1985 their fans had the chant 'sheepshagging bastards, you're only sheepshagging bastards' directed at them, to the tune of 'Guantanamera'. The chant caught on, and Aberdeen became known as 'the Sheepshaggers'.

What rival fans don't realise is that the Aberdeen fans, the vast majority of whom, presumably, aren't prone to bouts of bestiality, started calling *themselves* the Sheepshaggers. A small cottage industry was formed to produce hats and scarves with pictures of sheep on them. The fans now join in with the sheepshagger song whenever away supporters start it up. Indeed, according to their local fanzine the ironic self-deprecation of the Aberdeen fans engendered by the whole episode has led to them gaining a new positive sense of identity.

There is an enormous amount of rivalry between fans in the North

East and each team has an insulting nickname for the other team's set of supporters. Newcastle fans call Sunderland fans 'the Mackems', which refers to the old shipbuilding industry in the area. Sunderland inhabitants would make the ships and then they were taken away by rich businessmen. Thus the people of Sunderland became known as the Mackems, and the businessmen as the Tackems. Mack 'em is local dialect for 'make them' in case you hadn't cottoned on.

Hartlepool supporters are known locally as the Monkey Hoyers. This dates back to a story emanating from the Napoleonic Wars. A French ship was wrecked off the coast of Hartlepool, but there were no survivors bar the ship's mascot, a monkey dressed up in a military uniform. The townspeople, who had never travelled very far out of town, were convinced the poor animal was a Frenchman and hanged it. The club's fanzine, *Monkey Business*, has been named in deference to the story, another example of taking on an insult to defuse it. Newcastle fans have given themselves a name which has filtered into general usage: the Toon Army. A lot of Southerners don't realise what 'Toon' refers to; it's simply 'Town' in Geordie dialect. It's where you gan doon to sink a broon.

Liverpool fans are known as the Kop, or the Koppites, as the more vociferous amongst them traditionally congregated on the terrace at Anfield, officially called the Spion Kop. Liverpool's wasn't the earliest Spion Kop; the name was first used as a nickname for the bank of terracing built in 1904 at Arsenal's old ground, the Manor Field, to commemorate the Boer War battle in January 1900 where 322 British soldiers were slaughtered on the top of a hill. Many of the Arsenal supporters were veterans from the war. The name became fashionable for football stands at a time when many were being built: the Liverpool stand was built in 1906; in 1908 Birmingham City called their new 48,000-capacity main stand the Spion Kop too. Liverpool fans took on the name because in the 1960s and 1970s the terrace culture that grew on the Spion Kop (including their witty songs and their mass scarf-waving, more of which later) was phenomenally influential on other teams' fans. Nowadays, sadly, their supporters have quietened down, and the nickname is, I feel, slowly drifting out of use.

- 14 -
From the Old Invincibles to Fergie's Fledglings – Team Nicknames

In 1888-89 Preston North End dominated English football in a way no side has managed since. Their team, composed of Scotsmen who passed the ball instead of dribbling it and an English centre forward called John Goodall (nicknamed Johnny All Good) won the double that season, winning eighteen of their twenty-two matches and drawing the other four, scoring seventy-four goals and conceding just fifteen. Moreover, they won the Cup without conceding a goal, beating poor Hyde 26-0 on the way, still a first-class record in England. This was the first-ever double in England and the side that won it deserved a nickname. They will forever more be known as 'the Old Invincibles' for obvious reasons.

Certain outstanding sides get the honour of a nickname, though not all of them are complimentary. The Sunderland side that graced the field in the 1940s and 1950s were nicknamed 'the Bank of England' – not only because of the strength of their team, but also due to the amount of money that had been used to put it together. Money, by the way, can't always buy you success: in 1949 the Bank of England crashed out of the FA Cup to 5000-1 outsiders Yeovil Town, in a match which is still remembered as one of the all-time FA Cup shocks.

Sometimes it's David rather than Goliath that gets the nickname. The North Korean side which beat Italy 1-0 in Middlesbrough in the 1966 World Cup (and which the country took to their hearts) were nicknamed the Diddy Men. Ken Dodd at the time had an act with some diminutive characters of the same name. The 1971 Colchester United side that beat Leeds United was nicknamed Granddad's Army because seven of the players were over thirty, including former England international Ray Crawford, who scored two goals. (*Dad's Army* was an extremely popular TV show at the time.) A Southampton side which virtually the same Leeds team beat 7-0 in 1972 was dubbed the Ale House Brawlers by Bill Shankly after a bruising encounter between the Saints and Liverpool.

There is a whole school of alliterative nicknames for young sides who have been nurtured to greatness by a particular manager. Drake's Ducklings started the trend off. In the 1950s Chelsea manager Ted Drake started up a successful youth team and the side which won the League in 1955 was extremely top heavy with players from the scheme. Unfortunately many of them couldn't fulfil their early promise and by the beginning of the next decade Chelsea were in Division Two. The team that Matt Busby built up around the same time, which included the likes of Duncan Edwards and a full-head-of-hair Bobby Charlton won the league in 1956 and 1957 and looked destined to dominate European football until that tragic and well-documented air crash in Munich in 1958. The Busby Babes were no more. Nearly four decades later Alex Ferguson nurtured a similarly young team which dominated English football in the 1990s. A similar nickname quickly surfaced: Fergie's Fledglings ruled the roost. Any other manager looking to do the same thing should make sure first that he can find an alliterative young-animal noun. Keegan's Cubs? Evans' Eaglets? I think Ruud Gullit's buggered.

Alliteration is also used to describe two of the most influential sides in the history of football: the one which finally destroyed English notions of supremacy and the one that restored them thirteen years later. The Hungarian side (led by Ferenc Puskas and including the talents of deep-lying centre forward Nandor Hidegkuti) left Wembley in November 1953 on the right side of a 6-3 win which most people reading the late editions of their papers assumed was a misprint. The side became known as the Magnificent Magyars, and magnificent they were; the following year England went to Budapest to get revenge and were stuffed 7-1. In 1966 England manager Alf Ramsey, who played in the first of those games, found himself with a home-based World Cup to win and a dearth of top-class wide players. 4-2-4 became 4-3-3, and the Wingless Wonders were born.

- 15 -
Smeggy Smith and Other Players' Nicknames

One day in the summer of 1997, sitting in my office researching this book, I wondered out loud why former Arsenal and England striker Alan 'Smudger' Smith was nicknamed Smudger. Were all Smiths called Smudger? Was it because, as 'smiths' they had dirty hands and smudged everything? Or was it a personal thing? Had Alan been the sort of schoolboy who got ink all over his shirt-cuffs?

'Why don't you ask him yourself?' said Jim whom I work with, handing me his contact book open on the letter 'S'. He'd accidentally written the name of the man who won the 1995 European Cup Winners' Cup for Arsenal's number down twice. The first number read Alan 'Smudger' Smith. The second read Alan Smith (Smudger). Clearly this was a man whose nickname had stuck.

Smudger answered the phone almost immediately. 'I don't know,' he said in that in-need-of-a-Tune Midlands accent of his. 'I think it's just because it starts with S-M.' Then he went on to tell me a little jewel of an anecdote that made my day. 'I was called Smeggy at Leicester, not Smudger. One day there was an evening match at Watford, so I went along after training. I took Tony Adams along with me. The Leicester fans spotted me and started singing "Smeggy, Smeggy, give us a wave". They wouldn't shut up until I did. Tony's bloody called me Smeggy ever since,' he moaned.

When footballers and ex footballers talk about other players they rarely use their real names, and often bastardise them. Thus it's never John Barnes, it's Barnsey; it's never Phil Thompson, it's Thommo.

Sometimes you have to shorten the name before adding the suffix, sometimes you just add it on to the end. So Robson is shortened to Rob before becoming Robbo, whereas Giggs immediately becomes Giggsy.

This hasn't just happened recently (think of Lance-Corporal Jones, or Jonesy, from *Dad's Army*), and it's not restricted to football (ditto). But because footballers are so high profile, and because football is the major area where working-class culture gets a widespread airing, it's become known as a football phenomenon.

Whether to put a 'y' or an 'o' on to the end of the name isn't a haphazard process. It depends on the final consonant before the suffix is added. Any sibilant (s, sh, z, ch) requires a 'y' as in Rushy and Scholesy. Other consonants which also take a 'y' include 'd' (Gouldy), 'p' (Sharpy), and 't' (Wrighty). The consonants n, m and b take an 'o' ending (Tommo, Robbo, Deano). In the last example the first name has been used instead of the surname, probably because 'Holdsworthy' is a bit of a mouthful.

Some players, especially of Italian origin, don't need to have nicknames made for them as their names already comply. Grimandi is used as God meant it to be used, as are Vialli and Lombardo. Sometimes if the name is already a nickname it's further shortened: so Batty, for example, becomes Bats.

The practice isn't just used for players – it's also attributed to other people in the game, such as Motty (John Motson) and Statto (Angus Loughran, *Fanstasy Football*'s statistician). The latter actually breaks one of the rules I have made (it should be Statty) but the fact is that it has been created by the media rather than naturally evolved, and thus isn't genuine.

Such nicknames aren't just used by players. Supporters also feel that they can refer to 'their' players using affectionate tags, just as they feel they can use 'we' as a subject pronoun for the club. One of the guys in my office is a Chelsea fan, and he's forever going on about Wisey. It makes me sick, because I've got a thing about Chelsea. I hate them. But if Wise got back into the England team, and started doing well *I'd* start calling the guy Wisey, too, so any complaint I make is quite hypocritical.

One player who breaks the rules I have just invented (and if you study grammar you'll find that just about all 'rules' have been similarly imposed on the language, hence all the exceptions, so don't judge me too harshly) is Paul Merson, who has become known as Merse or, to adoring Arsenal and Middlesbrough fans 'the Merse'. An incident involving Merse taught me that footballers' nicknames, like all nicknames, can only be used by those who qualify to use them (ie, those who are close to the person involved). Once I was working at the England training camp before one of the Venables friendlies preceding Euro 96. The players were walking off the pitch after a morning of coaching. As Paul Merson passed by, quite a well-known journalist, whom I won't mention by name, said, obsequiously, 'Hi, Merse'. Merse just glared at him and carried on towards the changing room. Point made.

Many players' nicknames come from their personal attributes or strange habits. Well-endowed players, for example, often get given a nickname in deference to the size of their penis. Any player called Nobby (like Brian Horton when he played for Brighton) probably falls into this category. Most people assume former Chelsea hard man Ron 'Chopper' Harris was given this nickname because he was prone to chopping down opponents with his tackles. Not a bit of it; his teammates gave him the moniker because he was particularly well-endowed in the wedding tackle department.

Another common misassumption is that former Arsenal, Juventus and Ireland midfielder Liam Brady was nicknamed Chippy because of his penchant for delicately lofting the ball. Wrong again. The guy couldn't stop eating chips. Wouldn't happen in this day and age of dietary enlightenment.

Some players get nicknames from the way that they play. Remi Moses was affectionately known as Dogshit at Manchester United, because he got everywhere. On the other hand Wimbledon's Andy Clarke is referred to as Jigsaw. Why? Because he goes to pieces in the box. Cue the fox glove.

Amongst footballers, just like amongst any large groups of young men who spend an inordinate amount of time in close proximity to one another, piss-taking and name-calling is rife. Players talk about 'slaughtering' each other. Sometimes this takes the form of vandalism, such as the cutting up of suits and shoes. A lot of the time it's simply calling each other by silly nicknames. Some of these nicknames don't need much deciphering. Both Darren Anderton and Steve McManaman are known by the other players in their team as Shaggy; and it's true, they do both look a little like the *Scooby Doo* character minus the bumfluff. Other nicknames are much more complex. Newcastle's Warren Barton, Rob Lee revealed in a recent interview, is known at the club as the Dog. Why? Because he wears expensive clothes and thinks he's the dog's bollocks, that's why.

Piss-taking amongst footballers isn't a new thing. Chelsea's first goalkeeper William Foulke, who weighed in at up to twenty-two stone during his professional career, was nicknamed Cheesecake by his team-mates. His response was, apparently, typical of the man, who once got up early and ate the whole team's breakfast: 'I don't mind what you call me, as long as you don't call me late for lunch.'

Nicknames can come from all sorts of places. Sometimes they are from other famous namesakes. John Barnes is nicknamed Digger Barnes after the old fellah in *Dallas* (though some are of the opinion that it is rhyming slang made up by racist Liverpool fans. Such racism certainly existed – when Barnes arrived at the club some lowlife sprayed 'I'd rather be dead than see a nigger play in red' on one of the walls outside Anfield). French defender Basil Boli was renamed Basil Fawlty after a nightmare period at Rangers. Liverpool goalkeeper David James was known as Calamity James after a butter-fingered end to the 1996-97 season. Strict Spanish ref Manuel Diaz Vega is better known in his home country as Darth Vader.

Other names are childhood names that have stuck. Dixie Dean was called William Ralph Dean and he hated being called Dixie. It was a name he acquired as a child, not as a footballer, possibly because he had crinkly black hair which he tried to grease straight, possibly because of a childhood game called Digsie Dean in which you could dig your nails into another child's back while tagging them.

Gazza was originally called Gassa by his friends, just like his dad had been, but it was unwittingly changed by a schoolmaster from Sunderland who couldn't pronounce it. Ironically things turned full circle when the football 'humour' magazine *Sweet FA* ran a strip cartoon about a Geordie footballer who couldn't stop farting, called Gassa.

Some nicknames are simply derived from players' own names.

Dragan Dzajic, the Yugoslav outside left from the 1960s and 1970s was nicknamed the Magic Dragon. The brilliant Austrian forward Ernst Ocwirk was renamed Clockwork Ocwirk. 1980s Spanish striker Emile Butragueño was nicknamed *El Buitre*, Spanish for the Vulture. And, closer to home, Tommy Docherty was blessed with a nickname that couldn't have suited the homespun philosopher more: the Doc.

Sometimes players try to invent their own nicknames. The most famous example is Paul Ince, who liked to be known as the Guv'nor and tried to get all his team-mates to call him it. According to Mark Bright, who recently interviewed him for *Total Sport* magazine, Ince used to answer his phone with the words 'Guv'nor here'. Ince is now trying to get rid of the name, which is maybe why Liverpool players have started using it; something that never happened at Manchester United. Ince's latest nickname was made up by Paul Gascoigne during the Italy-England World Cup qualifier in Rome when Ince had a white bandage on his head, and it's stuck much faster than the Guv'nor. Bandage or no bandage it seems as though England's latest hero will have to put up with being called Guinness for some time. Making up your own name often doesn't work out right. Former Brighton and briefly England hero Steve Foster tells a funny story about Les Sealey, his goalkeeper whilst at Luton. 'One day he announced he wanted to be known as the Cat,' Foster recalls. 'We'd be playing a match and you'd hear "the Cat's ball!"and Les would come for it. But he didn't always get there so Mick Harford christened him Tiddles.'

If you can't make up your own nickname and your team-mates haven't bothered, there's always the chance that the press will step in and have a go. Thus most of the historical nicknames that we have been passed down for players aren't of the Giggsy or Chopper variety.

Nat Lofthouse, for example, was dubbed the Lion of Vienna by the press after helping England destroy the Austrian 'Wunderteam' in 1952. Now I've no doubt that this wasn't what his team-mates called him. Anyone who said in training ' 'Ere Lion of Vienna, pass us the ball' was looking to get shoulder-barged into the Irish Sea.

Nevertheless there is a certain reverential old-fashioned charm about many of the press-created nicknames that we have inherited. One of the leading figures of post-war football, Ferenc Puskas, who would now probably have been named by the tabloids something like Porky Puskas for his ample girth, was known as the Galloping Major. His team-mate at Real Madrid, Alfredo di Stefano, was known as the White Arrow. There's poetry in these names, born of the deference for the men's skill. Mozambique-born Eusebio was known as the Black Pearl for the colour of his skin, Russian goalkeeper Lev Yashin the Black Panther for the colour of his shirt. Some of the names have a charm and naivety that wouldn't be possible in this day and age. Alec Jackson, the old Huddersfield and Chelsea winger, was known as the Gay Cavalier. Len Shackleton was called the Clown Prince of Soccer, Portsmouth's Jim Dickinson was known as Gentleman Jim because of his fair-minded style of play, and John Charles was called *Il Buon Gigante* 'the Gentle Giant', by Italian fans because he was never booked, a name which travelled back up with him when he returned to Britain. My favourite old-fashioned press nickname is one given to Luigi Riva, the 1960s and 1970s Cagliari and Italy striker who was known, rather poetically, as the Rumble of Thunder.

The modern British press, especially the tabloids, is a little more mundane in its choice of nicknames. Usually they are alliterative and only last as long as they are relevant. 'King Kev' can easily lose his crown. The two which have really stuck are for successive England managers. The first is the nickname Turnip which was used in the *Sun's* systematic attempt to oust Graham Taylor from his position as national manager during the 1994 World Cup qualifying campaign (see chapter 41). The second is a name which is inspired in its simplicity and has stuck ever since – it had already long been attributed to Terry Venables when he got the job as England manger. He acquired it, in fact, when he got the job as Barcelona manager in 1984 and became, forever more, El Tel. I'm looking forward to Shearer moving to Spain and getting renamed after an Israeli airline.

Part Four
On the Park

- 16 -
'On the 'Ead, Son' – Talking a Good Game

Despite having a worse-than-mediocre record since I took over from Clive (four wins, three draws, ten defeats), as I write I am still the player-manager of Clissold Park Rovers. One of the many things I have to do in this role is to shout instructions, constructive criticism and encouragement to 'my' players throughout the match. One thing I shouldn't do is get into slanging matches with our goalkeeper and lose track of the ball, nearly letting the opposition in to score; but that's another matter.

I'm not the only one on the pitch shouting; some players are quieter than others, but everyone needs to keep up a constant barrage of shouting and instruction. It's a team game, after all, and one of the important parts of being a team is letting your team-mates know what's going on.

In my short playing career (this is the first time I have played eleven-a-side football for a team competing in a league) I have had to learn a whole new language; one that I previously had a passive knowledge of, but not an active one. Playing in London I have picked up a Southern dialect of football talk – in other parts of the country some expressions will be different.

One thing that you have to learn is the register of on-pitch football talk. Sometimes I get this wrong and end up sounding like a bit of a wally. Recently our right wing back, Mike, lost the ball with a careless pass during an important game. Angered by his mistake he upped his aggression and won the ball back. 'Well redeemed,' I shouted, only to receive a glare and a few choice words back. At half time I asked him what his problem was. Because I hadn't been speaking in the right register he hadn't understood me, and had assumed I was criticising him. What I should have said was 'well won' or 'well in'. In the tense atmosphere of a game, he would have recognised these stock words and been fired up by the praise. The word 'redeemed' didn't belong in the context of a football match and therefore (despite the fact that Mike, a barrister, was well aware of what the word meant) didn't have any meaning for him. I might as well have been yelling in Turkish.

One of the earliest bits of pitchspeak that you learn is the phrase 'man on'. This is directed at a member of your team who is in possession of the ball, and roughly speaking it means 'there's an opposition player coming up quickly behind you who is likely to rid you of the ball if you don't do something about it'. By the time you're three syllables into shouting 'there's an opp...' your team-mate has been robbed, so a shorter phrase is necessary. It's a little like shouting 'timber!' in a forest or 'fore!' on a golf course. I've often wondered how many fewer players would be dispossessed from behind if football had invented a one syllable warning, but it's too late now. The Newcastle crowd, by the way, shout 'man on' during matches, which shows that a large proportion of them have been football players themselves.

'Man on' is a warning; other instructions used in football matches are in a similar shorthand. Many of these terms are used to instruct the player in possession where you are, so he can give the ball to you. 'Line it', 'line ball', 'down the line' or 'knock it line' means that you are screaming down the wing ready to receive the ball. 'Square ball' means that you are to the side of the man with the ball, 'back door' that you are behind him. 'Switch it' means that you are right on the other side of the pitch. 'Give and go' or 'little one-two' means that you want the ball, but you are willing to give it back to him if he carries on running. Sometimes you feel that another team-mate is in a good position to receive a ball from you. In that case you could say 'John's free' or 'John's good'. If you want the ball yourself, and you're called Trevor, you could shout 'Trevor wants'.

If you are in a position you feel you can score from if you are given the ball your instructions tend to take on more urgency. They might be where you want the ball in relation to yourself ('on me 'ead/nut', 'on the volley', 'to feet'); instructions as to where in the box you are ('near post, back stick') or simply instructions to get the bloody thing across ('cross/knock it in', 'get it in the box'). If the player looks like he isn't going to carry out your instructions, or if he's just lost the ball by dilly-dallying around too long, 'for fuck's sake' is a common tag to these expressions.

Sometimes you feel that your team-mate is in a good position to score himself, but that he needs some encouragement to do so. 'Have a dig' usually does the trick, though 'dig' can be replaced with 'poke', 'go', 'shot' or even 'pot'. Alternative ways of saying this are simply shouting 'shoot' or 'hit it': the latter, especially in London and environs, is usually reduced to ''i' i''.

The defence has its own language. If the opposition get a throw-in, corner or a free kick in your half you have to make sure all the opposition attackers are marked by a defender. 'Grab a shirt' or 'mark up' usually suffices. If you see an unmarked man, you shout something like 'who's on seven?' or 'who's on baldie?'. 'Goal side' ensures that your players are the right side of the players they are attempting to mark. If the opposition get the ball, and look like taking a shot, you need some fool to get in front of him to block it; 'Close 'im down' is the shout required. If your clumping left back gets the ball and you want him to put it into touch, 'get rid' is the requisite term. If, however, no opponent is in the near vicinity 'time' is the call. (Before our Clissold Park left back Danny gets annoyed, by the way 'clumping left back' doesn't refer to him.)

When you play the 'flat back four' system in a 4-4-2 formation, it's important to push the attackers up to as near their halfway line as possible, so they haven't much room to pass the ball about in and they are more likely to get offside. 'Push up' is the shout, making sure that the other defenders keep up with you.

One time it's highly necessary to communicate to your team-mates is when you call for the ball. Simply shouting 'my ball' is considered to be a foul as the opposition might have thought that one of their players shouted it. Therefore you shout 'John!' or 'John's ball!' (if your name, of course, is John). Another verbal foul (and both are seen to contravene the laws on obstruction) is to shout 'leave it' when the ball is about to go off the pitch. What you must shout is 'leave it, goalkeeper', 'leave it, Giovanni' or 'leave it, yellows' to indicate who you mean to let the ball run. As simply 'leave it' is the natural thing to shout, you often have to add the last word as an afterthought, sharpish, before the referee blows his whistle and gives the opposition an indirect free kick in a very dangerous position.

It's highly important for the team captain or player-manager to keep encouraging his team to play well and keep their heads up. 'Come on, yellows, we can win this one' is the sort of thing that usually comes out. Sometimes the encouragement can border on the desperate. At 3-0 down I've actually heard myself yelling 'just two goals and we're only one behind', which didn't work at all – we lost 6-0. It's also important to ensure the whole team is talking to each other, which gives rise to my least favourite piece of football language. I've yelled 'talk to each other' and 'keep talking', but I've never, and I hope I will *never*, plumb such depths as to shout 'plenty of bunny'.

Each team has at least one player on the pitch who has the brief of yelling instructions and encouragement to his players. The most famous in professional English football is Peter Schmeichel who has developed a Manchester accent with which to berate his defence. Schmeichel, who I've been told (by Ryan Giggs, no less) is exactly the same off the pitch as on it, has given himself the role of 'keeping the defence on its toes'. This means that he screams his head off at a quartet of millionaires when he is called on to do anything. The most entertaining thing about Manchester United (a highly entertaining side, it must be said) is Schmeichel's reaction when they concede a goal. But he reserves his most vitriolic abuse of his defenders when he himself makes a rare mistake. The best occasion was when he kicked a goal-kick straight into touch and proceeded to harangue his defence for it. Other great shouters of our time include (and it's noticeable that they both play in the same position) are Peter Shilton and Bruce Grobbelaar, who once got so irate with the young Steve McManaman that after giving him an earful of abuse he gave him an earful of the palm of his hand, too.

The hoarsest people after games, however, are usually the managers. Until 1994 'coaching from the sidelines' wasn't permitted at all by FIFA rules, which didn't stop managers from doing it. It was probably the most ignored rule of the lot – in the 1970s Malcolm Allison, sick of simply yelling instructions from the side of the pitch, actually ran on to it and pushed winger Alan Whittle five yards further up the pitch from where he had been operating. And we all saw Graham Taylor's antics on the bench in the Channel 4 *Cutting Edge* video where, as well as giving the nation the catchphrase 'do I not like that', managed to say the word 'fuck' more times than his team managed to string passes together.

For the World Cup in 1994 FIFA decided that making managers shut up was an impossible task and wrote what they imaginatively dubbed the 'technical area' into the rules. This is a space which stretches one metre to the side of the dug-out to one metre from the edge of the pitch, in which the manager can stand when the game is in progress and yell to his heart's content. The area is sometimes painted on to the grass, but is usually up to the referee's discretion. The manager can thus talk to his midfield and attack – but will find his goalkeeper beyond even foghorn-voice range, which is why West Ham manager Harry Redknapp took to sending the ball-boy round to keeper Ludo Miklosko with his tactical instructions.

- 17 -
That Deaf, Dumb and Blind Kid Sure Plays Mean Football

Talking on the pitch has always been pretty important, which is why deafness is a major handicap in football. This was recognised as early as 1917, when it was written in the *Sportsman*:

> *It is a decided handicap to any player if his sense of hearing is not acute. The occasional calls from his captain as to tactics are liable to be missed and those short, sharp words or cries by which one player appeals to another in a sudden contingency, necessitate quick hearing if they are to be effective.*

This problem was overcome by Tommy Boyle, the minute Burnley centre half of the 1920s. Boyle was a 'talker', one of those players who needed to keep a constant barrage of chat going through the match. He had problems, however, with the Burnley outside right Nesbitt, who was stone deaf. It is understood that Boyle invented a kind of sign language to communicate with this team-mate. Sadly the details of what signals he made for which contingency have been lost.

In November 1997 the *Sun* reported on Rotherham Deaf FC, who lost 45-0 to local rivals Rotherham Rangers. The prime reason stated was that they had just devised a new offside system but it didn't work because they couldn't hear their manager when he shouted for them to move up. And when they did move up they couldn't hear the referee's whistle to find out if the trap had worked or not. Oh, and they also started the match with eight men. In typical upbeat *Sun* fashion the piece was ended with a quote from a spokesman from their opponents, 'Those deaf lads are a credit to football. They never stopped battling.'

Communication is of prime importance in blind football, too. I watched the Blind European Championships in Banbury in May 1997. If you've never heard about this version of the sport you'd be forgiven for wondering how it can be played at all. But it can. And it was an uplifting privilege to witness it.

The plastic ball is filled with 150 ball bearings to enable the players to chart its progress when it is near them. A bleeper is placed centrally behind the goal to let strikers know where to shoot. The six-a-side game is played on a 60 by 40 metre pitch. The goalkeeper is sighted, but his movement is restricted to within a three-metre box. All the other players are blindfolded so partially sighted players have no advantage. In the game of blind football the one-eyed striker would be virtually unstoppable.

There is much more sound during the matches than there is in a sighted match. Each player is constantly yelling his whereabouts to his team-mates. There is a coach on each touchline telling the players where to run.

Banbury had seen its worst storms for years when I went there, and the pitch was a quagmire, which had, as captain Dave Clarke later told me 'severely restricted England's passing game'. The result was that the ball kept on stopping and losing its sound. The players would wander around, to the instructions 'left a bit, two paces forward, right a bit' until they found the ball, then play would resume. Sometimes, when nobody was anywhere near the stationary ball, and wandering round in increasingly desperate circles, the referee would pick it up, shake it a couple of times, then roll it back into play.

There is a 'rolling substitutes' allowance, and when I arrived at the ground, two of the England subs were standing behind the posts of the Italian goal. 'I'm a post,' shouted one, when England were on the attack. 'I'm the other post,' shouted another. As the half-time whistle went, the England coach told the subs to stop this, because they were only confusing matters. 'We're only telling him where the fucking posts are,' came the reply.

Thanks to this unique form of communication the game worked, and was played with great spirit. There were no dirty players, but a few were rather over-enthusiastic, and the referee had to ignore (it was difficult to stop myself writing the obvious bad pun there) a number of accidental fouls. However, the event, which was won by Spain, who beat France 6-2 in the final, was competed for with a good deal of sportsmanship. And a good deal of humour, too. At one point an English striker, looking to cross the ball into the box, accidentally kicked it straight into touch. The referee gave a corner. '*Pure tu sei ciecco*, referee?' yelled the Italian goalkeeper. (Are you blind, too?)

- 18 -
Language, Please

An important part of sighted players' on-the-pitch language is swearing. Professional players' do it all the time – so much so that *Match of the Day* regularly get deaf viewers who can lip-read writing in to complain.

The most common target for this sort of abuse, of course, is the referee. Players swear at the referee all the time. The subject was documented several years ago when the TV series *Out of Order* wired up Premier League referee David Elleray at an Arsenal match. Before the game Elleray told the players that everything they said would be recorded and might later be used as evidence against them, but they still swore their way through the game.

I rang Elleray up to find out about the incident, and he told me that the programme had distorted the incident a bit to stitch Arsenal up by adding bleeps even over pre-9-o'clock-watershed adjectives. But yes, it was true that players swore all the time.

It isn't actually against the rules for players to swear, because if it was, says Elleray, there would never be any room in the early bath. 'The rules actually state that players shouldn't use "offensive, insulting or abusive language",' he explains, 'and we have the capacity to give players yellow cards or send them off if they break these rules.'

It's an interesting ambiguously phrased law, because what is 'offensive' depends on the offendability of the referee. 'It's a question of interpretation,' Elleray continues, 'you have to make a distinction between industrial language, that a player might use in his everyday life talking to his girlfriend or his mates, and actual abusive language. So if a player says, "oh f-ing hell, that wasn't a corner" you'd let it go, but if they said "that wasn't a corner, you *%$@!" you wouldn't. You also have to judge the manner in which it's said, the sort of body language that goes with it, and its audibility. I don't often have to send players off, but it happens occasionally. In 1997 I sent Duncan Ferguson off for going too far. Obviously I can't tell you exactly what he said to me.' Obviously.

Of course complaining about the referee's decisions is by no means a new part of the game, though perhaps the language used was not always quite so abrasive. In 1957, for example, Leicester City's Johnny Morris got suspended for two weeks for suggesting that the referee needed to buy himself a pair of glasses.

Touching the referee, on the other hand, is right out of order. In October 1997 Arsenal midfielder Emmanuel Petit was sent off for pushing the referee in the chest. In 1991 Bulgarian striker Hristo Stoichkov was banned for two months for stamping on the referee's foot while playing for Barcelona in a Spanish Cup match. In 1912 referee William Ernest Williams was attacked and killed in the changing rooms after a match between two teams in South Wales.

The referee isn't the only person on the pitch who gets intimidation aimed at him. What is known as 'sledging' in cricket has got a rather less colourful moniker in football. Insulting another player is known as giving him verbals. Garth Crooks has recently spilt the beans on the subject in *Goal* magazine. There is a famous incident from an FA Cup tie in the 1980s when a top-flight player announced that he'd slept with an opponent's wife so loud that all the other players heard. The referee, who would have been justified in booking the insulter (for obstruction, incidentally) let play go on as a corner was in progress. The next thing he knew he was stopping play to call for a stretcher. The 'cuckold' had exacted his revenge and the ref hadn't seen anything. The crowd, who hadn't heard the comment, remained none the wiser as to the reason for the moment of madness.

Well-paid players are likely to sidle up to underpaid ones and say 'How much are you on then?' Brian Honour of Hartlepool complained after a Coca Cola Cup match between the North Eastern minnows and Premiership club Sheffield Wednesday that Carlton Palmer had sidled up to him during the game and asked him how he got by on £300 a week, and whether he wanted to see 'one of my cars or houses'. International players might ask unrecognised ones to 'put your caps on the table'. Young players get a lot of stick with comments like 'How many games have you played?' and Alan Hansen's famous 'you win nothing with kids' delivered at a particularly undermining moment.

If an opponent is playing badly you can insult him with comments like 'you couldn't trap a bag of cement' or 'don't bother tackling him, he'll just give it to you if you stand next to him'.

Some players use racist comments to put their opponents off. The issue was highlighted in 1996-97 when Ian Wright accused Peter Schmeichel of insulting him by referring to his colour. The *News of the World* employed a lip-reader to work out exactly what the Danish keeper said. If Wright had decided to pursue the matter further Schmeichel could have found himself in bigger trouble than he was already in. Wright stated that the problem was much worse in the Sunday Leagues, where he started his playing career. In the same season Bari FC, a team of Asian players, was fined £200 for getting involved in a fight with their opponents after a match which was heavily punctuated with racial abuse. One of the opposing team is alleged to have stated 'let's have a Paki-bashing spree' before the game and things got worse from there, with a fan at one point letting his dog loose to attack an Asian player. The problem of such abuse is being tackled by an organisation set up specifically for the purpose, appropriately named Let's Kick Racism Out of Football.

Verbals aren't a new thing. Tommy Lawton, the Everton and Chelsea centre forward of the 1930s and 1940s recalled of his early playing days, 'Alf Young, who was England's centre half, was playing against me, and he said, "Are you young Lawton?" I said, "Aye, I am." "Well now, I'm just warning you. Now thee can go past and the bloody ball can go past, but thee and the ball are not going past together. I've heard you can go a bit, and I believe that, but you're not as big as me and I'll be sure to bring you down to my speed." '

And Jimmy Greaves writes in his autobiography *This One's On Me* that gritty Bolton defender Tommy Banks used to say to Chelsea winger Peter Brabook, 'If thou tries to get past me, lad, thou will get gravel rash.'

Players can communicate their messages without talking. It's common practice for full backs to 'soften up' the opposing winger with a crunching tackle early in the game to show him that he's not in for an easy match. Some players go further and do an 'over the top' tackle where they pretend to go for the ball but miss it and crunch into the opponent's leg instead. Flying fourteen-stone men landing in your shin via their studs hurts a bit, even if you are wearing shinpads. Another trick, made famous by Vinny Jones with Paul Gascoigne as the victim, is to squeeze your opponent's testicles. This move was also performed by Spanish international Michel in a Spanish league match with Colombian midfielder Carlos Valderrama the target. Unfortunately for Michel the TV cameras picked up on this and, in former Ireland international Michael Robinson's top-rating show *Lo que el ojo no ve*, replayed it time and again to the music of *The Sting*. The fans started singing 'Michel Maricon' – Michel is a homosexual – from the terraces and his career was never quite the same again. Robinson, in case you were wondering, got into Spanish TV after playing out his career at Pamplona club Osasuna and now is one of the most popular TV presenters in the country.

Usually verbal or physical intimidation suffices but occasionally matters boil over to the extent that players start to do their talking with their fists. It's nothing new: back in the 19th century the *Oswestry Observer* noted that 'sometimes a kick on the shins would lead the two men concerned to abandon the game until they had decided who was the better pugilist'.

Kevin Keegan and the late Billy Bremner were the protagonists in the country's most famous punch-up, though Bremner hardly deserves his notoriety, having done nothing. In an otherwise dull Charity Shield game in 1974 Liverpool were on the attack but Keegan was dispossessed by Johnny Giles, who, as the ball went upfield, followed his tackle with a left hook to the chin that sent Keegan crashing to the floor. When he got up Keegan wrongly identified Billy Bremner as his assailant, and started to attack him, held back by his team-mates and opponents. Giles had escaped from the scene. The referee sent both Bremner and Keegan off.

The Leeds side of the 1970s were well known for their unwillingness to take prisoners, and were involved in another famous punch-up a little over a year later in a match against Derby County. Francis Lee was tackled on the edge of the box by Norman Hunter, then, as he was getting to his feet, thumped in the head by the Leeds defender. It took four players to stop Lee from getting his revenge, and the referee sent off both players. He should have made them go off one at a time, because Lee was still fuming. On the way to the tunnel he suddenly erupted, swinging his arms round like a little kid who hasn't got his way and connecting a couple of times with Hunter's head. Again he had to be restrained.

Individual flare-ups can quickly lead to whole teams getting involved in the action as happened twice in consecutive seasons to George Graham's Arsenal. In November 1989 they were involved in a twenty-one-man brawl with Norwich City at Highbury, which was only the hors d'oeuvres for their 'Battle of Old Trafford' dust-up a year later. It started with Mark Hughes being sandwich-tackled by Anders Limpar from the front and Nigel Winterburn from the back. The ball fell loose, and Brian McClair, possibly attempting to kick it, instead connected with Winterburn, who was still lying on the ground. Seeing their comrade thus maltreated, the rest of the Arsenal team (except for David Seaman) decided to seek revenge. McClair was punched by Limpar, pushed by Michael Thomas and Paul Davis, throttled by Thomas and shoved over the touchline by Tony Adams. United didn't stand by and watch though, with Paul Ince, in particular, trying his damnedest to exact revenge. Arsenal were deducted two points and United one but the punishment didn't worry the London team, who took a stranglehold on the League, which they won by seven points, losing only one match (2-1 to Chelsea) in the process.

Fights between opposing players is one thing, but we're talking major communication breakdown when two players from the same team start laying into one another. Charlton's striking partners Mick Flanagan and Derek Hales had one memorable fracas in the 1970s, and in October 1997 Eyal Berkovic and John Moncur had a bit of a set-to. The most recent memorable example of 'friendly fire' was when Blackburn were competing in the Champions League away to Spartak Moscow in November 1995. Champions Blackburn were a side in decline after the loss of their inspirational manager Kenny Dalglish to that mysterious place they call 'upstairs' (which turned out in his case to be the golf course), and were having an awful time in an easy-looking group. In the second half David Batty and Graeme Le Saux both went for the same ball – neither got it with Le Saux tripping over his team-mate and the ball going into touch. The death of the ball gave the players the chance to vent their fury. Batty said something to Le Saux (and as yet nobody has revealed what it was) which made the wing back thump him in the ear so hard that his fingers had to be bandaged up afterwards. Blackburn lost the game 3-0 and with it their slim chances of qualifying from the group.

- 19 -
Which Way to the Diving School?

One of the more heart-stopping moments in England's World Cup qualifying decider against Italy in Rome in September 1997 was when, in the second half, Alessandro del Piero, fresh on the pitch, ran into the English 16-yard box and, seeing Tony Adams stretch a leg out, went flying into the air, looking for a penalty. Luckily for the Englishmen the referee was near enough to see that the player was speaking his body language with a forked tongue; Adams had never touched him. This sort of behaviour has become so common in the game that FIFA have recently legislated against it and del Piero got a yellow card for his play-acting instead of a penalty.

It would be short-sighted to imagine that diving is unknown in the English game: in the 1970s *Match of the Day* opened with a sequence that showed Welsh winger Micky Thomas win a free kick from a dive, then turn round and wink at the camera to admit his cheek. However, it's true that it has become much more widespread over here since 'the new influx' of players in the mid 1990s. Particularly noted for his penchant for, as Jimmy Greaves once put it 'doing a Jacques Cousteau', was German striker Jurgen Klinsmann, who joined Spurs in the summer of 1994. Klinsmann had, in the preceding season, got Milan defender Alessandro Costacurta sent off in the European Cup semi final for a foul that never was. I interviewed Klinsmann just before his Spurs début, when he was busily engaged in a PR exercise to win over his critics. From the dastardly German dive-bomber who'd helped knock us out of Italia 90 he became a sweet man-of-the-people who drove a Volkswagen Beetle and wanted to hitch-hike round America. 'Which way to the diving school?' he had asked London journalists in one of his first press conferences, provoking inches of copy about exceptions, rules, Germans and senses of humour. 'I don't dive,' he told me, more brusquely, when I asked him of his reputation, sitting on a park bench in Tottenham's leafy Mill Hill training ground. But although he did, and he knew that I knew that everybody knew that he did, somehow everybody forgave him for it and he became an unlikely hero. And, for sure, the only time he dived in this country was during his goal celebrations, as an ironic wink at his past misdemeanours.

- 20 -
'I Didn't Touch Him, Ref'

In this day and age of multicultural and international football you'd think that players would need to start doing some sort of course in sign language to be able to communicate with foreign referees with whom they share no common tongue. Not at all. Players have been doing it for years.

Think of Tony Adams. What is the most enduring image that comes to mind? Him on his haunches delivering one of his 'Russian dance' tackles? Him rising high in his box to head the ball away? No, I'd lay a wager that it's him, back in the George Graham days, lifting an arm in the air to claim for offside.

The 'arm in the air' claim is one of the many impulsive body-language statements that players make to the referee when they want him to give a decision their way. Many of them are made when the referee has blown the whistle against that player who has commited a foul. Picture a post-foul scene: the 'offending' player is communicating to the figure in black who, having blown his whistle, is running towards him. His opponent is writhing on the ground in pain (another form of body language, often acted). There are various sign statements open to the player. Try doing the actions and you'll get what I'm on about. Hands pushed in front of the body, palms outstetched, fingers pointing up, shoulders slightly hunched means 'whoops, look, I didn't mean any harm. Please don't book me.' Hands up in the air soldier-surrendering style, shoulders hunched, means 'OK, I fouled him, but it wasn't that bad, please don't book me'. A circle made with the index fingers of both hands means 'I went for the ball'. Arms pushed horizontally outwards and away from the body, hands together, palms downwards means 'the bastard dived'.

In Italy gesticulation is just as commonplace on the pitch as in the piazzas. One of my fondest memories of a football player's body language after a foul was when David Platt, newly signed for Arsenal in 1995 after spells at Bari, Juventus and Sampdoria, fell to the ground and got angry with the referee for not giving him the decision. He put his hand to his mouth and moved it back and forth in a classic Italian gesticulation which means 'you cannot be serious'. It looked a bit silly in North London. It looked much more appropriate when Alessandro del Piero did it in Rome.

- 21 -
Celebrations

Back at the beginning of this book I told you about being interviewed by a reporter at the end of one of Clissold Park Rovers' games in Hackney Marshes. That day there was a pack of reporters from the national and local press, the radio and the television at our Thames League Third Division game because we had just become the first-ever team to hire a choreographer to devise a goal celebration routine for us. It was a bit of a publicity stunt: I was writing a cover story on the subject of celebrations for *FC* football magazine.

Choreographer Kate Brown, a friend of a friend, who had previously worked on the football-inspired dance routine Over Two Legs, arrived at Hackney Marshes about an hour and a half before kick off – the bulk of the team got there with about three quarters of an hour to go. We didn't in effect have much time to learn our routine. But Kate had some ideas in mind. The scorer, she said, was to fall backwards into the arms of the four biggest players. Des, our centre forward, was chosen for the task. I took a shoulder – the other three either a shoulder or a thigh – and it was remarkably easy to hold him over our heads, arms fully straightened.

Then came the silly bit. The rest of the team was to do a pirouette behind us. We all practised, the cameras zooming in. We formed into pairs: the smaller of which took a flying feet-first leap into the air. His partner had to let the leaper's feet fly over his outstretched arms, then catch him, one hand under the arse, the other behind the back, as he fell. On catching the guy we had to spin round 360 degrees, twice. There was a lot of falling over, but in the end we got the gist.

Not content with that, Kate wanted us to practise star jumps, again in pairs. The smaller guy had to jump into the air, legs apart, arms raised diagonally into the air, with the bigger guy behind him lifting him up to give him extra height.

The whole routine, then, goes like this. The scorer runs to a phalanx of four players, turns his back to them, and drops into their arms. They hold him up horizontally and he waves his arms about. Meanwhile, behind him, the other six players (including the goalkeeper, who has run the length of the pitch) have to do two-man pirouettes and star jumps in unison. Remarkably, on the second take, it all came off. Unfortunately, that was only the dress rehearsal.

We kicked off with a strong wind blowing into our backs. But we were nervous; we had never been under such intense pressure to win, or at the very least score a goal. The photographers and TV crews were lined up behind our opponents' goal, in much the same way as they congregate behind the goal Manchester United are attacking at Old Trafford. On 23 minutes we got a corner. When the ball swung in a push in the back of Paul, our centre back, was spotted by the referee who blew for a penalty. Clive stepped up and took it – he placed it to the left, the goalkeeper (who had been a pro at Dundee United) dived to the right. Goal.

The celebrations were chaos. We raised Clive above our heads, but the goalkeeper didn't bother to turn up and the pirouetting and star jumps were a disaster. The experiment, in effect, was a failure – the routine was too complex to fulfil in the middle of an important match. And it was knackering. We scored another goal in the first half, and did another half-hearted celebration, but Daz came back in the second with two wind-assisted efforts of their own – and after each one ran to the cameras and swan-dived, Klinsmann-like, to record their own impromptu celebration.

To say that the country went goal-celebration crazy afterwards is a bit of an exaggeration; but the issue was discussed in several newspapers and magazines and we were called upon to recreate our routine live on TV twice: on the early-morning *Big Breakfast Show* and the late-night *Under the Moon*. Newspapers were ringing me up in my office for interviews. One Sunday two international camera crews turned up at Clissold Park to our jumper-for-goals kickaround – only to find there were only seven of us and I'd forgotten the shirts. They went ahead anyway.

- 22 -
A Short History of Goal Celebrations

In a way the issue was ripe for debate, which is why our little stunt got so much publicity. It's difficult to pinpoint the first scorer to eschew the typical knee-jerk hands-in-the-air response to his goal, but it's quite easy to work out why a player has more to celebrate than he used to. The phenomenon has risen sharply, in parallel with the amount of TV coverage the game is getting – and the money that goes with it.

Denis Law used to point a single finger into the air in the 1960s. Stuart Pearson clenched an aggressive fist in the mid 1970s. Mick Channon developed his bizarre windmill arm around the same time. Hugo Sanchez perfected the mid-air somersault in the 1980s – then we had Roger Milla's corner flag shuffle, Lee Sharpe's corner flag Elvis, Peter Beagrie's Hugo Sanchez, Jan-Aage Fjortoft's aeroplane, Paul Merson's lager lout, Ravanelli's shirt-over-his-head sprint, and many, many more. On realising the success of his two-gun salute a few seasons back Ian Wright decided to deliver an original routine every goal. He must lie in bed thinking about it at night. It's all a far cry from the Stanley Matthews shake-of-the-hand-and-now-let's-get-on-with-it technique.

My favourite celebration of all was by Faustino Asprilla after he scored against Metz in the UEFA Cup in December 1996. Not satisfied by his usual hand-spring somersault and fist in the air routine, 'Tino' (surely the most entertaining player, in more ways than one, in the Premiership) ripped his top off and ran to the corner flag. He then speared the shirt on to the flag and raised it above his head, waving it at the fans. He was booked under new FIFA 'excessive celebration' rules. Thankfully FIFA hasn't gone the whole hog, as the American NFL did in the 1980s, and ban celebrations entirely (giving it the nickname the 'No Fun League').

Nowadays it seems that individual celebrations are no longer enough. Football is a team game, and the person who finally puts the ball in the net has often applied the finishing touch to a move created by a number of team-mates. What's more, the whole team shares in the joy of an important goal, so the whole team should be given the right to display it by celebrating.

We can see the genesis of team celebration in the 1970s when goalscorers began to be mobbed by their team-mates and the moral majority started complaining about long-haired louts kissing and cuddling. This routine was turned horizontal in Italy in the 1980s when the goalscorer lay on his back and waited for his team-mates to form a pile on top of him, a routine famously mirrored by the Euro 92-winning Danish side.

But these celebrations were pure expressions of joy – they weren't formed in order to be of any aesthetic value for the audience. Oddly enough the first 'choreographed' team celebration was performed by a team that wasn't at the time noted for its aesthetic qualities. Wimbledon were involved in a tough penalty shoot-out with Liverpool in the League Cup in 1994. When Neil Ardley scored their winning goal he wheeled off from the box, his arms spread like an aeroplane. The rest of the Crazy Gang ran from the halfway line and, instead of jumping on him, got into formation behind him, arms outstretched, Red Arrows like.

It's unlikely that the Brazilian national team saw coverage of the match, but they pushed team celebrations on a notch in the World Cup in 1994. Bebeto, having scored Brazil's second goal against Holland in the quarter finals ran towards the touchline and, to mark the fact that he was celebrating the birth of a new baby as well as his third goal in the competition, started doing a cradling motion with his arms. Team-mates Mazinho and Romario decided to mimic him and performed the same action either side of him. It looked sensational.

Team celebrations started taking shape in the English League the next season. Jurgen Klinsmann celebrated his first goal in the Premier League by diving towards the corner flag, arms outstretched. On his home début against Everton he scored again. He also dived again. This time his team-mates, realising what he was going to do, followed suit.

Non-League Aylesbury celebrated an FA Cup first-round win in Newport (IOW) with mock Klinsmann dives, then, after a goal by striker Cliff Hercules that put Kingstonian out of the competition in the next round, performed a 'duck walk' that they'd worked out on the coach to the match, which involved going down on the knees and waddling whilst flapping their arms by their sides. The walk received a lot of attention and was repeated in the third round against QPR at Loftus Road – although the players performed it after the match, which they lost 4-0.

Further combinations followed. Ryan Giggs and Paul Ince, aping a routine originally performed by American footballers in the NFL, danced a little duet after a Manchester United goal. In the FA Cup in 1996 Watford celebrated their equalising goal at home to Wimbledon by performing a 'Dead Ants' celebration, lying on their backs and waving their legs and arms in the air. Disgusted Wimbledon striker Mick Harford stomped through the celebrating Hornets. The same season Tottenham's Ruel Fox celebrated a goal against Coventry by rubbing his legs, aping *Shooting Stars*' Vic Reeves and Bob Mortimer. In 1996-97 Sunderland celebrated a Michael Gray goal at Highbury by patting their heads and holding their noses: the celebration was in tribute to injured skipper Kevin Ball, who, as he explained afterwards 'had thinning hair and a larger-than-average-sized nose'.

It was all good clean fun – but nothing that had the Royal Ballet shaking at the knees – until Chelsea's Roberto Di Matteo scored against Middlesbrough on the opening day of the 1996-97 season, that is. The Italian midfielder lay on the ground on his side and left elbow and raised his right hand into the air. Dennis Wise, Jody Morris, Dan Petrescu followed suit, Erland Johnsen created a bit of balance by pointing his left hand in the other direction and Frank Leboeuf missed the plot completely, sitting on his bum with both arms outstretched. It quickly became the most famous goal celebration in the game. Until Clissold Park Rovers turned up on the scene, that is...

- 23 -
Come on You Barnet – The Language of Hair

Back in the days of baggy shorts and big ears it was unheard of for players to have any type of haircut apart from a traditional short back and sides. The only difference in footballers' cuts was how much Brylcreem was used and which side the parting was on. How things have changed. Nowadays footballers' hair is an important signal as to the sort of player they might be. And there's some diversity as to what signals they are trying to get across to the fans and opposing players.

With all the diversity around you've got to feel sorry for the players who are losing it. Or have you? 'He's got no hair, we don't care' sang the Wimbledon fans whenever their hero striker Alan Cork got the ball in the 1980s. They didn't seem to care that he didn't score more than two or three goals a season, either. Now it seems like every team's got a baldie and every set of fans sings the song. And if they haven't got any real baldies, they've like as not got a fake one. Ex Blackburn striker Derek Dougan started the whole thing off when he turned up to the 1960 FA Cup final with a completely shaved head. It didn't help him – they lost 3-0 to Stan Cullis's Wolves. Dougan's alliterative cousin Dion Dublin took the look into the modern era when he was playing for Cambridge – the all-brute-no-skill Marvin Hagler air it gave him deceived defenders and the slightest jink meant he was through on goal. A number of black players followed his lead – not least of them Ian Wright – and now white players are doing it, even though it makes them look daft. At Juventus Gianluca Vialli swapped his curly mop for a number zero all over, presumably to make him look more mean. His

Chelsea team-mate Frank Leboeuf followed suit when he reached London. It makes you wonder why Bobby Charlton ever bothered inventing the Bobby Charlton cut. Who did he think he was trying to fool, anyway?

But Bobby's brush-it-over technique wasn't a (bald) patch on Ralph Coates's devious locks. Coates was the first man ever to use his barnet as a tactic. The canny 1970s Tottenham winger had an exaggerated Charlton which was carefully groomed over his receding-by-the-minute pate at the beginning of the game. In a carefully rehearsed move he'd receive the ball, shimmy his hips, and with a quick burst of pace leave most of his hair in the place he'd been standing seconds before. Lunging full backs were left tackling thin hair as he broke free to deliver a telling cross for Jimmy Greaves to bundle the ball into the net. Trainers bust a gut telling defenders to watch the ball, not the hair, but to no avail.

Another popular all-or-nothing look is the come-and-'ave-a-go-if-you-think-you're-hard-enough Action Man realistic hair option sported by the likes of Sunderland's 'diminutive' midfielder Lee Clarke and its inventor Steve Bull, who's had as many haircuts at the club as he's scored goals, and as few styles as he's had clubs. Consistent haircut, goes the theory, consistent performance.

From one extreme to another. Back in the early 1970s the saying went 'more hair, more flair' and every team worth its salt had a midfield genius with dandruff all over his knees. Charlie George was the epitome of the style, using his flowing locks to help balance him as he hung in the air before volleying the ball home. There are still advocates of the style nowadays, although it doesn't always work. Darren Peacock's dragged-through-the-Arsenal-defence-backwards look may have been all very well in the nightclubs, but it always used to get in his eyes causing him to fluff backpasses and leave opposing attackers unmarked with alarming regularity; once he got himself an elastic band and started sporting a ponytail he became one of the better defenders in the Premiership. The beginning of the 1996-97 season saw the arrival of two long-haired Czech internationals on the scene, Patrik Berger and Karel Poborsky. Berger tied his back with an Alice band that had opposing fans whooping with homophobic glee. Poborsky, perhaps to deflect any ridicule, seemed to tie his up with a bit of old string. Talk about ugly challenges.

The liberated philosophies of the 1960s and 1970s led to another remarkable phenomenon that rocked footie to its foundations. The FA made a law change awarding points not according to results but according to how big players could grow their Pop Larkin mutton chops. *Match of the Day* ran 'sideburn of the month' competitions which were regularly won by George Best until Malcolm MacDonald came along. His love handles were so long they nearly met at the bottom of his chin and they were so thick you could hang three Burnley defenders from each one.

Luckily the FA saw the error of its ways in the late 1970s and changed the rules according to the fashion dictates of the era, devising a system whereby in the case of a draw away perms counted double. Stan Bowles started the whole thing off and pretty soon headers became a rarity as players didn't want to mess their hair up. Kevin Keegan gleefully swapped his shaggy dog and sideburns for a lovely bubble perm, became a pop star, then jetted off to play in Germany. When he came back nobody told him perms were out and he carried on sporting one until the end of his playing days. When somebody did tell him he jumped into a helicopter and said he was leaving the game for good. It took him nearly ten years to show his face again. I'll never forget the time when I arrived to watch Brighton play in 1979 to find that Peter Sullivan, our veteran moustachio'd Irish winger, had got himself a perm, meaning that of the eleven that started the game, only Brian Horton didn't have curls. And he didn't have much choice.

David Armstrong, at the same time Britain's most expensive and least hairy footballer, was in the same boat, receding so fast that you could actually see a difference in his hairline from the start of the match to the finish. At the other end of the scale Wolves' naturally curly defender George Berry got well irked that everyone was copying his waves and grew his afro to ridiculous proportions to keep ahead of the pack which gave him a huge advantage in the aerial battles he was so partial to.

The early 1980s saw the economy booming and players starting to get wideboy flicks to help them and their agents swing multi-million-pound deals. Everton suddenly became the best team in the country due to having the most flicks per squad, and north of the border Damon Grant lookalike Charlie Nicholas scored fifty goals a season for Celtic, regularly wheedling his way past defenders with a shrug of his cheque-book, before moving down south to Arsenal, where he vowed not to get it cut until he scored ten goals in a season. It grew and grew and grew, and by the time he moved back over the border he looked like the wideboy of Borneo.

By the late 1980s the recession had hit again and everyone had had enough of the nonsense. Gary Lineker sported a 'boy-next-door' look that kept his name out of referees' notebooks but regularly on the score-sheet. His England team-mate Chris Waddle took ages to twig on, managing to cut the top and sides short, but forgetting to tell his barber to lop off the back, leaving an absurd plume trailing over his collar and looking like a dodgy German tourist. He was crap, and roundly booed whenever he got the ball. When he did cut the back off in the middle of the 1990 World Cup, the inverse Samson effect came into effect; he became the best player in Europe and England nearly won the World Cup. Unfortunately nobody told Graham Taylor he'd been to the barber's and he left him out of the England team.

Now we're in the nervous 1990s and the whole thing's gone haywire again. We haven't quite hit the heights of the silly 1970s, but nowadays at least there's a lot more diversity; it seems anything can happen in footballers' hairdressers', and usually does. Jason Lee is a case in point. The poor boy tied his dreads up in such a way that the whole deal resembled a pineapple on his head, a fact that was noted with much mirth by David Baddiel and Frank Skinner on their late-night show *Fantasy Football.* National ridicule followed, Lee couldn't walk past a school without the kids chanting 'he's got a pineapple on his head' and he dropped down the divisions – not forgetting to take a trip to the barber on the way.

Perhaps the whole silly business is summed up by Paul Gascoigne, who has settled into a more natural look after a series of misdemeanours that would have seen him locked up in a less liberal society. Perhaps worst of all – and I'm forgetting the hair extensions here – was his bleached stubble look that became quite fashionable for a short time both on and off the football pitch. Still, it didn't look as bad as Andy Townsend's bottle-blond look in the 1994 World Cup. Townsend himself admitted he'd made a mistake. 'I asked for a Valderrama and they gave me a Val Doonican,' he said afterwards.

- 24 -
Collar Co-ordination – The Language of Clothes

There are many other forms of body language that help players distinguish themselves as individuals on the pitch – and it's usually the flair players who feel that they have to, despite the fact that they stand out from the others anyway. Traditionally such players (Charlie George, Tony Currie, Glenn Hoddle) proclaimed their genius by letting their socks fall down to their ankles and untucking their shirts, but FIFA have legislated against such sloppy behaviour (honest!) and nowadays players need to be a bit more subtle in their self-identification.

Eric Cantona, one of the most gifted footballers to have played in this country, used to turn his Manchester United collar up to give himself a James Dean look on the pitch. Neil Ruddock used to annoy the hell out of him during Liverpool-Man U games by turning it down for him whenever he was in range. Rumours that he left United because of their new choice of floppy, unturnuppable collars in 1997-98 proved unfounded. Ian Wright went the other way with his Arsenal collar until a design change stopped him in his tracks. He used to tuck it inside his shirt which gave him a curious 1970s-round-collar look. Emile Heskey, as well as some of the other Leicester players, took to slicing the bottom of the 'v' on their collars to make it look more open. Or was that the stitching just coming undone?

Another way of asserting your independence is with your boots. A couple of idiosyncratic cartoon players (there was a gypsy kid I remember in *Tiger* magazine and the big-breasted Red Indian Brown Fox in *Billy the Fish*) used to wear no boots; I've done it in kickarounds, and I wouldn't advise it – you tend to wimp out of tackles and it stings when you blast the ball. Incredibly enough, though, in the 1930s a Celtic player, an Egyptian called Abdul Samir, used to play with bandages round his feet. In the 1950s India qualified for the World Cup, but pulled out when they were told they wouldn't be allowed to play in bare feet.

There has been a spate recently of players wearing coloured boots to help them stand out from the crowd, whether they be in the top flight (Paolo di Canio, Benito Carbone, John Barnes) or right at the bottom of the football league. Brighton's Robbie Reinelt scored the goal that saved them from losing their league status with a red-booted foot – the boots had been a birthday present from his girlfriend, Lisa.

This sort of behaviour isn't a new thing. Alan Ball and Peter Taylor wore white boots in the early 1970s, and Herbert Chapman, innovator extraordinaire and winner of five League Championships as manager of Huddersfield and Arsenal, used to sport yellow boots in his playing days.

Other accessories have been sported by maverick players. Savo Milosevic used to wear a bandana while he was a national hero playing for Red Star Belgrade (and Yugoslavia). Wisely he chose not to wear it when he came to Aston Villa. Jens Knudsen made the bobble hat a vital fashion accessory in the Faroe Islands when he wore one for the Isles' first official international against Austria. The Faroes won 1-0 in one of the greatest shocks of international football history. Soon, however, manager Alan Simonsen banned the hat in a bid to make the team seem more professional.

Steve Foster, Brighton and later Aston Villa and Luton's gargantuan defender, wore a characteristic white headband throughout his career. At one point Fozzie was partnered by Eric Young – who also wore a headband, though his was brown. Both claimed that the article was there to protect scar tissue, though it might be argued that it helped Foster head the ball. It obviously saved a few brain cells...nowadays Foster is doing very nicely thank you as a players' insurance agent.

Feyenoord forward Joop Van Deale, who would no doubt argue he didn't belong in this list because it was out of necessity rather than fashion, used to play in specs. Feyenoord got to the final of the World Club Cup in 1970 against Argentine side Estudiantes – and sub Van Deale scored, only to have his glasses ripped off him and stamped on by an Argentinian defender. The Dutchman had the last laugh – his turned out to be the winning goal.

Another recent phenomenon of players who want to individualise themselves is to wear message-bearing T-shirts under their club shirts – and certain companies have been quick to capitalise on the fact.

As far as I can find, the player who started the craze off was Paul Tait, who, after winning the Auto Windscreens Shield at Wembley in 1995 for Birmingham City (with, incidentally, the first-ever 'golden goal') ripped off his shirt to reveal another underneath bearing the message 'Birmingham shit on the Villa'. It didn't ring true as City had just scraped a victory over lowly Carlisle, but who's arguing?

Shirt messages needn't just be expressions of tribal aggression. When Inter Milan played Torino in 1995 both teams wore a set of Greenpeace shirts which Inter's Nicola Berti promised they'd reveal when a player scored a goal for either team. Luckily the match didn't finish 0-0 – Torino's Rizitelli notched a rare goal and another blow to French President Jacques Chirac's nuclear testing in the South Pacific.

In 1996-97 Robbie Fowler and Steve McManaman quite rightly decided that the Liverpool dockers' strike wasn't getting enough public attention, and both wore T-shirts supporting the action. When Fowler scored he ripped off his shirt, and was later fined £900 by UEFA, who are wary of football being used for political ends. It was the first time some of the national papers even mentioned the strike.

UEFA had no such problems with Dennis Wise, though, when he pulled up his shirt to reveal a message to Gianluca Vialli, who was sitting on the substitute bench. Scrawled on the shirt were the words 'Cheer up Luca, we all love you'. Vialli had been moping about being a reserve. Similarly Ian Wright, shortly after being quoted as saying he was ready to leave Arsenal, apologised publicly to his team-mates with the under-shirt message 'I love the lads'.

Middlesbrough's sponsors grew a little worried when Ravanelli and his shirt-over-head goal celebration routines hit the North East. When the camera panned in to the Italian's ecstatic headless chicken routine, the logo on the Middlesbrough shirt was no longer visible. The solution was easy. Ravanelli wore a 'Cellnet' T-shirt under his shirt. Similarly Nike contacted one of their stars, Ian Wright, when he was two goals away from breaking Cliff Bastin's long-term scoring record for Arsenal of 178 goals. Wright scored a hat-trick against Bolton to bag the record, and after his first goal pulled up his shirt to reveal the slogan '179 – Just Done It!'. Yes, that's right, his first goal. Never mind.

Players often try to make a statement with their dress sense off the park as well as on it. It's nothing new, though until the abolition of the maximum wage in 1961 they had to cut their cloth according to their means. Colin Moynihan describes in his book *The Soccer Syndrome*, 'The Chelsea footballers were not dandies in those days. They dressed as well as they could afford on a £12-a-week maximum, which came into effect early in 1947, long overcoats with slightly spivvy shoulders, polished, solid shoes and gaudy ties.'

Nowadays top-flight players earn at least £12 every ten minutes (including sleeping, drinking and crapping time) so they can afford rather more flashy gear. 'I usually go out after the game wearing a normal suit,' said Liverpool goalkeeper David James in 1996, before defining what he meant by normal: 'Armani, Versace, the same as what the other players wear'.

James is a good example of a new phenomenon which has hit football – players as fashion models. Other footballers to saunter down the cat-walk include David Ginola, Phil Babb, Dean Holdsworth and Iain Dowie. OK, so maybe I was being economical with the truth about Dowie. Football flirted with fashion in the 1960s, when George Best opened a gear chain and the Chelsea players were often to be seen in the hyper-trendy King's Road – but that was nothing to nowadays when the two fields are practically blurring their distinctions. Off the pitch Chelsea have launched a successful designer-gear label and football shirts are verging on the trendy; in 1997 Norwich hired top fashion designer Bruce Oldfield to formulate their latest yellow and green kit.

Even Barry Venison, who used to wear gaudy suits with hundreds and thousands of flecks to match his highlighted Options-nightclub hair for his TV appearances, has seen the light and worked out a much more acceptable sombre intellectual look when called upon to be a pundit on Sky.

- 25 -
Managerspeak

Fashion and such apart, players are predominantly paid to express themselves by kicking the ball. Managers have to make do with words. So players who make it as managers tend to be those who are more articulate.

Before every Clissold Park Rovers game I get the players together and explain to them who's playing where and what tactics I want us to use. Then I try to encourage them, to get them fired up for the game. I do this rather self-consciously – although everybody wants to win it's not the done thing to be too earnest before a game of Sunday League football. I remember laughing at my predecessor Clive when, before our first-ever game, he produced a chart showing everybody's position in the formation he'd chosen. It was going too far.

In professional football there is no such thing as getting too serious. Although you could tell that to Jack Charlton. I was told the following story by Chris Waddle whilst preparing for an interview with the former Ireland manager. Waddle was lined up with the other Newcastle players the day before a vital Newcastle match, and Charlton was running through the tactical approach that he wanted to use for the game. 'Suddenly,' said Waddle, 'a car screeched to a halt by the side of the training pitch and a guy came running out. "Jackie, Jackie, there's troot in the Tweed," he shouted. Jack stopped talking and got straight in the car to go fishing. End of pre-match talk.'

Things are done a little more seriously in Iraq. Saddam Hussein's son Uday was so desperate for Iraq to qualify for the World Cup in France in 1998 that he sent the national team to a pep talk – at the nearest torture camp. The team had just lost 2-1 at home to Kazakhstan and were about to face their neighbours again in the return leg. The camp was normally used to perform such unsavoury deeds as branding deserters on the forehead and chopping their ears off. Players were whipped across their backs and the soles of their feet in an attempt to get them worked up for the match. Uday, who is head of the national soccer movement and President of the Olympic Committee, ordered the torture from his hospital bed having been crippled by an assassination attempt. However, it didn't have the required effect on his players and they lost the match 3-1, meaning they were beaten both on and off the pitch.

Former Liverpool manager the late Bill Shankly has become legendary for his inspirational team talks, but he was rather more subtle in his methods. Once he sent a scout all the way to Hungary to spy on the opposition in the Reds' next European match. In the dressing room before the match he asked the scout to talk about what he'd seen. After about a minute he interrupted the talk. 'That's enough about the opposition,' Shankly said. Another method he had at Anfield was to lay out a pitch full of Subbuteo players which represented the opposition. One by one he would pick the figures up and put them in his pocket with a comment. 'Goalkeeper – past it,' he'd say. 'Left back – overrated. Centre back – shouldn't be in the team.' And so on. Denigrating the opposition was one of his favourite tricks – at Carlisle, his first managerial post, he used to say, 'Boys, I've just seen them coming out of the coach. They should be in hospital. The centre forward can hardly walk.'

At halftime in our Sunday League matches everybody is much more serious than they are before the match. So much so that it's difficult to stop the meeting we have by the side of the pitch from becoming a inaudible cacophony of simultaneously voiced opinions. This is the time when the manager really comes into his own. His job is to communicate to the players what they have been doing wrong and how to amend it. And to fire them up so they approach the second half in the right mood. It's not a job I'm very good at. I'm not hard enough.

The halftime talk at professional matches is usually a no-go area for journalists, which is a pity because many a story could be picked up there. 'Flying teacups' is a euphemism for the sort of aggression that managers sometimes employ to try to get the best out of the players. It's a sign of the immense power that 'gaffers' have over their charges that one man can completely lose his temper and have eleven others sit quietly and listen him out. When asked what in the world he was most frightened of, former Scotland Under 21 player Gerry Creaney said 'manager Craig Brown at halftime'. Gerry Francis, after a game of two halves against West Ham in 1995, said afterwards 'what I said at half-time wouldn't be printable on the radio', whatever that was meant to mean. Alex Ferguson said in his 1996 book *10 Glorious Years,* 'All I have to say is "It's teacups time", just mention the word, and the players are all ducking for cover. In truth I haven't slung a teacup for years. The last pot shot was at Gordon Strachan, and I missed.'

An anonymous former 1970s Nottingham Forest player remembers that Brian Clough wasn't the calmest of men in the interval. 'Cloughie was screaming and shouting one time, then he threw something through the window. We were all showered with glass but still nobody moved. Archie Gemmill was tiptoing around pulling glass out of our hair.' The one time journalists, or documentary-makers to be exact, *were* allowed into a dressing room at halftime it was to see Leyton Orient manager John Sitton berate his players for being 1-0 down at home to Blackpool on 7 February 1995. Suddenly losing his temper he sacked his captain Terry Howard on the spot, talking about 'the straw that broke the camel's back' and challenged his centre half to a fist fight there and then. God knows what would have happened if there *hadn't* been any cameras there. Howard, who ended up cowering under the bench, was given a free transfer to Wycombe Wanderers three days later.

Some managers don't use such draconian measures to motivate their players. 'That ranting and raving stuff goes in one ear and out the other. If you talk to people they listen,' said then-QPR manager Ray Wilkins in 1995. By the end of the year he was out of the job. Former Celtic manager Jock Stein used a bit of amateur psychology to motivate his winger Jimmy Johnstone in a first-leg European tie at Parkhead. After an indifferent first-half performance, Stein told Johnstone, who was terrified of flying, that there would be no need of a second leg if Celtic won by three clear goals. Johnstone (apparently) believed him, and was outstanding in the second half, which Celtic dominated, scoring four goals.

Perhaps the most inspiring manager-to-player speech was made by Alf Ramsey in the period before extra time in the 1966 World Cup Final at Wembley. The England players must have been completely demoralised as West Germany had equalised seconds before the final whistle. I met Bobby Charlton at the launch of a TV show he was hosting in 1995 and managed to arrange a quick interview with him. I asked him what Ramsey had said to the players in the short period of time he had with them. No histrionics in this case. 'You've beaten them once; now go and do it again. Look at them, they're knackered,' was the general gist of it. You all know the result.

As well as communicating with their players, managers are expected to communicate with the media. Premiership managers are usually well versed in saying the right thing to the press, which usually involves saying as little as possible. Some of them are particularly well versed in the art of doublespeak. Doublespeak, according to linguist William Lutz is 'a blanket term for language which pretends to communicate but doesn't'.

A good example of this was the interview that Kenny Dalglish gave to the press a day before Newcastle's ill-fated trip to Eindhoven to play PSV in the Champions League in October 1997. When asked whether Newcastle's Italian defender Alessandro Pistone would be fit for the game he replied, 'You'd better ask the physio that question.' When asked whether Pistone had travelled with the team he said, 'I don't know.' Being manager of the team he was well aware of the answer to both questions – but he was unwilling either to communicate the truth or to admit that he was unwilling to communicate the truth.

In managers' defence doublespeak is necassary on two counts – firstly because sometimes it is wise to keep your team and formation a secret from your opponents who might change their tactics accordingly if they are privy to that information through the media. Secondly because, as we all know, the media are apt to blow what is said out of proportion, so managers tend to be careful with their words.

If some managers are wary of the press, others are aware of how to use it to their advantage. Manchester United manager Alex Ferguson is a master at this technique, which has been dubbed 'kidology'. The best example came in the 1995-96 Championship run-in, which Manchester United were contesting with Newcastle United. Newcastle had had a twelve-point lead in the race, but had slipped badly in February and

March, picking up four out of a possible eighteen points whilst United were on a run that saw them win ten out of eleven games, only to slip up and lose at Southampton. On 17 April both teams had home games: Newcastle were playing Southampton, Manchester were playing Leeds. Leeds were Newcastle's next opponents, twelve days later (the FA had caused a break in the tension by organising an England match against Croatia on the 24th). Both teams won tense matches by 1-0 – United's victory was against a tenacious ten-man side who needed to put forward Phil Masinga in goal after having keeper Mark Beeney sent off. It was a surprise that Leeds played so well; they went to Old Trafford on the back of three consecutive defeats. After the match Ferguson used the post-match interview to wind the Leeds players up to perform to similar heights against his rivals. 'If they played like that every week,' he growled, 'they'd be up near the top. You wonder if it's just because they are playing Manchester United. Pathetic, I think. We can accept any club coming here and trying their hardest as long as they do it every week. No wonder managers get the sack.'

Twelve days later Newcastle scraped another 1-0 win, the third on the trot, to keep themselves in the title race despite Manchester's 5-0 thrashing of Nottingham Forest the night before. Afterwards Keegan was asked by the Sky interviewer what he thought of Ferguson's comments. Keegan had clearly been upset by them, and wasn't able to contain his feelings. 'When you do that, with footballers, like he said about Leeds,' he said, tears in his eyes, '...I...I've kept really quiet but I'll tell you something, he went down in my estimation when he said that. We have not resorted to that. But I'll tell you...you can tell him now if you're watching this. We're still fighting for this title and he's got to go to Middlesbrough and get something and...and...I'll tell ya honestly...I will love it if we beat them...love it!'

Newcastle didn't 'beat' them, and you could tell from the interview that they weren't going to; Keegan had 'lost it' and was in no fit state to guide his players to the title. Newcastle drew their final two matches; Man United beat Middlesbrough 3-0 in the last game at Ayresome Park and the title, part of a 'double double' went to Old Trafford.

Part Five

The Fans

- 26 -
By Far the Greatest Team?

---

26 April 1997 was an extremely emotional day for me. It was the last match Brighton and Hove Albion were to play at the Goldstone Ground, before the place was demolished and turned into a shopping centre thanks to the greed of a couple of shameless capitalists. It was just over twenty years before that I'd seen my first-ever football match at the ground and I'd soon become a regular. Although my visits had tailed off dramatically in the late 1980s and 1990s as I lived abroad and in London, it was a place in which I had invested a great deal of time and emotion.

To add tension to all the poignancy, Brighton were fighting for their Football League lives. They were lying bottom of Division Three with only two matches left; this one against Doncaster Rovers and another against Hereford United the following week. Both were fellow strugglers. Brighton simply had to win that day to stay in the League. The ground, which was visibly falling apart, was as packed as it could have been – 11,341 were there to pay their last respects, to complain at the injustice of it all, and to urge the Albion on. Historically speaking it wasn't much – I'd been in a crowd of over 30,000 at the Goldstone in 1977 – but it was much better than usual. Crowds had gone under 2,000 that season, albeit after a boycott had been called. If the quality of play on the pitch wasn't up to much, the tension of the occasion made it an absorbing contest. Albion finally scored after 67 minutes, with a close-range blaster from Stuart Storer. It was just after the goal that I heard the song. I'd heard it at every Brighton match I'd ever been to, and at most other matches in this country besides. It came from the Brighton singing end, the North Stand, where I would have been if I had been able to get a ticket there. I'd have lent my full voice to the song, too. It went like this:

And it's Brighton Hove Albion
Brighton Hove Albion FC
We're by far the greatest team
The world has ever seen

It was the 'by far' bit that really cracked me up. The reality was that Brighton, who won the match 1-0 and drew with Hereford 1-1 the following week to send United down instead of them, were by a whisker the second-worst, rather than the worst, team in the Football League. There are only maybe two or three post-war teams that could claim to be the best the world had ever seen: Puskas's Hungary side that beat England 6-3 and 7-1 in 1953 and 1954 and should have won the World Cup in 1954; Pele's Brazil, who claimed the Jules Rimet trophy for good after beating Italy 4-1 in Mexico 1970 to record their third World Cup win; and Cryuff's Holland of the early 1970s, who introduced 'Total Football' to the game and should have won the World Cup in 1974. And any one of these would be hard pressed to claim that their supremacy made them 'by far' the best team ever.

Now there is a lot of irony on the football terraces, but as far as I can see this song is sung straight. In other words the fans are boasting about the quality of the team rather than trying to make the other spectators laugh or even wryly smile. It says a good deal about the blind passion of fans that they can allow themselves to get away with such gross exaggeration without a teeny bit of a twinkle in their eye. But it's a great song to sing, specially the 'by far' bit where your voice goes up on the word 'far'.

As long as there have been football fans there have been football songs. But before the 1960s these songs tended to be simple club anthems, or local songs sung before the match, often to the accompaniment of a brass band.

At some clubs you can still hear the legacy of this early club anthem singing. If you go and see Barcelona at the Nou Camp Stadium the brass bands have been replaced by a tannoy system, but it's a moving experience to hear the massed fans singing their club hymn in unison, *'Tot el camp es un clam, som la gent blaugrana...'*

Brighton fans have adapted an old military anthem, traditionally played by brass bands before the game, and made it into a terrace favourite – 'Sussex by the Sea' is one of the oldest songs still sung on the terraces. It goes, for the record, like this:

Good old Sussex by the Sea
Good old Sussex by the Sea
Oh we're going up, gonna win the Cup
For Sussex by the Sea

Line three in the original song, which is still sung on non-footballing crowd occasions such as at the Bonfire Night celebrations in Lewes, originally goes 'and we'll tell them all that we'll stand or fall' and is a good example of a phenomenon which is crucial to the understanding of terrace chanting, copsasis. Copsasis refers to the adaptation of the words of a popular song which make it relevant in a different setting. Copsasis, as everybody who has written about it has to say, has got nothing to do (etymologically speaking) with the Liverpool Kop. But coincidentally it was on that famous terrace where football chanting really took off.

According to the University of Huddersfield's Steve Kelly, who has carried out a good deal of research into the history of football songs, the first real football chant derived from a system of rhythmic clapping the Liverpool fans used to practise in 1962, which they had picked up off a record called 'Let's Go' by the Routers. They would clap twice, three times, four times, then twice again. Try doing it quickly but rhythmically, allowing a brief pause between every set of claps and you'll recognise the sound. After a while they started replacing the last two claps with the words 'St John': the surname of their Scottish centre forward hero, Ian. Football chanting was born, and started to grow into a wildly unpredictable individual who, sadly, is now starting to go a little grey.

At first the Kop mostly sang hits of the moment; The Beatles were extremely popular of course, and 'She Loves You' was a great favourite as was the Scaffold song 'Thank You Very Much', and Gerry And The

Pacemakers' 'You'll Never Walk Alone' which has now become so popular a football anthem it's not only sung all round the country but in foreign countries, too.

'There is in Liverpool a school of indigenous verse – known as the Kop Choir, which produces, as it were spontaneously, verses to suit every situation that might occur within the game of football,' wrote P Moloney in his *Plea for Mersey* and the Liverpool fans proved him right by singing the hit of the time 'Careless Hands' when Leeds keeper Gary Sprake accidentally threw the ball into his own net. In 1965 Liverpool reached the FA Cup final, and beat Leeds 2-1. Their fans, on live television, chanted:

We've Won the Cup
We've Won the Cup
Ee-Aye-Addio
We've Won the Cup

and the whole country was aware of the phenomenon. Terrace chanting was soon to go nationwide.

The terraces were the perfect setting for such singing. If you have missed the experience of being part of a massive, swaying football terrace crowd you will never quite understand the feeling of unity that it engenders and how singing is the perfect expression of this unity. For several reasons fans sitting in seats sing less than fans on terraces: the division of fans into seats makes a crowd less of an amorphous crushed-together whole, more a collection of individuals; fans who used to congregate together in one part of the ground are more likely to be divided from one another as they have to sit in the seat which corresponds to their ticket number; the very act of being in a seat makes you less likely to sing – how many church choirs have you seen singing sitting down? Add to this the demographic difference in the average match-attending football fan nowadays to his counterpart a decade ago (thanks mainly to the increase in prices), and what you have is much quieter football grounds. Arsenal were so worried by the lack of atmosphere at their stadium, which was becoming known as 'the Highbury Library' that in 1997 they tried to start up a special singing section in the ground.

However much the football song has been affected by the all-seater-stadia-only-in-the-top-flight ruling, it must be said that it is still alive and well, if a little less raucous than before. In the lower divisions the terraces still exist, and when they are full and the fans find full voice it brings to mind the good old days of the 1970s and 1980s. Also away fans, who are more likely to sing for many reasons (to assert their identity in alien surroundings, to make up for their small number by making as much noise as possible, and because passionate fans who are prepared to travel are more likely to sing) often create a good deal of noise at whatever level their team are playing. Even sitting-down top-flight home fans still sometimes burst into song – albeit usually only when they are winning.

Singing fans have usually got a very wide repertoire of songs which are almost entirely 'copsatically' formed, from pop songs, folk songs, music hall songs, classical music, hymns, carols and advertising jingles. Many songs are common to most clubs' fans, but each club has its own songs or its own versions of universally-adopted songs. If you want to read about each individual club's set of songs you'd do well to get a copy of *Dicks Out 2*, which is organised in this manner.

My aim, having recognised that a lot of football songs are almost Pavlovian responses to situations which arise on the football field and the moods they engender, is to work out what fans sing in which circumstances, and what the songs are designed to demonstrate.

- 27 -
Abuse

One job that a singing end feels it has to perform is to abuse the other team and its fans and players. In the 1970s and 1980s, when terrace violence was much more common, this abuse often led to physical violence between fans. Now it's largely a ritual, though when it's aimed at individual players the intention is to put that player off so he plays badly.

Abusing the other set of fans can take many forms. The most obvious is to attack them by ridiculing their geographical background. Teams from rural areas are almost always greeted at some stage with this song, performed in a mock country accent:

I can't read, and I can't write, but it don't really matter
Because I come from Norwich/Ipswich/Exeter/Plymouth
And I can drive a tractor

The song is usually followed by a chant of 'ooh ahrr'.

A more recent development, which began in the 1980s, was to accuse rural supporters of bestiality, particularly with sheep, usually by chanting 'sheepshaggers, la-la-la' twice, with the first 'la-la-la' going up in tone, and the second going down.

Urban-based fans have to put up with their fair share of criticism. The most common song aimed at them is one (I believe) originally directed at Liverpool fans by Portsmouth fans, sung to the tune of 'In My Liverpool Home':

In your Liverpool slums
You look in the gutter for something to eat
You find a dead cat and you think it's a treat
In your Liverpool slums

The most comic version of this song I heard was when I went to Monte Carlo to see Newcastle United play Monaco in the UEFA Cup in 1997. The fans, hugely jolly despite an inept performance by the team, were singing:

In your Monaco slums
You look in the gutter for something to eat
You find a dead lobster you think it's a treat

The North/South divide is another stimulus for insulting chants. When a player from a Southern team is fouled by a Northern opponent, for example, the crowd often chant 'You dirty Northern bastards' hardening the 'a' to mimic the opposing fans' accents. At Brighton back in the 1970s, a quiet period in the match against a Northern team was often punctuated by a rendition of Dvořák's *New World Symphony*. Why? The music was used to paint a picture of Northern simplicity in an advert campaign by Hovis.

In 1991 I went to see Brighton play Wolves in the old Division Two. Because I was going with a friend who supported Wolves I was in a much-to-be-dreaded position: I was 'in the wrong end'. So I suppressed a smile when the Brighton fans, as yet unhit by the recession, started waving credit cards at the Wolves fans, singing, to the tune of 'You'll Never Walk Alone':

Sign on, Sign on
With a pen...in your hands
And you'll never work again
You'll never work again

I was still able to laugh, though, when the Wolves fans let their retort be heard: 'At least we're not gay.'

Sometimes fans abuse opposing fans (and teams) about their lowly status. Some clubs with rich histories and big fan-bases consider themselves to be 'big' clubs and their opponents to be of lower status to them. One common chant from such fans is to sing 'Who the fucking hell are you' to the tune of 'Bread of Heaven' as their opponents run on to the pitch, pretending never to have heard of their existence. This chant, by the way, was turned on its head by Scunthorpe fans a few years ago when, on the opening day of the season, their team ran on to the pitch with seven new faces in the team.

Fans can also abuse opposing teams for their league status, especially if they are remotely threatened by relegation that season. 'Going down, going down, going down' is often heard, or, if a local rival is in the same position, to the tune of 'Guantanamera', 'Down with the Villa/Tottenham/Plymouth, You're going down with the Villa [etc].' (At the Bruno-Tyson fight in Las Vegas in 1996 Bruno fans chanted 'down with the Bolton, you're going down with the Bolton' at Tyson during the weigh-in, as well, incidentally, as 'get your hair cut for the lads' to Don King. Neither man obliged.)

Some songs don't account for any idiosyncratic difference in the opposition. 'You're going to get your fucking heads kicked in' is a common threat which dates back to the 1970s, along with 'You're going home in a county/city/fucking ambulance'. I heard the most original version of this chant sung, surprise surprise, at Brighton in 1977. It had become 'You're going home like Sandy Richardson' – Richardson was a character in the soap *Crossroads* who was wheelchair-bound.

Another common insult, originally claimed by Manchester United supporters but by the late 1970s pretty universal, was, to the tune of 'Distant Drums':

> *We hear the sound...of distant bums*
> *Over there, over there*
> *And do they smell [clapping rhythms]*
> *Like fucking hell [more clapping]*
> *Over there, over there*

Nowadays the first two lines of the song are largely passed over.

Football fans like to feel that they are 'good fans' and that their club produces 'good fans' in general. Being a good fan means going to all the matches, home and away, and making a lot of noise when you do. The more away fans the better. It's thus considered an insult to question the opposing supporters' fan credentials. If the other fans are travelling supporters and are not many in number, this could be done by chanting 'is that all you take away' to the 'Bread of Heaven' tune, or, to that old fave 'Guantanamera', 'come in a taxi, you must have come in a taxi'.

If the other fans are quiet their counterparts let them know, with:

Can you hear the Palace sing? (no-o, no-o)
Can you hear the Palace sing? (no-o, no-o)
Can you hear the Palace sing?
I can't hear a fucking thing. No-o No-o.

Away fans, often more vociferous than their home 'opponents', often insult them, when quiet, with the chant 'you're supposed to be at home'. If the home fans react to the barb with a song, the away fans retort with a high-pitched 'woooh' to suggest that the song has been sung by a bunch of not-yet-men whose voices haven't broken.

Sometimes opposing players are singled out for abuse. The most simplistic form of this is simply to boo the player in question whenever he gets the ball. This can be stimulated by the fact that the player has done a particularly bad foul earlier in the game, or has left the club acrimoniously. Paul Ince is booed every time he gets the ball at West Ham because, before leaving the club for Manchester United in September 1989, he posed for pictures in the press wearing a United shirt. A Man United shirt that is.

Certain players become unpopular with the team's fans, but the situation has to get pretty bad before his own fans switch from grumble-mode to boo-mode. In December 1997 Manchester City fans started a campaign of hate against their captain Kit Symons after a series of under-par performances. As I write this manager Frank Clark has taken the player's captaincy away from him 'for his own good'. By the time you read this he will almost certainly be at a new club. There you go, there's my head on the block. England players are sometimes booed at Wembley if they aren't deemed good enough for national selection, especially when their names are called out by the tannoy guy. This used to happen to Chris Waddle – before he got his hair cut – and to John Barnes.

Back to opposing players: the most common insult is to question their sexual prowess by chanting 'Johnny Smith's a wanker, is a wanker' or, to the tune of 'Let's all do the Conga':

Johnny Smith's a wanker
Johnny Smith's a wanker, la-la-la-la, la-la-la-la

(I apologise here to any players called Johnny Smith, I picked the name at random.)

If an opposing player misses an easy chance he is told, again to the tune of 'Guantanamera', 'score in a brothel, you couldn't score in a brothel'. When Justin Fashanu became the first gay footballer to come out, his brother John, particularly hated by opposing fans for his aggressive style of play and nicknamed 'Fash the Bash', often got told, 'score with your brother, you couldn't score with your brother'.

I was thirty, by the way, before I heard the song 'Guantanamera' on a collection of Latin American songs. For a second I wondered when the guy had been to the footie in England to pick up the tune. It's one of many cases when the copsasis has turned full circle and the derivations are more famous, in this country at least, than the original.

Particularly prone to insults are players who used to play with one club on the field, but have moved to another. As well as much choicer insults he might be greeted with, ''Allo, Fulham reject, Fulham reject, 'allo', even if it was him who decided to leave Fulham for greener fields.

Fulham fans will also use the same song to insult a player who has moved to that day's opposition from local rivals Chelsea.

Certain players get whole songs made up to insult them. My favourite is sung by Newcastle fans about Sunderland manager Peter Reid, who was likened to a chimpanzee in Skinner and Baddiel's *Fantasy Football*. I first heard it when I was following Newcastle in the UEFA Cup Monaco, and it became the song of the trip.

Understanding that 'head' in a Geordie accent is pronounced 'heed' and bearing the tune of 'Yellow Submarine' in mind, altogether now:

In the town where I was born
Lived a man called Peter Reid
And he had a monkey's heed
Peter Reid, monkey's heed

(Chorus) Peter Reid's got a fucking monkey's heed, a fucking monkey's heed, a fucking monkey's heed (ad nauseam)

When Reid, incidentally, was asked during an interview with *Goal* magazine what he thought about Skinner and Baddiel's comparison between him and a monkey he said, to his great credit, 'I think they're fucking spot on.'

Local teams come in for a particularly large amount of 'stick' from their rivals' fans, even when they aren't the opponents that day. Each team has one other club which they hate, and which figures in their songs.

The figure of hate is usually, though not always, the nearest neighbouring club. Sometimes the hatred isn't reciprocated because the object of scorn already has a natural enemy. Chelsea fans, for example, direct their venom at Tottenham, whereas Tottenham sing about Arsenal. Similarly Crystal Palace and Brighton developed a healthy disrespect when they were rivals in the 1970s and 1980s (and Palace were the nearest team to Brighton). Palace's hatred has waned with time as their rivals have dropped down the divisions, but Brighton fans still sing about Palace.

The most simple form of this abuse of local rivals is in the chant:

We hate Palace and we hate Palace
We hate Palace and we hate Palace
We hate Palace and we hate Palace
We are the Palace haters

A bit more complex is the song:

Allo, allo, we are the Brighton boys
Allo, allo we are the Brighton boys
And if you are a Palace fan surrender or you die
We all follow the Albion

Sometimes teams rather cleverly take one team's anthem and change the words to make it insulting to that team. The best example of this, to the tune of 'Glory Glory Hallelujah' is Arsenal fans' (unusually) brilliant:

The famous Tottenham Hotspur went to Rome to see the Pope
The famous Tottenham Hotspur went to Rome to see the Pope
The famous Tottenham Hotspur went to Rome to see the Pope
And this is what he said 'Fuck off!
Who's that team they call the Arsenal?'

Arsenal fans also chip in with another funny (if obscene) anti-Tottenham song, to the tune of 'My Old Man':

My old man said be a Tottenham fan
I said, 'fuck off, bollocks, you're a cunt'

In both these songs I love the fact that the fans are relating a supposed dialogue.

This sort of local rivalry is generally pretty harmless as fans usually mix quite happily with fans of rival teams in non-football situations; there are rarely potentially volatile racial or political reasons for supporting one team over another. One strong exception is in Glasgow, where the Rangers fans sing Unionist songs (such as 'I was born under a Union Flag' to the tune of 'Wandering Star') and Celtic fans sing Irish rebel songs.

However, when fans collect together to support national teams, because countries generally have real traditional enemies rather than just imaginary ones, fans' songs tend to get more overtly political.

England fans are a case in point. In 1981 England played Holland during the Falklands conflict. 'What shall we do with the Argentinians, what shall we do with the Argentinians, what shall we do with the Argentinians, Early in the morning' came the chant, with the sinister adjunct, 'bomb, bomb, bomb the bastards'. Another chant which is commonly heard on the way to England matches (though rarely in the stadium where there are never enough numbskulls to get it going) is 'no surrender to the IRA'. I'm being negative in tone here because I believe that things get dangerous when patriotism starts turning into nationalism. In a similar vein, if rather more funny, is the anti-German chant, to the tune of 'The Campdown Races':

Two world wars and one World Cup, doo-dah, doo-dah
Two world wars and one World Cup, doo-dah-doo-dah-dey

If teams are bored of taunting the opposition fans, they often turn on fans from their own club who regularly inhabit different parts of the ground. At Brighton the North Stand used to sing 'can you hear the South Stand sing?' In the Stretford End at Manchester the fans sing, to the tune of 'Nick Nack Paddy Whack':

Left side sing, right side fight, tunnel are a load of shite
La, la, la, la, la, la, la, la, la

At St James' Park, Newcastle, which is so popular a venue nowadays that there is a three-year waiting list for season tickets, but where crowds got as low as 8,000 before the arrival of Kevin Keegan, the Gallowgate End sing to the Leazes End. 'Where were you when we were shite?'

Sometimes the crowd turn on their own players. This can manifest itself in the slow hand-clap, which accompanies a bad performance and tries to shame the fans' team into action, or by booing. Teams who have not been deemed to have tried their best are often booed off the field at half or full time, often to the accompaniment of the song 'what a load of rubbish'.

If performances are particularly bad and the team starts dropping in status, or selling its best players and not replacing them, the board inevitably comes under pressure. The most simple way the crowd voice their dissatisfaction is by shouting 'Swales out', 'Chase out' or 'Pleat out' according to the object of their scorn. Brighton, in the 1996-97 season, devised a whole song against two of the executives responsible for the sale of their ground, sung to the tune of 'My Darling Clementine':

Build a bonfire, build a bonfire, put Bill Archer on the top
Put Bellotti in the middle and then burn the fucking lot

Derby have a song celebrating the demise of one of their former chairmen, who was not popular at the club, a certain Mr Robert Maxwell. When he was still at the club the fans used to sing 'he's fat, he's round, he's never at the ground, Maxwell, Maxwell'. Nowadays, to the tune of 'What Shall We Do With The Drunken Sailor', the song goes:

What shall we do with Robert Maxwell (x3)
Throw him in the ocean
Heave-ho and overboard (x3)
Now the bastard's drowning

The songs mostly fall on deaf ears – sometimes, however, they hit their mark. Jack Charlton left Newcastle after a pre-season friendly in which a small minority of Newcastle fans were calling for his head after a dull performance against Sheffield United. Crucially his wife and kids were there at the stadium. Similarly a former Lincoln City chairman said of his resignation in 1984: 'It wasn't so much the death threats or the vandalism, but when you are sitting with your family in the directors' box and you hear a couple of thousand people chanting "Gilbert Blades is a wanker" you think it's time to go.'

- 28 -
Songs of Praise

When fans are feeling optimistic after a good spell of football from their team or a goal or two they often, literally, sing the praises of their team. One common anthem, to the tune of 'Land of Hope and Glory' goes:

We all follow the Albion
Over land and sea (and Palace)
We all follow the Albion
On to victory

Rod Stewart's 'Sailing' has been hijacked by most clubs, and turned into an anthem:

We are Brighton
We are Brighton
Super Brighton
From the South

Millwall fans have turned this on its head with a song celebrating their almost universal unpopularity:

We are Millwall
We are Millwall
No one likes us
We don't care

One song which shows fans' ability to transform their team's title, however many syllables it contains, into three beats is the chant, 'We all agree...Brighton and Hove Albion are magic.' In this case the fans condense their six-syllable name into a four-syllable 'Brightnovalbion' to fit the song. Wolverhampton Wanderers manage to fit seven syllables in. Arsenal fans fit their two-syllable name into the same structure by becoming Ar-se-nal.

It's at this sort of point in a game that the club anthem comes out. Most teams usually have a special song which they reserve for particularly rosy moments when the tension of a match has been broken by a couple of goals' lead. This is where Newcastle fans will sing 'The Blaydon Races', Tottenham fans will indulge in 'Glory Glory Tottenham Hotspur', Liverpool fans will raise their scarves to 'You'll Never Walk Alone', and Norwich fans, bless their hearts, will sing their anachronistic 'On the Ball, City', written in 1905, which goes:

Kick off, throw it in, have a little scrimmage
Keep it low, a splendid rush, bravo, win or die
On the ball, City, never mind the danger
Steady on, now's your chance
Hurrah! We've scored a goal!

Many of them *can* drive tractors, apparently.

One of the simplest songs in virtually every club's repertoire is the 'army' song, which I first heard at Brighton as 'Alan Mullery's blue and white army' but which has also involved Jimmy Melia, Chris Cattlin, Barry Lloyd, Liam Brady, Jimmy Case and Stevie Gritt. The only difference between one set of fans' version and another is the colours and the name of the manager. Its simplicity is offset by the fact that it is, in effect, a duet, with half the fans singing 'Alan Mullery's blue and white army' and the other half repeating it, starting the first syllable of the manager's first name (in this case the 'A' of Alan) just as the second syllable of 'army' is finishing. The first set of fans then do the same, and so on, and the song can last for minutes. It usually takes place in a lull in the game and is a way for the fans to entertain themselves when there is nothing going on on the pitch. It is almost always stopped by a piece of exciting action which captures the attention of the crowd. There is no rational decision as to which line you sing – you just take up the rhythm of one or the other – the person next to you might be taking up the other part of the duet.

Newcastle fans perform a similar duet which again needs two sets of singers as the second line of the chant starts right on the heels of the first. One part of the crowd sing 'Toon! Toon!' and the others respond with 'black and white army'. Then the Toon Tooners start up again and so on. Again it can go on for minutes and become quite hypnotising, instantly whipping up a frenzied atmosphere which will (the fans hope) have a positive effect on the players on the pitch.

Fans sometimes keep their good humour even if their team is losing. One Saturday afternoon in 1979 I arrived at the Goldstone Ground at halftime for the game against Preston. My feelings were mixed when I asked somebody the score and we were winning 4-0. I'd obviously missed a brilliant first half. The Brighton crowd were singing the name of a Preston defender, and I worked out exactly what it meant. When I asked who'd scored I was proved right. He'd hit two own goals.

There weren't many Preston supporters in the little triangular enclosure Brighton used to pen the away support into, but those who had turned up were having a right old time of it, singing and jumping up and down. It was my first experience of that great trait of the British fan: humour in the face of adversity. 'We're losing 4-0 but we're gonna win 5-4, 5-4, 5-4,' they were chanting. I've seen examples of the same thing happening ever since with fans whose team was being thrashed – especially (like Barnsley fans in the 1997-98 season, for example) if they were used to the situation. We won 5-1, by the way.

In 1995 Ipswich famously lost 9-0 to Manchester United, as I write the biggest defeat since the start of the Premiership. The next match after such a thrashing is always difficult – Ipswich were away to Tottenham. Again they were beaten easily, this time 3-0. Their fans decided this would be a good time to show they could take the odd disaster on the chin. '3-0, we only lost 3-0,' they sang.

And pity the poor Crystal Palace fans who went up to Anfield in 1989 only to see their side whomped 9-0. As was the custom in those days, the fans were kept behind for half an hour in an otherwise empty stadium to try to minimise violence outside the ground. To their great credit, they reacted with the sort of gallows humour so common amongst football fans, chanting, 'Liverpool, Liverpool, you're not singing any more.'

Talking about Liverpool (and there's a handy link) we have seen that in the 1960s the Kop used to sing songs which didn't necessarily have any direct reference to football; this trend has continued, although nowadays there is often a touch of post-modern irony to the proceedings.

Often the song was simply a chart hit at the time when the club was doing well. It's said that Bristol Rovers actually predated the Kop by some six years singing 'Goodnight Irene' on the terraces after beating Manchester United 4-0 in the FA Cup in 1956. The song is still heard at home matches.

Similarly Kilmarnock fans, after a famous victory in 1973, started singing 'Paper Roses', which Donny and Marie Osmond had just made number one in the charts. They still sing it when things are going well today. Away fans usually retort with 'stick your roses, stick your roses up your arse'.

Since the late 1980s, Stoke City fans have been singing the Tom Jones' hit 'Delilah' at Victoria Park. This bucks the trend as it wasn't a hit at the time. The story goes that a particularly vociferous fan, nick-named TJ for his love of the Welsh crooner, used to sing the song in the pub before the game, and the other fans used to join in. Then one day he started it up at a match, everybody joined in, and now it is the Stoke City anthem, given an airing at least once a match.

Other teams which have hijacked pop songs and used them, in their unadulterated form, as anthems are Nottingham Forest, who sing the Righteous Brothers' 'You've Lost that Loving Feeling', Manchester City, with Bob Dylan's version of 'Blue Moon' and Swansea, who sing Andy Williams' 'Can't Take My Eyes off of You'.

It's not only pop songs which become club anthems. West Ham fans have been singing the popular Victorian music hall number 'I'm For Ever Blowing Bubbles' since the 'White Horse' final in 1923; a game doesn't go by at Newcastle without 'The Blaydon Races' being sung; Chelsea fans give a great performance of 'One Man Went To Mow' and Grimsby supporters have made the *It Ain't Half Hot Mum* theme a standard.

Sometimes fans start singing a traditional song, but change the words at the end to turn it into a football chant. One favourite is 'Molly Malone' which becomes, at Old Trafford:

In Dublin's fair city, where the girls are so pretty
I first set my eyes on sweet Molly Malone
As she wheeled her wheelbarrow
Through streets broad and narrow
Crying M-U, M-U-F, M-U-F-C, O.K

Watford fans sing the same song, changing the 'through streets' line to the more local 'from Watford to Harrow'. Reading fans in the early 1990s went a little further:

In Brisbane's fair city
where the girls are so pretty
I first set my eyes on sweet Kylie Minogue
She wheels her wheelbarrow
Through streets broad and narrow
Singing
I should be so lucky
Lucky lucky lucky
I should be so lucky in love

In a similar vein, Nottingham Forest fans have been known to bastardise the carol 'Away in a Manger' like this:

Away in a manger,
No crib for a bed
The little lord Jesus
Woke up and he said
We hate Derby and we hate Derby, we hate Derby and we hate Derby

- 29 -
Hero Worship

When I went to my first Brighton match when I was twelve in 1976 I stood in the Chicken Run, the large East terrace, where the old men and young kids went. Everybody between thirteen and thirty, it seemed, went in the North Stand, the singing end. My graduation there, halfway through my second season, was an exciting time, especially the singing. Even though my voice hadn't broken yet, and I was well aware that it would be letting the side down if I raised it above a mumble, I pretty soon learnt all the words to all the songs, though there was a transition period when I only knew the easy bits, the one-liners.

My favourite song was the one they sang about Peter Ward, which was immediately pickuppable. It was sung to the tune of 'The Quartermaster's Stores' and it went:

He shot, he scored, he must be Peter Ward
Peter Ward, Peter Ward

To my delight, when Ward missed a shot, the song became rude:

He shot, he missed, he must be fucking pissed
Peter Ward, Peter Ward

I think to this day Peter Ward is the biggest hero I ever had, much bigger than Strummer or Kerouac ever were. It was the same, I think, for everybody else; his was the first name chanted when the players ran out and were kicking the ball about pre-match. But pretty much every player got a chant. 'Spi-der' we'd chant at Ian Mellor until he gave us a wave. Peter Sullivan would get 'Sully'. Brian Horton would get the chant 'Nobby 'Orton'.

The first-ever modern football chant, as we have seen, was directed at an individual player and the trend has left a rich tradition of songs, used when the player in question ran on to the pitch, when he scored a goal, or simply when he performed an action characteristic to his game. One of the earliest was the Stretford End's tribute to their hero Denis Law, to the tune of 'Lily the Pink':

We'll drink a drink a drink to Denis the king, the king, the king
He's the leader of our football te-e-eam
He's the greatest centre forward
That the world has ever seen

Pretty soon his forward partner George Best had a song, too, again stolen from a popular hit of the time:

Georgie Best, Superstar
How many goals do you think you'll score?

The song was picked up by opposing fans and, for the first time, we had a team's chant altered by opposing fans in order to insult the opposition, becoming:

Georgie Best, Superstar
Walks like a woman and he wears a bra

Even Nobby Stiles, the toothless unfussy destroyer, got a song of his own, to the tune of 'Alouette':

Nobby Nobby, Nobby Nobby Nobby
Nobby Nobby, Nobby Nobby Stiles

Over the years hundreds of players have been given their own song: and if they haven't their fans can chant their name in the ubiquitous 'there's only one Johnny Smith' (sung, of course, to the tune of 'Guantanamera') which reared its head in the 1980s and hasn't ducked down since. The only time the chant became at all amusing was when there were two Gary Stevenses playing at the same time for England.

Some players fit a song perfectly thanks to the rhyme or rhythm of their name. Thus, in the 1970s, Manchester United fans would sing:

Lou, Lou, skip to my Lou
Lou, Lou, skip to my Lou
Lou, Lou, skip to my Lou
Skip to my Lou Macari

Current Liverpool fans have found that Steve McManaman's name fits perfectly to the tune of 'Ma Na Mah Na' (think of the Muppets) and that Jason McAteer scans nicely into that intensely annoying Spanish Euro-hit 'Macarena' by Los Del Rio:

He runs down the wing and his name is McAteer
He runs down the wing and his name is McAteer
Whooa McAteer

Newcastle chip in with their song for Belgian international, Philippe Albert, which I'm sure he hasn't worked out. It's sung to the tune of 'Rupert the Bear' and goes:

Philippe, Phillipe Albert
Everyone knows his name

I've got three favourite name songs. The first was chanted by Tottenham fans in the early 1990s about their Moroccan international midfielder Nayim. It's not 'Nayim from the halfway line' (to the tune of 'Go West') which they still sing at local derbies to celebrate his forty-yard lob which helped Real Zaragoza beat Arsenal in the 1995 Cup Winners' Cup Final. It's far better than that. To the tune of 'Chim Chimenee', and playing on the fans' nickname 'the Yids' (see chapter 13) it goes:

Chim chimenee, chim chimenee chim chim cheroo
Nayim was an Arab and now he's a Jew

My second is the song that the Manchester United fans gave to their hard-tackling midfielder/central defender Paul McGrath. Before you sing it in your head, remember that, in the Irish fashion, he doesn't pronounce the 'th' at the end of his name. It goes to the tune of 'Oops Upside Your Head':

Ooh ah Paul McGra
I said ooh-ah Paul McGra

The song was taken up by the Irish fans, who loved the player who became hugely important to their team in the glory days under Jack Charlton. There's a lovely story around it. In 1990, when the Irish team came home from the Italia 90 World Cup, the whole of Dublin went to the airport to greet the players. Cars were driving over the central reservation and down the fast lane of the wrong side of the motorway to beat the traffic jams and get a glimpse of their heroes. It has been estimated that 500,000 people congregated in the city to celebrate the team's return. The player they wanted to see most was their black defender, Paul McGrath, and they were chanting his song ad nauseam.

By a strange coincidence Nelson Mandela was also due to arrive that day, and when he landed at the airport, before the Irish team, he was startled to see that so many fans had turned up to greet him. When he stood up on the balcony to wave at them, however, he was a little confused to hear 'Ooh-ah, Paul McGrath's Da' chanted at him. 'Da' is Irish dialect for Dad.

The third, as I've already mentioned, is the one about Peter Ward. Which is why I'm glad that the Brighton fans are still singing it. And amused. Terrace song culture is so rich at the moment that a current trend has started up for the singing of retro songs. One the funniest sights I have seen, on the night before Newcastle played Barcelona in Spain in November 1997, is a pissed Geordie fan, isolated from his mates, sombrero askew, standing in a bar in the grotty Barrio Chino in Barcelona. He was singing, 'We've got Terry Terry Terry Terry Hibbit on the wing, on the wing.' Hibbit played the last game of his second spell at the club back in 1980.

- 30 -
The One-liners – And the Birth of Chants

As well as songs crowds also come out with 'one-liners' – chants which are sparked by particular events on the pitch.

One situation which always triggers a stock response is the goal kick. Back in the 1970s as soon as I went to matches I was aware that when the opposition keeper took the kick the whole stand behind him would chant whoooooooooaaaaaaaa to try to put him off. In the 1980s this became a little more subtle (if that's the right word) by the addition of the words 'you're shit' afterwards and a guttural aaaaaaaaargh to cap things off. This has been attributed to West Ham fans, though the first time I was aware of it was at Highbury in the mid 1980s.

Leyton Orient fans have gone a stage further by going completely quiet after the goalkeeper's kick, then, when the ball hits the ground, shouting 'boing' and jumping around.

Here are some other one-liners and the situation on the pitch which stimulates them:

'The referee's a wanker' – after any questionable decision, interchangeable with 'who's the bastard in the black?'

'Boring, boring Arsenal' (or any other opposition who are using stifling tactics away from home)

'Here we go, here we go, here we go' (otherwise known as the Earwig song, which is from Sousa's *Stars and Stripes*) – used when the team looks like scoring.

'Always look on the bright side of life' – you've given up on the match

'Calm down, calm down. Calm down, calm down' – the opposition fans (usually Liverpudlian) thought their team had scored

'Are you Palace in disguise?' – when the opposition is playing so badly you feel you must liken them to your local rivals

'What's it like to be outclassed?' (interchangeable with 'easy, easy') – you feel your team is hugely superior to the opposition

'Come on, you Reds' – general encouragement, often used in promising situations, such as a corner

'Score in a minute, we're gonna score in a minute' – when your team has been attacking and looks like putting one past the despairing dive of the keeper

'Bring on the dustbin' – after an opposition player has been injured

'Attack, attack, attack attack attack' – used when your team has been on the defensive too long. Sometimes changed, when you're 1-0 up with a few minutes to go, to *'defend, defend, defend defend defend'*

'Get into them' – again born of frustration from a passive display by your team

'Alan Hansen/Elton Welsby/Jimmy Hill, you're a wanker, you're a wanker' – when the game, which has reached a dull patch, is being televised. Interchangeable with *'Are you watching...'* plus name of rivals

'Sing your heart out for the lads' – encouragement to your fellow fans to sing up, especially if the match isn't going well

'Sign him up, sign him up, sign him up' – when the ballboy catches the ball cleanly or gives it a great hearty thump

'Who's ate all the pies? Who's ate all the pies? You fat bastard, you fat bastard, you've ate all the pies' – directed at any fat person who is noticed by the crowd

'1-0 to the Arsenal' – letting the opposition know the score, to the tune of 'Go West'

Arsenal fans first started this last chant song to celebrate the defensive style of their manager George Graham, having heard Paris St Germain use the tune to chant their club name in the 1994 Cup Winners' Cup. It really caught on when the Gunners beat Parma by that score in the final of the competition. Pretty soon the tune, which is simple to remember and easy to apply any lyrics to, became a staple for a number of football chants for supporters from all clubs. Other tunes which have a similar factotum versatility are 'Abide with Me', (which used to be used to let your opposition know the score) and, as we have seen, 'The Earwig Song' and 'Guantanamera'.

Some of the tunes are used over and over again, others are specifically hijacked for a particular song. Either way the words accompanying them don't spontaneously invent themselves on the terraces. The song has to be conceived before it's sung. And each club has a handful of fans who make up songs, often while they are drinking together before away games.

Travelling on the tube to see a West Ham-Newcastle match in October 1997 I witnessed this process in action. Newcastle had just beaten Barcelona at St James' Park in the Champions League with a hat-trick from their gifted striker Faustino Asprilla. It was one of the most glorious results in the club's history. Soon afterwards the Newcastle-based building society Northern Rock floated, giving thousands of Geordies cash windfalls. How to spend them seemed obvious. The return match was scheduled for six weeks later. In the bit near the door of the train on its way to Upton Park tube station there were five Geordies, all a bit drunk, all incredibly good humoured. 'And we're off to sunny sunny Spain...' sang one. '...with Tino Asprilla,' joined in another, off the cuff, and they all burst out laughing. 'Hang on, I think I've got the next line,' said the guy who'd thought of the second, his eyes looking to the ceiling. 'And we're going from Luton on the plane...with Tino Asprilla.' Again they burst out laughing. They were trying to work out the fourth line when the train pulled into the station. 'We're going to beat the Barca again' seemed to be the favourite. Later on, in the seats a few rows behind me, I heard the song get its first public airing. On its second there were more voices joining in. I'd love to say that by the end of the match the whole stand was singing it, but that didn't happen.

It showed me, though, the process that goes into the creation of a football song. It's a kind of sub-art – songwriting with a ready-made tune and subject matter. All you have to do is find the words to fit in the rhythm. When French forward David Ginola arrived at Newcastle, the chant was obvious. Ginola rhymes with Lola, the name of a famous Kinks song. 'Ginola la-la-la Ginola' became a Toon Army classic. If the song is popular it gets picked up by more and more people and, via the TV or exposure to away fans, by other teams too, if they can tailor it to their own needs. What do you think, for example, that Chelsea fans sing about Italian star Gianfranco Zola? Most songs never make it to stage one, that is, being accepted by enough fans to make it audible to the whole stadium. If one does, however, it may remain around for weeks, or months, or – if it is deemed a classic – even years. The guy who started the first Stretford End song in the mid-1960s, to the Hispanic tune '*Campa no Llores*', 'Aye aye aye aye, Charlton is better than Pele' must get a glow of warmth whenever he hears any of the myriad songs starting 'we all agree...'

- 31 -
The Sound of Silence

After a run of luck with the trains and a scoot up Wembley Way I got in my seat just in time. Elton John's 'Candle in the Wind' was just beginning.

Now all the Diana fever had largely passed me by. I wasn't of the radical-chic 'glad she's dead' brigade, but on the other hand I couldn't bring myself to feel weepy. I didn't know the woman, after all.

The *Sun* wrote the next day that 75,000 people sang 'in clear loud voices the words that will forever provide a loving, lasting memory of the Princess'. Actually a few people joined in with the chorus but nobody seemed to know the other words – the song hadn't even been released yet. What was strange was the way that people had brought candles with them. Others held their lighters in the air like Italian pop fans. Mine stayed firmly in my pocket.

What did move me though was the minute of silence that was held before the match. I had supposed it would be the most effective one I'd ever heard and I was right. The referee blew his whistle and 75,000 people practically held their breath for a minute. There was the odd muffled cough, a watch alarm going off, the clunk of a couple of badly behaved seats, the zoom-whirring and clicking of various cameras (as if you could photograph a silence) – and that was it. Such a big silence (I mean one kept by so many people in such a confined space) is nine and a half months pregnant. It's palpable. It's very, very quiet. And when the referee blew his whistle to end it everybody instinctively did what they usually do after one minute silences in football crowds only more so; we let out a huge unfettered roar as if, after such a silence, we felt that we had to celebrate.

It was the first time I'd felt really moved about the Diana news since I'd read it in a newspaper a couple of Sunday mornings before. But any poignancy soon evaporated. This was because of the tannoy guy they were employing at Wembley, and it wasn't the first time he'd got under my skin.

Like all tannoy guys the tannoy guy was just a voice – but it was one of those smooth smarmy Southern voices you hear on cheap radio DJs. It wasn't just him directing the mourn-along-with-Elton singing either, although he *was* hugely inappropriate for that task. It was the fact that he took it upon himself to direct the football singing too. That really irked me, as it had in Euro 96. 'Here's one I'm sure you'd all like to sing along to,' he smarmed. 'It's called "Three Lions".'

Now Wembley-going England fans have always had a problem with their singing. The fact is that they don't usually congregate more than once every two or three months (tournaments apart) and the result is that a strong 'terrace' culture hasn't developed. Apart from the obvious 'Engerland, Engerland, Engerland' and a bit of rather old-fashioned 'clap clap, clap clap clap, clap clap clap clap England', they very rarely indulge in much spontaneous singing at all. Many of them, you can tell, don't regularly go to club matches.

The truth is that the tannoy guy's plan worked. He put the record on, and the crowd dutifully sang along, at least to the chorus bit they knew, and waved their flags. It was very loud really, although you could still hear the music behind. It must have looked good on the telly. Then came 'You'll Never Walk Alone' and again the crowd sang along, although at a rather quicker pace than the record.

Now my problem wasn't that I didn't like the sound of the guy, and, after all, he had managed to get the whole stadium singing. Well, not entirely, anyway. What I really hated was that he was, for me, betraying the whole deal about football singing. As we have seen, football crowds have many moods and their songs reflect these moods. Telling the crowd what to sing is disenfranchising the crowd from their right to *choose* what to sing.

I have a worrying vision of the future. Already some of the bigger clubs are starting to get more money from commercial spin-offs and television than from the fans that pay to watch the games. As TV gets more sophisticated; first with pay-per-view facilities, next with – who knows? – virtual reality options, bigger clubs will be relying more and more on a non-match-going customer base, who will be watching matches more and more from home.

The atmosphere at the stadiums is bound to suffer even more than it already has. But the match as a spectacle is bound to suffer, too, if there is no one there making any noise. So what will clubs do? Wembley-type terrace-songs-by-numbers might be a short-term option, but it does rely on the fans who turn up to actually sing. Canned terrace atmosphere is the next obvious step, though somebody had better can some quick while it still exists.

- 32 -
Siddoon – Post-Taylor Fan Behaviour

I don't really hate Sunderland, but peer pressure is peer pressure so I feel obliged to stand up.

I'm at Chelsea in the Newcastle end. Newcastle is my other team, the other woman. I was born there, and supported them since 1974, the MacDonald final. I go to their London matches – I suppose you could call me a Cockney Geordie. I always have to do a lot of explaining when people question me on my Southern accent and Northern team. Anyway, we're in the seats. Of course we are – it's a Premiership game. I hate seats, but you've got to live with them. I've been up and down all afternoon. Whenever there's a bit of action near us everybody stands up, and it's either do the same or miss everything. I'd rather stay standing at this point, but if you do someone shouts 'siddoon!' so gradually, as the action moves away again you sit down again, though not immediately. First you go into a half-crouch resting your bum on the rim of the upswung seat, and gradually you ease yourself down in unison with the people in front of you. Sometimes, if the ball comes back down your end unexpectedly you're up again before you've gone down.

Anyway, as if all this wasn't bad enough, in a lull in the game, the inevitable chant comes out. It's one of those songs which require action as well as words, and has been invented since the all-seater stadiums ruling.

'Stand up, if you hate Sunderland, stand up if you hate Sunderland, stand up...' to the tune of 'Go West'.

Within seconds I'm the only one left sitting. As I say, I don't hate

Sunderland, but I don't *not* hate them enough to be the odd one out in the whole crowd, so I reluctantly stand.

Once I'm there, however, I'm happy. I can see the game just as well like this. I'm more used to watching my football on the terraces, standing up. I suppose, higher up, you get a better view...Oh shit, they're singing again.

'Sit doon if you hate Man U, sit doon if you hate Man U, sit doon...'

Later on the Chelsea fans show us how to incorporate the seats into a song in a really effective way, the best bit of post-Taylor fan culture I've seen in the country. Ever since I can remember, Chelsea fans have sung 'One Man Went to Mow' on the terraces. They start with 'One man went to mow, went to mow a meadow, one man and his dog – Spot – went to mow a meadow' and then work their way up to ten. As they go further and further into the song more people join in because they know it's reaching its crescendo. This time, as Chelsea are leading 1-0 and in good spirits, it seems like the whole stadium is singing the song apart from our little area. Then, on the last verse, as they sing 'Ten men went to mow, went to mow a meadow' they all stand up and the increased lung capacity or whatever leads to the song nearly doubling in volume. 'Ten men nine men eight men seven men six men five men four men three men two men one man and his dog – Spot – went to mow a meadow. Chel-sea, Chel-sea, Chel-sea.' It's an awesome performance, though why they stop at ten and don't make the song football-relevant by making it eleven, I'll never know.

- 33 -
Actions Sing Louder than Songs

There's a long tradition of football fans incorporating actions into their songs. Perhaps the first case was the Kop in the early 1970s when they started raising their scarves above their heads between their outstretched arms with the song 'You'll Never Walk Alone'. At a time when a scarf was a vital accessory to a football match, the habit spread all over the country. We used to do it at Brighton. You couldn't see anything for a bit – which was why you did it at a quiet point in the match – but it felt great.

Some of the actions are very simple. When, for example, fans sing the 'By far the greatest team' chant, they hold their hands above their heads, ready to clap when necessary. At Brighton, when there is a corner, fans shout 'Seagulls' whilst pointing to the corner flag where the corner is to be taken.

Other actions are silly, almost comedy routines. When Woking fans get excited they jump up and down singing 'Woking Woking, boing, boing' until they get tired, a habit they passed on to West Bromwich Albion fans when they met in 1991 in the FA Cup. Or learnt from them, depending on whose version you believe. Grimsby fans chant the music of the American TV series *Hawaii 5-0*, whilst doing the action of a double-bladed paddler. Barnet fans do the twist. Even England fans got in on the act at Italia 90 by singing 'let's all have a disco' (to the tune 'Let's All Do The Conga') whilst lifting their arms up and down – a routine which captured the England players' imaginations so much that they performed it when receiving the tournament's Fair Play Award. This was a rare case of England fans being inventive, born of the fact that they had spent a long time together in Italy and had built up the sort of camaraderie only usually evident in club fans.

It was during the Italy World Cup that I first participated in a Mexican wave, a ripple across the stadium caused by fans standing up and sitting down at the same time as those in their vertical vicinity. Mexican waves were so called because they first became part of the football scene in the Mexico 86 World Cup. They were virtually impossible in England before the 1990s because of the terraces – people would have to sit down instead of standing up. At first it's quite exciting – you can see the thing coming towards you, then you stand up. Then you sit down again. The people in the press box weren't doing it, and we jeered them. After a while it pales, as you can imagine. I started siding with the journalists.

There was a theory going round that Mexican waves were like water in the plug-hole. They went round anti-clockwise in the Northern Hemisphere and clockwise in the Southern. It was discussed at length in the *Guardian*'s Notes And Queries. It turned out, however, to be a lot of fanciful nonsense. It just depends on whether the second person to stand up is on the left or the right of the initiator.

The only English stadium where I have seen the Mexican wave performed with any regularity is Wembley Stadium, at England matches, where, as I have previously mentioned, many of the fans are not habitual stadium-attenders. Football fans tend to eschew it as they have already developed much more complex ways of making their presence on the terraces known.

'It's a very English thing to be able to go nuts just at football matches. Lots of other cultures find lots of other ways of expressing themselves emotionally and then you find the English being most un-English at football matches,' says Nick Hornby, and, in a way, he's right.

Normally we are a nation of few performers and many spectators. In other European countries it's the other way round. On Shrove Tuesday, for example, the Italians, the Spanish, the Germans, the You-name-its traditionally get into fancy dress and have a carnival. Cities are packed with people in strange clothing – the people have become the spectacle. What do we do? We toss pancakes around, when we can be bothered.

However, being in a football ground allows us to lose some of our reserve. Like alcohol it affords us a release from our usual stiff-upper-lipness. In fact, we actually become exhibitionists – we put on a show for the other people in the stadium and for the players too. This is the major difference between armchair fans and match-going fans. The latter are part of the fabric of the game, the former are merely spectators.

Singing is part of the performance that fans put on. But an opera wouldn't be an opera without the props and the fancy-dress. Football fans, too, add a lot of visual signals to their performance. And at the same time as the singing is decreasing at matches, the visual language of fandom is getting more important.

- 34 -
Wearing the Colours

Before the last war, people used to go to football matches wearing their ordinary working clothes as they would most likely have worked on a Saturday morning. Gradually, however, the idea of 'wearing the colours' became more common, if at first only for big matches.

After the war, rosettes became a popular way of stating your allegiance – men used to work at the grounds selling them from boxes round their necks. By the 1950s a lot of fans had started wearing simple bar scarves, which you still occasionally see today.

In the 1960s skinhead culture was very influential on the way people dressed up for football matches. The skinheads wore big boots, jeans, T-shirts and braces and club-colour bobble hats with the bobbles cut off. Bobbleless bobble hats are still a very common sight at grounds.

In the 1970s everything went ape. Different types of scarf started appearing. There were college-style bar scarves with vertical rather than horizontal stripes. There were bar scarves with the innovation of a third colour and thin mock-silk scarves, which people tied round their wrists, with more intricate designs and slogans printed on them – usually the name of the club. Also, clubs started mass producing their shirts for fans to wear on the terraces.

My first shirt was a black-and-white striped Newcastle one with a round collar – the sort they wore in the 1974 FA Cup final. Unfortunately, I had grown out of it by the time I got to see a game at St James' Park in 1978 – and it had gone out of date. My second was a Brighton shirt with blue and white stripes, a V-collar and little Bukta symbols running down the arms. This I used to wear to matches in the late 1970s. A few people did the same, though not nearly so many as today. Looking back at pictures of the period it's difficult to spot shirts on the terraces. I also used to wear two scarves: one, a bar scarf, was knotted tightly round my neck; the other was mock-silk and I tied it around my wrist. I thought I looked brilliant. Fortunately there are no photos.

In the 1982 World Cup the world caught a glimpse of how effective shirt-wearing on the terraces could be when virtually all of the thousands of Brazil fans who had travelled to Spain wore their country's yellow shirts on the terraces. The result was spectacular – the crowd was nearly as exotic and exciting as the team they were watching. Football shirts started becoming more popular.

In the mid 1980s, however, after the Heysel disaster, English football fans didn't want to advertise the fact that they were football fans. Some people still wore scarves and shirts to matches, but the terraces ceased to be the colourful explosions they had been. Also the 'casual' football fan had been born. The casual fan wore designer label gear and didn't sport anything to identify himself with one club or another – partially in order to camouflage himself to facilitate fighting with casual fans from different teams. The style had started in Liverpool when, during the team's jaunts in Europe, a lot of their fans obtained expensive designer gear from foreign shops – Adidas, Lacoste, Puma, etc. Soon it became fashionable to *look* fashionable on the terraces, and colour-wearing fans were looked down on and nicknamed 'scarfies'.

Football, however, started regaining its credibility in the 1990s and shirt-wearing became acceptable again – especially at Arsenal when the club brought out a hideous yellow away shirt with blue chevrons all over it that became an instant classic. The casuals started to become a minority.

Nowadays such a large proportion of fans wear shirts at games that a backlash is inevitable. The fans have a large selection of different tops they can wear, with some clubs selling three different shirts at a time and changing the design of each at least every other season. People who want to stand out from the crowd can choose from any number of retro shirts – with designs dating back to the 1930s.

There are other personal statements people can make with their shirts, especially since the printing of players' names came in in the

Premiership in 1994. Most people simply have the name of their favourite player and his number. Some are more original. At a recent Newcastle game I saw a fat guy with 'JIMMY' and 'BELLIES' written over and under the number 10. Another old fellah with white hair had I AM 64 on his shirt. Aston Villa fans celebrated their Coca-Cola Cup win with shirts reading WEMBLEY 96.

A rather un-English seeming way of sporting the team's colours which has come into fashion recently is face-painting. As a rule fans who go in for this rather radical form of colours-wearing don't do it for every match. But it's becoming more and more popular at big cup matches and England games, having first reared its red and white head at the European Championships in Sweden in 1992. There are drawbacks, however, to face-painting. The paint tends to look better before games than after them – especially if your match-watching body language involves your hands being raised to your lips, foghorn style, or clutching your head in dismay. And if one of your team's colours is white, your teeth end up looking yellow. If you look for a moment at the cover of this book, you'll see a cretinous fan with his face painted and a blue wig on. That's me, that is. (Well, it saved paying a model to do it.)

The paint washed away in seconds after the photo-shoot. Fans face much worse drawbacks if they fancy a tattoo. Although having MUFC written across your knuckles is unlikely to help you in job interviews, you're pretty safe if you ink the name and/or badge of your club into your skin. Statistics have proved that you're much more likely to stick with your football team than your wife (or husband). And you'd be in good company – Fabrizio Ravanelli has a huge tattoo of his home-town former club Perugia on his arm.

But getting a tattoo of a player or a manager is somewhat short-sighted, however big a fan you are. One Newcastle fan became something of a minor celebrity in 1995 when he got a huge tattoo of Andy Cole on his thigh – just days before Cole was surprisingly off-loaded to Manchester United. Maybe he was among the hundreds of Newcastle fans who queued to get their Kevin Keegan tattoos removed at a special mobile unit of a tattoo-removing agency drafted into toon in February 1996.

- 35 - Banners From Heaven

One effective way for fans to make a statement is with a banner, which are making something of a comeback in the game.

The predecessors to banners were placards, which people used to prepare before big matches. In 1948 a Spurs fan went to Birmingham to watch the FA Cup semi final against Blackpool burdened with a placard reading, 'In fond remembrance of Blackpool, who passed out at Villa Park on March 13th. Funeral arrangements by Burgess & Co.' Burgess was the Spurs captain. It's worth a bet that the placard never made it back to London. Blackpool won 3-1 and Spurs didn't reach Wembley again until 1961.

In the 1950s an eccentric Arsenal fan used to go to all the matches carrying a big shield with the legend 'we Arsenal supporters say – may the best team win!!'

There was an explosion of banners in the 1970s and 1980s when it became de rigueur to take a funny one to any cup final you got to. Famous banners include an Aston Villa fan's caricature of Andy Gray in the League Cup final of 1977 with the caption 'He's here, he's there, he's every f**king where, Andy Gray, Andy Gray' echoing the song of the time (which has recently been revitalised at Chelsea in tribute to Frank Leboeuf). From the same year's European Cup final: 'Joey Ate the Frogs' Legs, Made the Swiss Roll, Now he's Munching Gladbach.' Liverpool full-back Joey Jones is the subject, St Etienne, FC Zurich and Borussia Moenchengladbach were his victims.

There was something in the air in 1977 – in the Home Internationals there was a Scottish banner reading 'Joe Jordan strikes faster than British Leyland'. Under a new government in 1981 left-wing

Spurs fans took a banner to the 1981 Cup Final with the slogan 'Maggie isn't the only one with Crooks at No. 11', referring to their forward Garth. Fans can also voice their dissatisfaction with banners. Ten Tottenham fans recently stated SUGAR OUT with a letter on each of eight cards held out in front of them, an original way of doing what countless dissatisfied fans have done before them. Another fan who thought of an original way of getting his message heard was a Barcelona fan with a grudge against the referee Brit Arceo, who in a previous match had given a dodgy penalty against the Catalan side. The fan released a pig dressed in a black referee's shirt on to the pitch with the referee's name written on its side.

Italian fans are particularly fond of banners. Each major club has several different gangs of fans called Ultras; each gang has its own *striscione*, a long thin banner made in the club colours with the name of that particular group of Ultras written on it. These are laid out on the running track in front of the fans before the game and are considered, rather like a military standard, to be valuable spoils of war much sought after by opposing fans.

Sometimes it's opposing players who are victims of banner abuse in Italy, sometimes it's opposing fans. Roma fans didn't do quite enough homework before producing a banner saying 'Paul Gascoigne you are big poofter' at a derby game when the Geordie midfielder was playing for local rivals Lazio. A typical Italian grammatical mistake, that, forgetting to use the indefinite article, which must have made Gazza smile.

More meticulous were the Inter Ultras group 'the Boys' who, during a Milan derby, unveiled a banner reading 'The show is about to start. Prepare to look in the mirror and see your shitty heads.' Then they produced a series of thirty-five black sheets with holes in them and did moonies through the holes.

Racist Padova fans were a little less subtle when they displayed a banner during the French nuclear testing in the South Seas in 1995 reading 'stop the nuclear tests in Muraroa – do them in Naples instead'. Many people in the Veneto area where Padua lies have long wanted the North of Italy to be a different nation from the South. The same issue brought a more right-on response from the Swiss national team who, in a rare case of players producing banners, held out a strip saying 'stop it

Chirac' before their international with Sweden.

The same year produced my all-time favourite banner, which I saw at Wembley in the Umbro Cup match against Brazil. The banner was carried by four young girls at a time when there was some debate as to whether Blackburn's Tim Flowers or Arsenal's Dave Seaman should be England's number one. 'Boys', it proclaimed, 'we prefer Seaman to Flowers.'

Apart from on banners, good football graffiti is difficult to come across – the best two examples, possibly apocryphal, are from Liverpool in the 1960s and 1970s and were both added to religious posters. The 1960s poster read 'What would you do if Jesus returned amongst us?' and had 'Move St John to inside left' scrawled next to it. The 1970s religious group who put up a sign saying 'Jesus Saves' up in town were just asking to have somebody write '...but Keegan nets the rebound' after it.

In the 1970s a spray-canned 'Chelsea Rule, OK' was a common sight around the country. Outside Cambridge station an enterprising fan had added his own message to this most formulaic of graffiti: 'Whereas Cambridge United exhibit traits indicative of inherent superiority'.

True graffiti artists aren't hidebound to painting on walls. Brighton fans in 1996 stole into the Goldstone Ground before what was potentially the last-ever game there, and painted 'Sack the Board' right across the half-way line, as well as adding 'less' to the word 'home' on the manager's dug-out. Just down the coast a year earlier before the local alien-invasion-crop-circle-conspiracy-theorists were scratching their heads when a 300-foot stick figure with a halo above his head representing Matthew Le Tissier appeared in a wheat-field in Cheesefoot Head near Winchester. Could some sort of superior intelligence have been suggesting to Terry Venables who to pick in the latest England friendly?

- 36 -
Fruit, Vegetables and Other Oddities

Sometimes fans can make visual messages without using words. Perhaps the most spectacular example of this were the Argentinian fans who in the 1978 World Cup gave their team (who were hosting the tournament) a magnificent welcome each time they came on to the pitch by throwing millions of little bits of paper into the air. This 'ticker-tape reception' as it was dubbed by the press (remembering its origins from American office workers celebrating from skyscrapers during parades) is one of the enduring images of that competition, especially as all the Argentinians' matches (including the final) were played on pitches which had become more white than green.

Of course, when the 1978-79 season started English fans copied the Argentinians, and I remember for a few early matches at Brighton, when people had actually organised themselves and got busy with scissors and newspapers before the game, it looked quite good. Tottenham fans, too, went big on the ticker tape in an attempt to make their two new Argentinian World Cup heroes, Osvaldo Ardiles and Ricardo Villa, feel at home. However, it soon pretty much petered out in this country, though you do see it from time to time, especially at cup matches. It must annoy the hell out of the people who sweep the stadiums.

In a way there was a British precursor to the ticker-tape welcome, though it was far less graceful or spectacular than the South American version. It is the bog-roll salute. The bog-roll is a brilliant trajectile to throw on to the pitch. It's soft, so it can't hurt anyone, and it unravels rather interestingly as it arcs through the air. Mid flight on a floodlit night is about as graceful as the bog-roll can ever get. It's cheap (unless you buy a brand name) and it's easy to smuggle into the ground.

('Honest, officer, there's never any left in the toilets, so I always bring my own.') It also has a down-to-earth, very British feel to it, and makes a statement about the quality of the football that the thrower is watching. In the 1970s bog-roll throwing was a much more common craze and goalkeepers would have to clear reams of the stuff from their goalmouth and put it into the back of their nets. But the retro roll throwers still find their way to the odd match.

Just as odd was the late 1980s inflatables craze. In August 1987 Manchester City fan Frank Newton took an inflatable banana to City's first home match of the season against Plymouth for a bet. It was a perfectly innocent gesture with no racist overtones. Newton had seen it at a friend's house, begged to take it home with him and had only been allowed to on the condition that he took it to Maine Road. Football has never quite been the same since.

Bananamania, according to an article that Newton wrote in City fanzine *Blue Print*, took a while to spread, and nearly died at Barnsley in March when 'Imre' (named after City striker Imre Varadi – it nearly rhymes) split. But he was patched up, and with a little help from *Blue Print*'s editor Mike Kelly, who urged his readers to start taking bananas to matches, the craze grew. At the last game of that season at Crystal Palace there were about fifty at the game. That could have been the end of it, but instead of forgetting about the whole thing, City fans had seemingly spent the summer scouring novelty shops for inflatable oddities. And at the first away game of the season, at Hull, the terraces were a sea of gorillas, giant golf clubs, skeletons, crocodiles and pink panthers. And every away game that season the phenomenon grew with fried eggs, paddling pools, inflatable dinghies and rubber sex dolls joining the fray. The beautiful thing about the whole craze was that the toys were completely irrelevant to the football – they symbolised nothing except the daftness of the fans that were carrying them.

The craze didn't exactly hit the country in the same way it hit Manchester but for a while, outside the capital at least, plastic inflatables were quite a common sight at football matches, especially at Grimsby, where fans took haddock to their matches to milk other fans' sing-when-you're-fishing type abuse.

Looking for sociological reasons for the inflatables phenomenon would be a little daft, but in the negative atmosphere surrounding football, which was at the time still scowling under a black post-Heysel cloud, their burst of colourful and inane humour was a welcome relief.

First the fruit, then the vegetables. In the same period that Manchester City fans were prodding inflatable things in the air Chelsea fans were throwing sticks of celery around whilst they were on their travels. Apparently the whole thing started at Brighton, where a clandestine club called the Caveman Crew used the vegetable as part of an initiation ceremony (use your imagination) whilst singing the song:

Celery, celery
if she don't come
I'll tickle her bum
With a stick of celery

The Crew were Albion fans and the song was heard occasionally on the terraces. By the 1988-89 season Chelsea fans had cottoned on to it and, before travelling to away games, they'd buy a few sticks of the stuff, which they'd throw on to the pitch in unison after singing the song, usually around the time that the opponents were attacking their end. We're not just talking one or two sticks here, we're talking hundreds.

The song is still sung at Stamford Bridge sometimes, though the police have banned celery from the ground. If that seems a bit steep, the draconian measures that Gilligham have taken to stop the vegetable passing through the turnstiles are even worse. Gillingham fans took up the song when their goalkeeper Jim Stannard was put on an enforced diet by the club. The keeper's official weight went up from 14 stone 2 at the beginning of 1995-96 to 16 stone 6 the following season, and though Stannard was, according to the official PFA players' guide, 'still surprisingly agile' for such a big man, the fans thought it was time to press the message home. Stannard was showered with celery, to the accompaniment of the song, every game – it's well known that the salad vegetable takes more calories to eat than it gives you. Gillingham didn't enjoy their fans' humour and threatened a life ban to anyone taking celery into the ground. So don't put it in your halftime sandwiches if you go down to the Priestfield Stadium.

Another victim of food abuse is Paul Gascoigne, who was showered with Mars bars when he returned to St James' Park after moving from Newcastle to Spurs in 1989. Gascoigne is reputed to be a big fan of the chocolate bar.

Taking food into matches isn't always such harmless fun. Certain racist fans occasionally throw bananas at black players – John Barnes used to have a lot thrown at him when he played at neighbouring Everton, who were slower to employ a black player in their team. I thought that this sort of behaviour had died out until I went to Brighton's last game at the Goldstone. The match, a tense enough affair anyway, was marred by a fight between Doncaster's (black) defender Darren Moore and Brighton striker Ian Baird which resulted in both players being sent off. To increase the tension further, a Brighton fan standing a few yards to my left started throwing bananas, one after another, at Moore as he remonstrated with the ref. The other Doncaster players were treating the bananas as a joke, and were volleying them so they disintegrated before hitting the ground. The insult served to make Moore even more angry than he had been and he kicked the side of the tunnel as he walked into the changing room so hard that people nearby jumped with fright at the sound.

Fans take some props into the ground for their aural rather than visual qualities. The traditional noise-maker, of course, was the good old rattle, which was originally a warning device used by the army in the Boer war and was what every teenager wanted to make in woodwork classes in the 1950s and 1960s.

Nowadays a rattle would be confiscated by the coppers outside the ground as an offensive weapon, which makes it all the more surprising that they let the Sheffield Wednesday band – their small group of supporters who bash drums and blow trumpets – into grounds. I'm not saying they're likely to attack anyone with their instruments. I'm talking about *their* safety.

When I read that Wimbledon wouldn't let the Wednesday band into Selhurst Park I thought 'spoilsports'. Then I went to Wembley Stadium to watch England play Moldova and heard the band for the first time. I realised, on the contrary, that far from being spoilsports the Wimbledon suits who'd refused them access had had the Dons fans' interests in mind. Wednesday, you see, have a one-tune band, and they play that tune time and time and time and time again. Originally sung by the German fans, the tune is a martial 'der der der' affair which is repeated over and again, allowing a two-beat pause between finish and re-start for the name of the team ('Eng-land' in this case, but usually 'Wens-day') to be shouted. The band, along with the tannoy man, who I have already mentioned, ruined my evening. I think that they should be strung up by their instruments and be made to listen to back-to-back tapes of their collected work for several days.

Before we move away from fans it's worth talking about the other way they communicate while they are watching matches; their personal commentary. This differs from fan to fan, but is pretty similar in one respect. Each fan's commentary is usually only audible to the people in his immediate surroundings but is addressed to the people on the pitch. Therefore it's not really a form af communication at all – it's really a venting of the spleen, a football version of the pantomime audience's stock response to given situations.

The personal commentary can be complimentary. 'Good ball' is a common stock response to, well, a good ball. 'Good tackle' and 'good header' speak for themselves. 'Well in' follows a fine intervention. 'What a goal' might sound a little outdated, but next time you see one of your players lash the ball into the net, listen to yourself for a second and out it will pop.

Sometimes bad elements of play from your team will provoke negative responses. 'What the fuck was that, Smith?' might follow a bad shot from your striker. Other forms of general abuse, which I don't need to spell out, are directed at players when they do things wrong.

Sometimes fans don their metaphorical sheepskin coats and jangly jewellery and shout manager-like instructions. 'Get your foot on the ball' can be used if your team is failing to connect their passes. 'Spread it wide', 'hoof it out' and 'shoot' are some of many possible instructions that fans give to players. At Stamford Bridge recently I actually heard one fan taking managerspeak as far as shouting 'get it in the mixer'.

The referee, of course, is the man with whom most fans want to perform this type of one-way communication. Part of the beauty of being a football fan is that for ninety minutes every fortnight you can completely bypass your normal standards of partiality, and the poor old ref is usually the victim of this collective abandonment of objectivity. They must be the most sworn-at people in the country, with traffic wardens coming in a close second.

The futility of the whole exercise (the only time spectators' individual cries are heard is when there are just a handful of spectators round the pitch) is really shown up when you find yourself shouting abuse at a referee who is several hundred or even thousand miles away, that's to say when you are watching the game on the television. I noticed this phenomenon in November 1997 while watching Italy play Russia in an Italian restaurant full of Italians in King's Cross, London. I was supporting the Azzurri because I used to live there, plus I was with my Roman girlfriend. At one point the ball hit a Russian hand. To a man (and Francesca) the people in the room stood up and shouted, in perfect unison, 'mano!' I was in unison, too, though being English I shouted 'handball'. The referee, or the collection of microdots representing the referee, didn't react to our plea.

Part Six

The Media

- 37 -
Programmes – The Clump on the Drain

In 1976-77 I lived with my mother and my older brother in a big house on an estate in a small rural village in Sussex. My brother was taking a year off before going to university. He used to go drinking every night and he'd come up to my room to talk to me when he got back. We got on very well. I used to lie awake waiting for him – I knew the sound of his gait, especially when he wore his cowboy boots. I was absolutely sure it was him when I heard the clump he made stepping on a drain cover just in front of our door.

I was completely obsessed at the time with football, especially the fortunes of Brighton and Newcastle. I was particularly impatient for my brother's return on nights that Brighton had played at home. He used to go to all the Brighton matches, and he'd bring me back the match programme. I treasured those programmes. I used to pore over them for hours reading the club news, the match statistics and the fate of the reserve team.

As I write this I've just been into the loft in the same house to look for the programmes. I spent a whole morning up there delving into old things from my childhood. I found toys, I found school exercise books, I found letters from old lovers, I found my old Subbuteo floodlights, I found my brother's cowboy boots – and I found my football programme collection. In *A la recherche du temps perdu* Marcel Proust writes at length about the taste of a madeleine cake bringing back floods of memory about his youth. Well, that was obviously in the days before match programmes.

Match programmes go back a long way. They are a direct desendant of match 'cards' which used to be given out at and before important games giving the essential details of the game, including the teams, team colours and umpires' and referees' names. These are valuable to football historians because they tell us a lot about the game: an 1875 match card from Wanderers against Queens Park in Glasgow shows, for example, that each team's players were distinguished from one another by the colour of their stockings (details of which were given on the programme) and that Queens Park played a system akin to the modern 4-3-3 formation. The legend 'Please do not strain the ropes' is added at the bottom. These cards are now extremely valuable commodities – a Victorian FA Cup final card recently changed hands at a Christie's auction for over £5,000.

It wasn't until the 1900s that teams started producing 'programmes' (named after theatre programmes) for their regular games – Chelsea were amongst the first to do so when they set themselves up in 1905 with their grandly named Chelsea FC Chronicle. There were no autocratic rantings, I'm afraid, from their Ken Bates equivalent Gus Mears, but there were some rather nice caricatures of such players as 'Fatty' Foulkes.

The two world wars, and the paper shortages that ensued, hampered the evolution of the football programme. Again it was Chelsea who broke the mould by producing the first magazine-type programme in 1948. Costing sixpence, it was a sixteen-page affair with action shots, and Portsmouth (the opponents) team photos. Arsenal and Manchester United soon followed suit.

By the 1960s all League clubs were selling magazine-style match programmes and by the 1970s quite a few people had started seriously collecting them. Nowadays collecting football programmes is a popular hobby and there are two large fairs every year which attract thousands.

Although design has improved over the years the content of programmes, team statistics apart, has remained on the whole pretty insipid and although some club programmes have taken on former fanzine writers to zap up their prose, no club is going to allow anything but the party line to be preached from their pages. With more and more information available from other media (remember that you used to need the programme for the halftime scores key and you actually read the team line-up, and not the local paper, to find out who was in the team) programmes might well be living out their winter years.

Before I looked through one of these Brighton 1976/77 programmes again I assumed that I'd got the whole deal sussed. That the material inside wasn't important, but that they represented actual physical evidence that you'd been to a match. That they helped you keep track of the games you'd been to. And that they were classic collection fodder for anoraks. And that that was about it.

I was wrong.

For your 10p you got four pages of glossy black, blue and white A4 paper, folded in half and stapled in the middle. The blue cover had three stamp-sized pictures on the front (that remained the same all season) and the legend 'Brighton & Hove Albion welcome Reading Football League Division III K.O. 7.45 p.m. Tuesday, 12th April 1977 Price 10p.'

The inside cover was Down The Tunnel – a jaunty look at a football issue, in this case how we take floodlighting for granted. 'One early disaster in 1966-67,' it reads, 'caused a Fourth Division match between Crewe and Lincoln to come to a halt and the visitors were possibly robbed of two points which might well have proved vital.'

Next are some match photos, both showing 'goalmouth scrambles', one at Brighton's end, one at the opponents'. Then a page of 'Albion Facts And Figures' – the results and statistics of recent matches, the league table, appearances and scorers – faced by another pair of match action pictures and captions.

The next pages are dedicated to 'our visitors' Reading, with a short history, the season so far, pen-pics, and a team photo over the middle spread. Robin Friday and Eamonn Dunphy are the only names I still recognise. Then we're into the back section with details about 'Tonight's Referee', competition winners, how to drive to Walsall, charter train arrangements, what was happening twenty-five years before and a list of matchball sponsors.

On the inside back spread there are the First Team Fixtures, with the scores, crowds and scorers, the results of the reserve team and the reserve team league table. Finally it's the back cover, with, of course, Tonight's Line-up, plus a little retrospective about previous clashes between the clubs.

I timed how long it took me to read it: fifteen minutes.

It's the First Team Fixtures and Albion Facts And Figures which were the key to my fascination with the whole deal, especially the fixtures. Nowadays these pages are sumptuous affairs with the fixtures down the left-hand column and the result, crowd and team for each match running across the double-page spread, with special annotations for scorers and players that were booked and sent off. This was a simpler affair with just the crowd, score and scorer. But it was still enough information to make you lose yourself in dreamland for long periods. Vitally it gave you the chance to indulge in looking back at the past *and* looking forward to the future, too.

Looking backwards enabled you to relive those past matches, even if you hadn't been to them. Albion 7 Walsall 0! Peter Ward with four goals, Ian Mellor with three, and all seven coming in the second half! But only 14,204 there. How many at the next match? 18,790 against Peterborough. That's better. Only 1-0, mind. And so on.

Looking forward gave you the chance to see what matches were coming up – what there was in store. Five away matches left and only two at home! An away game against Wrexham, rivals for promotion. We lost to them at home. What was the score now? Oh yes, 2-0. Dreadful. Last home match on 3 May against Sheffield Wednesday. There's no way I'm going to miss that one. How did we do at Sheffield? 0-0. Hmm, it's an evening match. Maybe I'll be allowed to go.

The match programme introduced me to the joys of football statistics – and twenty years on I'm still obsessed with them. Every week I spend half an hour on the Sunday paper results section, on the toilet so nobody can disturb me. But the joy of the match programme is that it gives you *your team*'s statistics and you can get lost in memories and expectations of your team's season. The chairman's notes, the articles on issues within the sport, the team-sheet which is probably wrong (or, in the case of the Premiership, merely gives you the names of the whole squad) the manager's message, Junior Jottings and Reserve Round-up, the whole of the rest of the deal is to keep you mildly amused on the train on the way home. It doesn't matter if it's quickly written, uncritical, watered-down rubbish. Put it in a pile with the others, stick it in the loft, and immerse yourself in the statistics section twenty years later.

- 38 -
Real *Roy of the Rovers* Stuff

Back in those days, there was precious little reading matter available on football. The newspapers reported on the matches and did the odd interview, there were a few magazines (more of which later) and there were a couple of comics – *Roy of the Rovers* and *Scoop*. For a while I got *Roy of the Rovers* every week. I tried *Scoop* but it was an inferior product and soon, as I remember, folded. It was by no means the last sports magazine to do so.

The earliest football strip cartoons were woodcuts made from drawings showing various episodes from games. One example, by W Ralston, exhibited in the FIFA museum, shows nine episodes from the first official international between Scotland and England in 1872. The quaint captions include 'A soft falling, fortunately', 'How's that, Umpire!' and 'Well done Mac!!', which shows a Scottish international performing an early form of the bicycle kick. This was in the early days of comics (or comicks) which weren't yet 100 years old, having first been published in magazine form in 1796 (with a collection of Hogarth's works).

The genre improved over the years, and an example from the 1899 Cup final, drawn by a Ralph Cleaver, uses the sort of perspective that wouldn't look too amiss in a modern-day football strip. The guy scoring Sheffield United's equaliser against Derby, in fact, is in exactly the sort of 'just-having-thwacked-the-ball' pose that Roy Race was to adopt so often in *Roy of the Rovers*.

The first sporting comic book was called *Sports Fun* and was launched on the back of the success of *Film Fun*. But even with the collaboration of Tom Webster (sports cartoonist with the *Daily Mail*) it was a flop. Strips like 'My funniest experience on the football field, by Fanny Walden the famous Tottenham and English international inside forward', and 'What I'd like to do to the referee when we win' by Stanley Fazackerly, Everton, failed to capture the imagination and, even after a revamp thirteen issues in, it never made it to issue thirty.

No football strip really caught the public imagination until the most famous one of the lot, *Roy of the Rovers* was launched on 11 September 1954 in *Tiger*, 'The Sport and Picture Weekly'. The strip is still cited by commentators when something extremely exciting happens in the game, and it's no surprise. Right from the start it was real Roy of the Rovers Stuff. The first strip kicked off with the legend...'Only two minutes to go in the local Cup Tie...and the score 0-0! With all his pals of the Milston Youth Club FC played to a standstill, centre forward Roy Race was the one member of the team still tireless and on his toes. Could he score before the final whistle blew?' Well, what do you think? And guess who was watching? A scout for Melchester Rovers!

Roy, of course, went on to become the most explosive centre forward in the game, although throughout the years Melchester Rovers were notoriously bad starters, partially because the team suffered from a series of kidnapping attempts on their best players by rival teams just before kick off. They won their first title in 1958 with a last-minute goal after being 3-0 down at halftime, and went on in much the same vein, with Race in the first team for an incredible thirty-nine years. The strip was such a success that on 25 September 1976 Roy launched his own football strip comic, which he celebrated with a phone-in ('Dial 01 261 6272 – Roy is waiting for your call!') and a free football chart. The storylines tried hard to keep with the times – Rovers entered into European competition, and started signing foreign players. Having become the first comic strip character in the country to fall in love, get married and have kids, Roy split up for a time with his lovely wife, Penny. But sadly, as sales dropped, the storylines had to get more dramatic to try to keep their readers' attention. In 1981-82 Roy was shot. In 1986 eight members of the team were killed by a terrorist bomb. In 1988 Mel Park, Melchester's ground, was hit by an earthquake during a match and Rovers had to play their home matches at Wembley. Finally, in 1993 Roy's helicopter crashed and it looked like the end for

Race. He lost a foot and went off to manage AC Monza in Italy.

Roy Race has helped introduce countless youngsters to football literature – myself included. It was there I learnt about some of the facets of soccer, and some of its terminology, too. I quote from a January 1978 issue in which Roy is playing as player-manager for England, who are facing Holland at Wembley Stadium. The team includes, for some reason, Malcolm MacDonald and Trevor Francis in the attack.

Commentator: ***Giles*** *to* ***Race*** *and out to* ***Vernon Eliot****...Now it's* ***Holland's*** *turn to chase back*
Crowd: ***England Englaaand!***
Caption: Vernon, playing in the position of an 'old-fashioned winger', cut in confidently!
Commentator: We've seen England's ***speed*** *and* ***fighting spirit*** *and now comes the* ***skill****...He's trying to get in close enough to make sure his cross is* ***accurate.***
Caption: It was a pinpoint ball, aimed at the far post!
Commentator: Lawrence! He's got in behind their right flank!
Nipper Lawrence: ***Where are you, Trevor?***
Trevor Francis: Right here, Nipper!
Crowd: ***Three one! Goal! Goaaaaaaal!***

Of course I was used to some of this tactics-speak from watching *Match of the Day* and the *Big Match*, but here, suddenly, I found I could study it at my leisure. And such terms as 'chase back', 'old-fashioned winger' and 'got in behind their right flank' became second nature, to be repeated when playing footie in the playground or on the green in the holidays.

One hilarious element of *Roy of the Rovers* – one I probably didn't pick up on at the time – was the cartoonist's difficulty in keeping the narrative going without disturbing the action or using too many 'boring' captions. 'The pictures aren't in themselves enough to tell the story, so you have to use various techniques to keep the readers informed of what's going on,' says Pete Nash, the cartoonist responsible for the *Sun*'s *Striker*.

One technique that Nash uses and is also used by some of the later

ROTR stories is to incorporate a commentator who is pictured occasionally, then represented by adding serrated edges to the speech bubble.

Another technique, and one which, with the benefit of hindsight was pretty risible, was the 'well-informed fans' method which had the fans creating the narrative. The fans in question were rarely pictured, they were represented by a speech bubble coming out of the crowd behind the action. The fans might let you know about the general shape of the game...

> *Great ball! Gerry Holloway's away! He drifted into the gap left by Fischer...*

About the state of Rovers' fortunes...

> *It's a good job Charlie Carter is on form! Melchester have only taken five points from their last seven games!*

Or just to keep the suspense going...

> *What's wrong with Roy? They're giving him chance after chance and he's chucking them all away. He's letting the team down!*

My favourite crowd comment of all is a short conversation between two German fans in Rovers' 1978-79 UEFA Cup clash against Rassberg, which borrows a cliché from the war comics to give us no doubt about the nationality of the fans in question.

> *Teufel. What will Roy Race do now?*
> *It is rumoured that Mervyn Wallace has many problems!*
> *So he will not be a threat to us!*

I grew out of *Roy of the Rovers* pretty quickly – I found later issues in the loft and in the 'My Marks out of Ten' little triangle at the end of every story my marks range from 0 to 3 with the later stories unread. Sales dwindled as strip cartoons became less and less popular and eventually *Roy of the Rovers* was taken out of circulation in 1993. Like a soap star deemed surplus to requirements Roy was written out of existence in that dreadful helicopter accident. However, when *Match of the Day* magazine went monthly in 1997 they started up the series again, bringing Roy back as non-playing manager of the team and focusing on the fortunes of his dashing son, Rocky Race. As I write, in a typical *ROTR* twist, Rocky is playing for local rivals Melborough after a bitter family row...

The series' unlikely cliff-hanging storylines and inflexible style made it ripe for parody; *Viz* magazine obliged with the tale of Billy the Fish. The first half of the strap-line for the strip revealed most of what you needed to know: 'Despite being born half man/half fish, Billy Thompson has made the Fulchester Utd no 1 shirt his own...' The second half traditionally went on to reveal the nature of the latest absurd storyline. For example, '...But now he has turned his back on the club in order to go to bed with Kylie Minogue in her Australian love nest.'

The strip did a brilliant job of mimicking the 'voice in the crowd' method of narrative delivery. Here's a typical matchtime conversation between three fans, each in a different stand.

Fan 1: The game appears to be slipping out of Fulchester's grasp.
Fan 2: I wonder whether Tommy Brown has an ace up his sleeve.
Fan 3: Yes. A strange new signing perhaps. Someone who he has omitted to mention so far.

The signing in question turned out to be Wing and Wang, a pair of Siamese twins who immediately went on to score an equalising goal which the referee decided to count as two goals. The signing wasn't that strange at Fulchester; manager Tommy Brown always had an eye for the unconventional. Other players to make the team included Johnny X, invisible since childhood after an unfortunate laboratory accident, and Professor Wolfgang Schnell, who could work out his slide-rule passes to a couple of decimal places.

As well as sending up *Roy of the Rovers*, the strip parodied football in general; Billy's haircuts, for example, included a long-at-the-back Chris Waddle and a golden-stubble Gazza. The storylines echoed some of the big issues in the game: dodgy agents, bungs, booze, the lot. The strip's joint task of taking the piss out of football strips in particular and football in general can be summed up by a quote from manager Brown in the *Billy the Fish Football Yearbook* of 1990:

> *As team manager my job has not been an easy one. I've been sacked, I've been slandered in the gutter press, I've suffered a fatal heart attack, been kidnapped and taken to Mars, undergone a sex operation and travelled back through time to caveman days. But that's football.*

The most-read footie cartoon strip is (arguably) *Striker*, which sits at the top of the funnies page in the *Sun*. The strip was the idea of journalist Pete Nash, who got the idea past Kelvin MacKenzie despite (as Nash, a self-taught cartoonist, admits) the ropey initial drawings. He told me on the phone of his plans to take *Striker* to the forefront of cartoon technology, by computerising the images – something which he reckons will have taken place by the time you're reading this book.

Striker is, in effect, *Roy of the Rovers* for grown-ups. 'I was looking round for ideas on a cartoon strip and I realised an adult football one had never been done,' says its creator. What Nash is trying to blend is traditional soap issues with the drama of football – so the cartoon drifts from the bedroom to the stadium. Never having been a *Striker* fan, I picked a few issues of the *Sun* from the pile in my office, put them in order, and became enthralled by the story that unfolded.

The earliest strip took place entirely outside a leafy mansion. The first square showed a power-dressed beauty leaving with a fat sweaty-looking man on the doorstep. He looked desperate and bewildered.

> *'Where are you going?' he says.*
> *'I'm leaving you, Eric. I can't take any more'*
> *'If this is about the liver and bacon casserole...'*
> *'It's not about that...it's about your reckless, inconsiderate behaviour and the strain you put me under...Goodbye Eric! You'll be hearing from my solicitor.'*
> *'Vanessa.'*

That's it.

Sometimes the action goes on to the pitch, and we are treated to a football match with the narrative written in captions. 'Joe comes close to scoring Warbury's first goal in Division One...But the Warriors are soon on the retreat...and a clever move leaves them trailing after just six minutes.'

Sometimes we get a mixture, with drama on and off the pitch in the same strip. Picture, for example, Eric the chairman, talking into a mobile phone in the executive box, with a match in progress behind him. 'Listen to me, you prickly old gasbag, Vanessa's my wife and I've got every right to speak to her.'

The next square flashes to a determined old woman with a phone to her ear. 'She's my daughter and I've got every right to protect her from violent bullies like you!'

Back to the chairman. 'Me? Violent? What has she been telling you?'

The final picture goes down on to the pitch and shows an opposing striker lining up a shot against Warbury's keeper, a thought bubble coming from his head. 'Number four coming up.'

Great stuff. That *Striker* has been successful in a period in which strip cartoons are in decline says a lot for the increasing popularity of football – and of Nash's ability to drag the genre from its stereotypes and move it into the modern age. I don't much like the sound of this computer-generated bit, though.

- 39 -
Shoot to Kill – Football Magazines 1977-1997

Back in the mid-to-late 1970s, the main reason I gave up on *Roy of the Rovers* was because *Shoot!* satisfied my lost-in-the-desert thirst for football stories much better. Instead of fantastic fictional last-minute-goal type stories, the magazine delivered the sort of nitty-gritty football stories I really wanted to read. I was becoming a student of the game and *Shoot!* was my teacher. I was realising that the sort of drama that was created on and around the pitch was far more interesting than invention.

I started getting the mag around 1976 but few of my early issues survive as, when I'd finished reading it cover-to-cover, I used to cut *all* the pictures out and stick them in do-it-yourself sticker albums. I've just read through an issue from November 1978, by which time I'd ceased my vandalism, and I was surprised by three things. The first was how serious the magazine was, the second was how much space was dedicated to words and how little to pictures, and the third was how much access they had to the stars of the day.

The News Desk released as many as twenty-eight items. There were four guest columnists – Gordon McQueen, Andy Gray, Ray Clemence, and Derek Johnstone who brought us 'Tartan Talk'. The issues discussed were such topics as how Manchester United had tightened up their defence, who was the better keeper – Ray Clemence or Peter Shilton, whether foreigners playing in the country were good or bad for the game and what the ideal age to retire was. By the time you got to Take a Break – It's Quiz Time at the back, you really needed it. There was very little concession to the average teenager's vocabulary – I vividly remember as a twelve-or-so-year-old looking up from my Rice Krispies and asking, 'Mum, what does, "the onus is on us" mean?' There was very little attempt to cater to a teenager's sense of levity. The football funnies weren't funny and the 'Focus On...' player profiles were answered in a completely deadpan way: 'Miscellaneous Likes: Good company, horse racing and golf.' People took the mag so seriously that there were letters of complaint after Frank Worthington wrote that his most difficult opponent was the taxman, his likes included 'birdwatching and browsing round hardware shops' and his favourite other team was Bolton market's half-holiday second eleven.

Today's *Shoot!* is a far cry from its 1970s cousin, and is representative of the dumbing down of youth culture that sociologists are going on about. It's geared to the kid with an attention span that has been cultivated by a TV zapper and a wide choice of rubbish on the screen – news is delivered in short, usually photo-led soundbites and even double-page-spread features (which are always broken up with a sidebar) are split into a number of digestible paragraphs. It doesn't discuss serious issues of our time, concentrating instead on simpler interviews with players. The only recognisable legacy from before is the 'Focus On...' section, which is still remarkably similar, down to the deadpan answers.

I don't want to sound too pompous and 'it was better in my day' here, because I think that maybe, especially at eleven or twelve, I would have chosen my magazine to have had more information delivered in shorter chunks. *Shoot!* has got more idea than it used to about what kids are like – and, with its rival *Match* having been breathing down its neck it's had to take every step of its development since I read it with an eye on the competition. OK, so it's less didactic – but is that what kids' mags are for?

More serious kids with a yen for issue-led stories have got another option nowadays, anyway, with the birth of the adult football mag. One of the longest-standing myths of the publishing world was debunked in August 1994 after Haymarket launched *FourFourTwo* with the strapline, 'It's not a matter of life and death. It's more important than that', and a warts-and-all close-up of England manager Terry Venables underneath. British football had its first adult-oriented monthly magazine. And it not only survived in the marketplace; it thrived.

FourFourTwo was like none other before it, in that it devoted more space to issues and interviews than the papers (or the children's magazines) ever had before. In the first issue they dedicated eight pages to an interview with Venables, six pages to one with Barry Fry, and performed an in-depth analysis of how to beat Manchester United. It indulged in a spot of nostalgia whilst looking ahead to the future. It told us about all the kits the teams would be wearing that season and about the Yugoslavian team that won 134-1 to sneak their league title on goal difference. It was just what football fans needed – an informed, detailed read written by fan-journalists who were as obsessed with the game as they were. It was much better written than the fanzines and more detailed than the dailies; 132 pages of end-to-end action. It was a godsend.

I remember buying the magazine in a Brighton newsagents and going down to the beach to read it. I felt like I'd bought a porn mag. An adult reading a football magazine? I put the cover down on my knees so no one could see. I was there a while.

It soon became perfectly normal for grown men to read football magazines in public. *FourFourTwo* got copied. In September 1995 bright young publishers Future brought out *Total Football* which was much more laddish, a kind of *Loaded* for footie fans. Two months later IPC launched *Goal*. *Goal* was much hipper than its predecessors – *The Face* meets *Roy of the Rovers*. In April 1997 BBC magazines, having tried and failed with an adult weekly magazine – *Match of the Day* – turned it into a monthly.

Pretty soon the situation had been turned on its head. We had a case of information overload. To read four football magazines a month takes some doing. I mean you've got to leave some time aside to actually *watch* the game, haven't you? On top of these four there were the specialist mags: *World Soccer*, *Football Europe* and *Football Italia* for the cosmopolitan fans, *When Saturday Comes* for the cynics, *FC* for the players. As if that wasn't enough each club started getting its own glossy mag – in 1997-98 only two Premiership clubs didn't have a monthly publication. *Manchester United* magazine is the biggest-selling of all the monthly football mags, unloading 20,000 issues a month in Thailand alone.

The long nature of interviews in thick glossy monthly football magazines sometimes puts players too much at their ease and they start acting like normal human beings. This was certainly the case when Karen Buchanan, founding editor of *FourFourTwo*, interviewed Stan Collymore, at the time in the Liverpool reserves after a big-money transfer from Nottingham Forest.

'If I felt now that I'd be stuck at Liverpool for the next two years and just be average and just go through the motions I would give up football tomorrow without a doubt,' he said to her, and she felt the statement to be so strong that she started off her piece with it. 'I don't know of any other industry that would lay out £8.5m on anything and then not have some plan from day one of how they are going to use it,' he continued.

The day after the article was published the *Sun* had a field day. 'Grovel or You're Off Collymore' read the headline on the back page, and quoted manager Roy Evans, who expressed his annoyance that Collymore should choose to 'go public and air his opinions like this'. It was one of the major stories of the week. Even the *Guardian* wrote that Collymore 'claims he is considering retiring from professional football'.

Buchanan is angry at how the daily press picked up on the story, and how Collymore got in trouble for, in effect, being honest.

'I thought he made a number of reasonable points about the way we treat footballers, the way we expect them to be and what our perceptions of them are,' she told me in a wine bar near my office in King's Cross where we'd arranged to meet to talk about the subject. 'They're supposed to be thick little pieces of meat that we buy and sell and not actually have any say or thoughts on it. When you get a player who steps out of line, that doesn't give the Stepford Wives line, then the rest of the press feasts on it.'

The fact is that Collymore refused to follow the usual clichéd football line and chose to speak his mind, which is not the done thing in football. 'The way Stan Collymore got treated, I think, was appalling,' she continued. 'He actually had opinions and we don't expect them to have opinions because that contradicts the whole language of football in the traditional press. You don't ask challenging questions because you don't want them to give challenging answers because it's all a nice, cosy little world.'

The result in modern football is that players, because of this sort of journalism, tend to be tetchy with the whole press for fear of being misquoted, or saying something that will lead them into trouble. Unfortunately as a magazine writer, largely unconcerned with dishing out dirt, I suffer from players' umbrella image of the press. Alan Shearer is a good case in point. All through the 1994-95 season I ghost-wrote a monthly column 'by' Alan for the sports section of *Satellite TV Europe* magazine. The job involved ringing the then-Blackburn striker every month and then getting blood out of a monolith while he played with his kids. Someone, somewhere, has taught Shearer to play his cards buttoned up in his top pocket, which is why he makes such a good spokesman for the England team – as far as the management is concerned.

Shearer was getting paid £250 per ten-minute phone call (which is remarkably cheap nowadays; I was recently quoted £5,000 for an interview with Fabrizio Ravanelli). I was on considerably less. But I was doing all the work. It's difficult to make 500 words out of ten minutes of largely monosyllabic answers, clichés and truisms.

I didn't meet Shearer in the flesh until about six months after we'd finished, when I went to the England training camp (by cycling across London to Paddington, getting on the train to Marlow, and cycling from there to Bisham Abbey. You should have seen the security guy's face when this sweaty guy on a sit-up-and-beg showed him valid press accreditation.) As he walked off the pitch I introduced myself. I felt we'd got to know each other quite well with our monthly chats.

'I'm Alex who did your column for *Satellite TV* magazine last season,' I said, or words to that effect.

'How are you doing?' he replied, and walked off.

Six months later I met him in an office in Huddersfield Town's Alfred McAlpine Stadium, a meeting his agent had set up for us. I was writing the cover story for the first edition of the FA-endorsed magazine *England*, which covered the England team in the run-in to the European Championships in 1996. As an England player, Shearer was obliged to do the interview. When he arrived, he didn't recognise me. 'Have you just signed for Huddersfield, then?' I joked. 'No, this is where my agent works from,' he replied, deadpan.

At one point I asked him what the worst part of his job was. 'Doing interviews like this,' he said. Three-quarters of an hour later I was glad to get out of the room and head back to London. I was forced to write an article about how difficult it was to interview Alan Shearer. 'Shearer has learnt his interview technique at the Gary Lineker School of Diplomacy, without taking the catchy soundbites option,' I wrote.

Shearer views interviews as his England colleagues viewed the Italy match in the World Cup qualifiers. He wanted to go in there, be defensive for ninety minutes, and make sure he didn't make any silly mistakes. Oh, for more Collymores.

- 40 -
From the Deranged Ferret to the Hanging Sheep – The Fanzines

The way for the adult football magazine had been crazy-paved by the birth and development of the fanzines in the 1980s. The term 'fanzine' was first used in the USA in 1949 to describe sci-fi mags produced by geeky kids, but these weren't a direct influence on the genre, and are, apart from their name, unimportant to our argument.

It's now over ten years since the birth of the football fanzines, and, partially because of the technological breakthroughs in desktop publishing, there are more than ever before. It's difficult to judge, because they rarely register themselves as publications in the British Library (which they could), but according to *When Saturday Comes* (who keep tabs on these things) there are currently up to 300 fanzines on the market in this country alone. The vast majority (with one or two notable exceptions) focus on the fortunes of individual football clubs.

Nowadays some of them are, in the quality of their design, virtually indistinguishable from the club programme, using glossy paper and colour photographs of the team. Others, more in keeping with the original ethics of the movement, are stapled-together photocopies of badly-typed prose and rough cartoons.

Although some of the glossier numbers are starting to become rather self-important and serious, the vast majority of fanzines are written with a certain amount of self-deprecating humour, and are unafraid of confronting the fan-based issues.

The first football-style fanzine, which came out in 1977, wasn't about football at all. It was called *Sniffin' Glue* and it was about the punk rock movement. It wasn't particularly well-written and was even more badly designed, but because it covered an area no mainstream magazines wanted to write about, it became pretty well-known. When the music papers fell in love with punk a year later it stopped; it had done its job.

Over the years there followed a number of imitators, including *Snipe*, which in 1985 gave away with one of its issues a football-related magazine of the same style, called *When Saturday Comes*, edited by Mike Ticher and Andy Lyons. This proved remarkably popular and soon demand outstripped the printer's supply.

Andy Lyons is still the editor of the magazine, which, without having lost its irony or (all of) its anger, has become a mainstream mag on sale in the newsagents. To find out some of the background I went to see him in the magazine's book-cluttered rooftop offices in Farringdon, London. A pleasant, soft-spoken, quite serious guy, Andy sat me down, made me a cup of tea, let me scrounge one of his colleague's cigarettes, and gave me a history lesson in fanzine culture.

There was a precursor to *WSC*, he told me, called *Foul*, which came out in the mid 1970s, put together by Cambridge graduates and financed, funnily enough, by Tim Rice. It put out thirty or so issues over a period of three years. It was quite similar to *Private Eye* as it looked inside Fleet Street at the sports journalists, as well as going behind the scenes of football matches and looking at styles of play. It was closed down when a journalist won a libel case against it. Then Saturday came.

Looking back on the early issues of *WSC*, Lyons now finds them rather ranting and angry, but realises that this attitude was much needed. 'The fact is that there was a gaping hole in the market: there had previously been nowhere for football fans to read about football fans' grievances – the mags like *Shoot* and *Match* were all about the players and teams, and the match programmes, produced by the clubs, were necessarily sterile.'

The style of writing was influenced by the music papers, 'especially the *Melody Maker*, and the way they were also interested in cult TV and popular films as well as music. Football fans are not only interested in football and nobody was reflecting that.'

'There must have been something in the air,' he remembers, 'because one week before we launched another fanzine, called *Off the Ball*, came out. There was a mood around at the time after Heysel that branded football fans as being hooligans and it simply wasn't true in most cases. We felt it would be good to correct that and show that a lot of us were normal, rational people. We wanted to reflect the informed point of view that fans might express to one another before and after games or in the pub.'

Soon *When Saturday Comes* had influenced a number of imitators. However, there was an important distinction between the original and its spawn: *When Saturday Comes* was about football in general, the others tended to follow the fortunes of one team.

Among this early batch of fanzines were the *Chelsea Independent*, *Leyton Orientear*, *Eagle Eye* (Crystal Palace), *Blue Print* (Manchester City) and *Flashing Blade* (Sheffield United).

Some excerpts of the early fanzines (which have been collected together in the excellent anthology *El Tel Was a Space Alien*) will give a good idea of the sort of humour and tone of the publications, which were generally type- and hand-written, photocopied and sold outside the ground before games.

The first issue of Charlton's fanzine *Lennie Lawrence* had a dig at the banality of match programmes with a badly drawn picture of a sexy blonde lying suggestively by a football. It said:

'Soccergirl has big tits and a Newcastle shirt. But what's she doing in the programme? Cross out eight words or phrases that describe the programme to find out.' Above the picture of Soccergirl there was a grid with lots of letters in it in which you can clearly read 'piss boring' 'dreary' 'dull' 'awful' 'tiresome' 'terrible' and 'pathetic'. Underneath the box it read, 'Answer: Soccergirl is in the programme to fill space.'

A refreshing aspect of the fanzines was that many of the jokes were at the clubs' expense, aimed at the players or even the fans (again from *Lennie Lawrence*):

Q: How do you confuse a Charlton forward?
A: Put him in the opposing penalty area.
Q: How many Charlton fans can you put in a Mini?
A: All of them
Q: What is the difference between the team coach and an open goal?
A: Andy Jones doesn't always miss the team coach

I love that 'always', by the way.

The *Chelsea Independent*, which is still being produced, showed similar irony when eulogising about the departure of the Blues' Scottish defender Doug Rougvie to Brighton. 'Predictably the move brought an angry response as Rougvie's fans flooded the Fulham Rd. to protest and an extra policeman had to be called upon to disperse them both.'

But there was a serious side, too, as the fanzines published opinionated editorials about how badly the clubs were run and policed. Fanzines were also able to approach issues that were too controversial for match programmes or football magazines to touch, such as racism in the crowd.

Some of the writing was pretty bad – fanzines were and are champions of the misplaced apostrophe, for example – but some were particularly good. Take this example from the Orient 'zine *The Orientear*.

'The following week we were beaten 1-0 at Hartlepool. The home fans taunted us with chants of 'Yuppies, Yuppies' and a rendition of the EastEnders *theme tune. We replied with 'We've got better regional stereotypes than you, Leyton, Leyton' and followed up with a continuous buddhist mantra whilst flicking desiccated onions from our burgers. A few days later we lost 1-4 to Rotherham, who have ex-O Tony Grealish, with beard.'*

Well it took my fancy, anyway.

The quality of the Orient magazine reflects an interesting trait that soon developed in fanzines. As a rule of thumb, the less successful the club, the higher quality of the magazine. 'The standard tends to be higher in lower division teams – they have to be more creative as there is less to write about and as things are usually going rather badly there is much more room for irony,' says Andy Lyons. 'Bigger club fanzines seem to be obsessed with the fact that they are a big club and shouldn't be losing so much. Smaller clubs tend to revel more in their misfortune because they are more used to it.

'A case in point was the Meadowbank Thistle fans who produced a funny inventive magazine called *AWOL* which was successful because there weren't many fans and most of them bought it. So they could print songsheets out for them to use on the terraces.'

Most fanzine editors report that sales actually increase when the team is doing badly. 'There is very much a floating fanzine reader who is more likely to buy the thing when his club is doing badly than when it is doing well as was shown by a recent Carling survey – Sunderland fans topped the list of fanzine reading fans in the Premiership in 1996-97, a season in which they ended up relegated. The cynical ideas in the humour stem from the sense of being let down and adjusting to the disappointment by laughing about it,' says Lyons.

By their very nature fanzines are the voice of the fans and they are written in an ironic, often self-mocking manner. The names often try to reflect this.

Arsenal *The Gooner/One Nil Down, Two One Up*. The first is the fans' version of the club nickname, the second a reference to the 1987 League Cup final win over Liverpool.

Barry Town *Only 38 hours to Vilnius*. A cross-reference with pop music culture, and the memory of Barry's glorious UEFA Cup run in 1996.

Blackburn *Loadsamoney*. A reference to Jack Walker's millions invested in the club.

Bolton *Tripe and Trotters*. An ironic play on the way the area is traditionally viewed by outsiders. Bolton are nicknamed the Trotters.

Burnley *Who Ate All the Pies?* Typical terrace chant.

Carlisle *Land of Sheep and Glory*. Plenty of self-deprecating irony here – Carlisle are known as the Sheepshaggers by other fans.

Coventry *In Dublin's Fair City*. Referring of course to their captain and hero, sax-toting Dion Dublin.

Derby County *Hey Big Spender*. Like Blackburn's, a reference to their chairman's wallet.

Doncaster Rovers *Keegan Was Crap, Really.* The young Kev was rejected by his hometown club, Doncaster, for being too small.

Dundee *It's Half Past Four and We're Two-Nil Down.* 'Nuff said.

Everton *When Skies Are Grey.* Deriving from the terrace song to the words of 'You Are My Sunshine'. Typical of the plaintive tone of most fanzines.

Gillingham *Brian Moore's Head.* This shows perfectly how fanzines often cross-reference with other areas of popular culture, especially pop music. 'Brian Moore's Head Looks Uncannily Like London Planetarium' is a song from the quirky football-obsessed post-punk band Half Man Half Biscuit. Moore has been a Gillingham director.

Hearts *Always the Bridesmaid.* A reference to the ultimately disappointing 1985-86 season when Hearts finished runners-up on goal difference in the League and lost the Scottish Cup final.

Leeds *The Hanging Sheep.* The Leeds City crest shows a sheep being weighed.

Lincoln City *Deranged Ferret.* If anyone can enlighten me to the meaning of this one I'd be much obliged. Maybe it's on the town crest, too.

Liverpool *When Sunday Comes.* Reflecting on the fact that because fixtures are nowadays ruled by TV schedules the Reds rarely play on Saturday any more.

Manchester United *United We Stand/Red Attitude.* This follows the theory that bigger clubs, with less to complain about, engender less need for irony. Dull names, or what?

Manchester City *Bert Trautmann's Helmet.* A reference to their former POW former goalkeeper, German Bert Trautmann, who broke his neck in the 1956 Cup final, but still played on.

Merthyr Tydfil *Dial M for Merthyr.* Another popular culture cross-reference.

Millwall *No One Likes Us.* From the Lions' fans' trademark song.

Norwich *Ferry Cross the Wensum.* You what?

Nottingham Forest *The Almighty Brian.* Cloughie's still revered at The City Ground.

Notts County *The Pie.* After their nickname (oddly Newcastle, the other Magpies, produce a fanzine called the *Mag*).

Partick Thistle *Sick in the Basin*. Beats me, this one.

QPR *A Kick up the R's*. A play on the club's nickname which reflects the nature of football fanzines – they are there to try to remind the clubs of the fans' rights.

Sheffield United *Great Chip Butty.*

Tranmere Rovers *Give us an R*. From the terrace song which spells out the club's name.

Wolves *A Load of Bull*. A play on the name of popular striker Steve Bull.

Wrexham *The Sheeping Giant*. See Carlisle.

A recent rant in *Goal* magazine had a go at the whole fanzine scene: 'the fanzine format is tired. Jokes about rival teams stolen from other fanzines with the name of the team altered to fit; poor cartoons seemingly drawn by someone with more than one thumb on each hand; editorial "think"pieces calling for the dismantling of the Capitalist State by next Tuesday...' it blasted, and I've heard the view that the mags have over-run their sell-by date expressed many times.

By Andy Lyons' own admittance fanzines have seen their best days. 'Now fanzines generally follow an established pattern,' he says. 'It was inevitable that they would eventually become formulaic. It's so much more difficult for them to take anybody by surprise any more. And a lot of the new ones simply aren't very good. They are done by kids quite often – it's just become something that you do, when you're that sort of age.'

However, having become an established form of football literature, Lyons believes that the fanzines still have an important role to play. 'They have become an important part of the fabric of football, which has helped to empower fans by giving them a voice. It's a third point of view – first there was the independent point of view from the newspapers, then came the clubs' point of view in programmes, then there were the fanzines which took things from the fans' angle.' Whatever the case, there's very little doubt that fanzines have been hugely important in the evolution of the language of football for two reasons.

Firstly they have brought fans' grievances to the fore, and made them much more widely discussed. 'Fanzines have empowered the fan,' says Lyons. 'They have given him a mouthpiece to express his views.

With the Premier League relying less and less on turnstile money for its income it is precisely the time when fans need to be empowered.'

Secondly, their humour and off-beat style has filtered through to more mainstream media and influenced the way football is presented. 'I wouldn't say the success of the show is a reaction to *A Question Of Sport*,' says TV presenter Nick Hancock on the popularity of his comedy sports quiz show *They Think It's All Over*. 'It's more like a natural progression from the humour of the fanzines.'

The translation of the sort of humour fanzines injected into the sport has influenced a number of football shows, including Sky's *Soccer AM* and BBC2's *Fantasy Football*. It has also, according to Lyons, even gone as far as influencing other forms of more mainstream sports writing.

'I suspect that younger broadsheet writers have been influenced by fanzines in that they have started to link football with other forms of popular culture,' he says. 'Moreover, writers who started off with fanzines are starting to work in other areas of the media. A lot have permeated into the press. Some have been employed by clubs to edit their programmes (for example at Exeter and Brentford). It's the same with unofficial web-site creators being taken up by the clubs to run the official sites.'

It's a good job that some experienced people have been let loose on the Internet. The fact that it is getting easier and easier to set up a web-site means that the variation in quality is getting bigger and bigger – if you do a simple engine search for a subject (let's say Andy Cole, for example) you're as likely to end up in some Scandinavian schoolkid's semi-literate tribute as anywhere else.

I was recently commissioned by *Manchester United* magazine to do a review of the best soccer on the net and I came up with the conclusion that footie sites largely fall into three categories: sites that make you laugh, sites that give you information, and sites that try to do both.

The latter are the direct descendant of the fanzine – and take the fan-based nature of the movement even further by being interactive (ie, allowing any other fans to contribute). A good example of this is the Reading site Hob Nob Anyone? (on http://www.i-way.co.uk/~readingfc

if you're interested) which gives you a fan's-eye view on all Reading's matches in the last four years, plus up-to-date news and gossip. Because there's no limit to space, accessing the site is like buying the latest fanzine and getting all the back issues free. There is a very silly and funny section called Strange Soccer Stories, which has made it on to lots of link lists and gets contributions from all over the world.

One good comedy site is produced by *When Saturday Comes*, and is called the Half Decent Web Site (http://www.wsc.co.uk/). Again its strength is its interactive nature – readers (viewers? accessors?) can send in their football dreams and have them analysed by 'Dr Dream' and illustrated with a little moving cartoon. Otherwise you can tell everybody about your top football-related romantic incident. Yes, you read that right.

What we football writers want most off the net, however, isn't laughs or idiosyncratic information about individual clubs. We want facts. We want statistics. We want the Internet to be like a vast global football *Rothmans* where, at the jab of a key or two we can access whatever information we need about whatever team, game or player we need to write about. Unfortunately that's not there yet – although the odd site such as the *Daily Mail*'s Soccernet (http://www.soccernet.com/) does give you detailed world and domestic news and statistics dating back to the beginning of 1995-96 and by the time you read this Danny Kelly's new comprehensive football guide, football 365 (http://www.football365.co.uk/) should be up and running.

The future of football on the net is frightening – the technology is already there for somebody to film an entire match and beam it live around the world with a commentary – as future TVs are likely to give viewers easy net access this may well be how our football is served up to us in time to come.

- 41 -
Anders Limpar's Brief – The Press

I arrived at Highbury two hours before the match started. I was the first journalist there. It only served to make me more nervous. It was 3 October 1992, the date of my first-ever football assignment, Arsenal-Chelsea. At 5 o'clock sharp I would have to file 400 words by phone to the *Irish Sunday Tribune*. I wasn't used to being a journalist in those days – the whole business filled me with dread. But there was no going back. About twenty minutes before the kick-off Bobby Moore sat at the same table as me. I was too shy to say hello to him, so I started reading my match programme. I never did meet the man.

The match was a dull affair with a thrilling ending. I scribbled notes throughout, and had already formulated much of the copy for a 1-1 draw when George Graham made a substitution. He brought Anders Limpar on. Within seconds the Swede had beaten his full-back and hit in a great cross to the far post that just left Ian Wright with the job of tapping the ball in from two yards and winning the match. I still remember, more or less, what I said down the phone, twenty minutes later, after frantic scribbling and much crossing out. '*Anders Limpar's brief was clear when George Graham told him to shed his tracksuit and get on to the pitch. He had five minutes to change one point into three and keep Arsenal's title challenge on the tracks...*' I remember wondering what the copy-typist was thinking of my prose, whether she was realising that I'd never done it before. And having to spell all the names out. 'Yes that's Graham with an "h". G-R-A-H-A-M.'

After I'd finished I had a drink at the bar (it was free) and wandered back to my seat to look out at an empty stadium. I lit a cigarette that felt like a Hamlet in the ads. I felt the same drained triumph as the night

I'd lost my virginity.

The next day I searched London for a copy of the paper and eventually found one in Finsbury Park Station. With a thrill I saw the by-line '**From Alex Leith** at Highbury.' My name in bold! Then with a shudder I read the opening paragraph.

'Arsenal striker Ian Wright was in trouble last night after allegedly making abusive gestures at Chelsea fans following his 85th minute winner in his side's 2-1 victory at Highbury.' The last half of the copy resembled what I had written but the piece, essentially, had been completely changed. I was crestfallen.

On Monday I rang up the sports editor. He told me not to worry. They'd read the news about Wright on the wire, and they had felt that they had to include it in the piece, although my original copy had gone in the first edition. He was being nice to me but I realised that the fact was that I'd missed the story. There'd been some scandal and I hadn't picked up on it. The drama of a late goal on the pitch was less important than the fact that Ian Wright was in trouble with the authorities.

It wasn't always like that. Back in Victorian times the average newspaper reader was hardly interested in the result, let alone any baulked-up 'scandalous' behaviour by the players. In early Victorian times the players' names wouldn't have been particularly familiar to the readers, anyway. Writers needed to concentrate on descriptions of play and tactics. 'The only thing which saved the Scotch team from defeat, considering the powerful forward play of England, was the magnificent defensive play and tactics shown by their backs, which was also taken advantage of by their forwards,' wrote a 'our correspondent' of the day on the very first international between England and Scotland in 1872.

There was also room for more speculation about the team. Another correspondent was worried that England's players were drawn from nine teams whilst Scotland had half a dozen representatives from Queen's Park. 'It was naturally thought,' he wrote, 'that the English, although showing fine individual play, would be deficient in working together, belonging as they did to so many clubs. But the game had not proceeded far when this illusion was dispelled like mist at the approach of sun, for the magnificent dribbling of the England captain, Kirke-Smith and Brockbank, seconded as it was by the fine back play of

Welch, Greenalgh and Chappell, was greatly admired by the immense concourse of spectators, who kept the utmost order.'

Victorian newspapers created their own clichés ('the leather orb', 'the enemy citadel', 'the guardian of the posts'), many of which can be explained away by the fact that copy writers were paid by the word. But in their defence, although the style of writing seems stilted now, they were doing just the job a newspaper writer should be doing. In the days before wirelesses they were giving news – and then explaining what had happened in more detail.

By the time wirelesses were more common the result of the match would have been much more widely known by the time the newspaper came out. So writers became expected to explain exactly *how* a result had come about. A look at a post-match report from *The Times* in 1948 after England's 4-0 win in Turin over Italy, shows that the writer clearly expects quite a deep knowledge of football tactics from his reader. Here are a couple of examples:

> *'After Mortensen snatched an early goal for England, the Italian approach play began to click smoothly and worry the English defenders out of their stride...'*
>
> *'...The Italians were very impressive in attack, keeping the ball low, with quick passes into the open spaces, but they failed inside the penalty area with hurried, temperamental finishing.'*

Notice how Mortensen's first goal is hardly described at all – the writer was much more concerned with giving an overall impression of the game than describing its crucial moments in detail. Lawton's second is given a little more space and shows us that some of today's football clichés are well rooted into the past. 'Franklin found Matthews, a through pass again reached Mortensen, who changed pace twice to gallop past Grezar and Parola and hook the ball back for Lawton to shoot the ball home like a thunderbolt.' There was very little glorying in what has gone down in history as one of the finest England victories of all time – the writer was at pains, on the other hand, to show how the result didn't really reflect what happened on the pitch.

That glorious victory in Turin took place in a time when Englishmen thought that their team was unarguably the best in the world. Pretty soon, however, a run of disastrous results was to shatter that illusion. We can glean a lot of knowledge about the state of the press by looking carefully at their reaction to England disasters over the years. In the early days of England catastrophes, there was very little of the sort of Rottweiler reaction we see nowadays. Walter Winterbottom had life a lot easier than Graham Taylor.

On 29 June 1950 England travelled to Brazil as favourites to win the World Cup. Despite never having played in the competition before, English players still considered themselves the world's best. They had got off to a good start in the tournament by beating Chile 2-0 in the Maracana. Next up was a seemingly easy match against the USA. Manager Walter Winterbottom picked a strong side: Finney, Mannion, Bentley and Mortensen were amongst the attackers. They all had an off day – England hit the woodwork eleven times and were kept out by some heroic saves by keeper Borghi whilst going down to a freakish deflected goal to lose 1-0. It was the most humiliating defeat ever to befall the side. Here's what John Thompson had to say in the *Daily Mirror* the next day.

> ***Bombshell for our World Cup hopes***
> ***England fall to US amateurs***
> *English soccer was humbled as it never has been before in the little stadium here today when America beat us 1-0 in the World Cup match. The Americans, who entered the cup on a 'hiding to nothing' basis and completely unfancied, were the better team, and fully deserved their victory...[on England's part] it was a pathetic show from a team expected to do so much.*

It's a highly critical account by a man who is obviously trying to be a good loser. But there are no calls for manager Walter Winterbottom's head, even after we were beaten in the subsequent match by Spain and thus knocked out of the competition (headline – Brilliant soccer, but goals? oh no!)

Just over three years later on 25 November 1953, England faced

Olympic champions Hungary in a prestigious friendly at Wembley. The team had never lost to a foreign side at home. But the Hungarians, led by the inspirational Ferenc Puskas, were playing a brand of football never before seen in this country, playing their centre forward Hidegkuti in a deep position which caused all sorts of confusion in the defence. 4-2 down at halftime, despite a fine performance from goalkeeper Gill Merrick, England ended up on the wrong end of a 6-3 drubbing having been taught a lesson in modern tactics. Here's what Peter Wilson had to say in the *Daily Mirror* the next day.

> ***The twilight of the (soccer) gods***
> *The lesson is clear. Our best is not good enough for the best of the rest nowadays. We must build and encourage the young men who kick a football on the commons and the broad spaces all over the shires of England and who kick a tin can in the cobbled streets of the city. It is no good bemoaning the past – although I trow that there will be many heavy hearts among those that remembered when English soccer was a hallmark of greatness through the myriad lands where this most international game is played – when the only question at the end of a home game against the continentals was 'how much did we win by?' The only possible answer is to build for the future, and to start building now.*

The response, then, was a largely positive one, a thoughtful appeal to sort out the problem by nourishing football's grass roots; again there are no calls for the manager's head.

England steered clear of disasters for another twenty years, although they shouldn't have lost 3-2 to West Germany in the 1970 World Cup. At least they had qualified for that tournament. In 1973 they came second to Poland in the qualifying group, which wasn't good enough to book a place in the finals. The crucial result was a 1-1 draw at Wembley on 17 October 1973. England were desperately unlucky, coming up against an inspired goalkeeper in Jan Tomaszewski. By this time the *Sun* was around. Here's what their reporter Frank Clough had to say:

The End of the World!
Soccer shocker: England are blasted out of the cup
Glory Glory Goodbye – It's the end for England
I can't find it in my heart to be critical of this England performance, disastrous though the result was. Most of them gave everything for England...So the question this morning is what does the future hold for Sir Alf Ramsey. Nobody likes to hit a man when he is in the depths of disappointment, but his entire future must be in the melting pot.

For the first time the manager's position is being put into question, Ramsey lasted two more matches but after goal-less games against Italy and Portugal he finally went in April 1974.

In the qualifying draw for the 1978 World Cup England and Italy, two of the great sides in world football, had the misfortune of being placed in the same group, with only one team to qualify. It was obvious from the start that goal difference might be crucial, so it was important to score a hatful of goals against the other teams, especially at home. England faced Finland on 13 October 1976, having beaten them 4-1 in Helsinki and seen them trounced six weeks before 6-0 by Scotland. At the end of a frustrating night, punctuated by booing from the large Wembley crowd, England were lucky to win 2-1.

Frank Clough, having blasted, 'Let's hit them for six: England's World Cup fighters are in a mean and magnificent mood for tomorrow's showdown against Finland'. on the morning of the match, wrote the next day:

England jeered after big flop
To be brutally honest England hardly deserved to prosper after the dreadful mess they made of matters.

At least a win is a win. Four years later, the country was in shock as a place in the 1982 World Cup looked in jeopardy – and the country had to face up to the possibility of three World-Cups-in-the-wilderness in a row after a 2-1 defeat to Norway, then nowhere near the world powers they are today. Here's what the *Sun*'s sports editor David Shapland had to say afterwards:

For God's sake, go, Ron
England were humiliated by the no hopers of Norway last night...it was a defeat that must spell the end of Ron Greenwood's career as England manager...You can throw your sombrero and suntan oil into the dustbin: England's glossy dream of going to Spain for the World Cup finals is now a million miles away... England are virtually out of the World Cup. Now we say that's the only course for Ron – OUT. And then England can start all over again to rebuild for the next finals in 1986.

Notice how the plea for the head of the manager has by now been moved into the headline, and is repeated in the main text, and how the standard of journalism has dropped with the use of clichés such as 'a million miles away'. England qualified in the end, by the way.

Greenwood retired at the end of that World Cup campaign, to be replaced by Bobby Robson. Robson's first job was to get England to the European Championships by qualifying ahead of unfancied Denmark. The Danes, however, were an emerging force, and outplayed England to hand them their first competitive defeat at Wembley Stadium. The *Sun* wasn't best pleased. And Robson came in for the sort of personal criticism that had never been seen before in the press.

Robson's Rubbish
After defeat for Danes send for Clough!
If the rulers of English football have any sense of shame or sense of justice they will order a symbolic lion to be stuffed, mounted, and sent for display in Copenhagen's civic museum.

Frank Clough had a selection suggestion for Robson. 'Bring in Luton's young striker Paul Walsh and put Martyn Bennett in the centre of defence.' Martyn who? Martyn *Bennett*. He played 180 games for West Brom in the 1980s.

Robson didn't qualify England for that European Championships, but he did manage to get them to the finals of the 1986 World Cup and the 1988 European Championships. Nevertheless, the tabloid press was still after his blood. The *Sun*'s John Sadler wanted him to behave in an unprecedented manner and resign in the middle of a tournament after bad finishing by Lineker and Beardsley led to a 1-0 defeat to the Republic of Ireland in the second of these two finals.

> ***On yer bike, Robson***
> *Bobby Robson's job as England's boss is on the line. Yesterday's disastrous European Cup opener in Stuttgart made that a cert... Disgrace to the name of England. A gutless spineless shower.*

Worse was to come for Robson after England were eliminated from the competition after a closely fought game against eventual winners Holland who won 3-1. England hit the post twice. Before the game John Sadler had given Robson a do-or-die message: 'Beat 'em or beat it, Bobby!' The reaction to the result was:

> ***Stuffed!***
> *With the right selections, made by the right man, England can still be one of the best footballing nations in the world.*

Nigel Clarke of the *Daily Mirror* joined in the Robson-baiting:

> ***Rubbish!***
> *Come on, do the honourable thing, Bobby GO NOW...On your bike. Bobby Robson must call up the FA this morning and tell them he intends to resign as England manager.*

Robson, though, refused to go, which made the tabloids behave more and more like a lynch mob. On 16 November 1988 England faced a tricky friendly in Saudi Arabia, and put in a rather lacklustre performance to draw 1-1. The tabloids were jubilant.

> ***England Mustafa New Boss!***
> *There can only be one fate for Bobby Robson. He must pay after English football was humiliated yet again. England's boss should offer his head today at the main square in this city of public*

execution. The team that finished the match? We should cut off the hand that picked an England team so poor that surely the FA can no longer ignore the obvious message from the desert: England Mustafa new manager!

The team he had picked, incidentally, included Seaman, Adams, Pallister, Pearce, Gascoigne and Beardsley as well as Robson, Lineker and Waddle. The vitriolic attack on Robson became pictorial as well as verbal; a dunce's cap and a fez were crudely superimposed on Robson's photo. It was a glimpse of things to come.

Robson, of course, took England to a semi final place in the World Cup in 1990 with a similar team, but, tired of all the pressure, announced his retirement after the tournament finished. He was replaced by a man who was fully aware of how savage the British press had become, Graham Taylor. Taylor hadn't seen nothing yet. Was he not going to like the treatment he was handed out. After a honeymoon period Taylor's selection policy and simple 'long-ball' tactics started making him unpopular. After qualifying for Euro 92, Taylor's men had drawn their first two group encounters and needed to beat hosts Sweden to go through. They lost, 2-1, and vegetable humour was born.

Swedes 2 Turnips 1
Sunsport verdict: Turnip in, Taylor. GO NOW. Graham Taylor should do himself and England one big favour today – Quit. English Football RIP Died a laughing stock, 1992

The next day a picture of Taylor's face with the top of a turnip superimposed on his head was printed on the back page of the *Sun*.

After a friendly defeat in Spain (Spanish 1 Onions 0) Taylor quipped 'I'm beginning to wonder what sort of vegetables they grow in Norway' before a vital World Cup encounter. He was soon to find out, when the *Sun* howled after the 2-0 defeat:

Norse Manure!
England manager Graham Taylor dropped us all in the Norse manure with the shambles of a side he put out against Norway...

Turnip has lost the vegetable plot – and he can't hold the respect of the players.

John Sadler chipped in:

Come on Keegan, your country needs you!... When did Graham Taylor ever play the game at a top level? Let him show us his caps and medals.

The *Sun* was on a roll – no newspaper had ever been so savage before, but nobody was doing anything to stop them, so the baiting continued. It also fuelled a hysteria in the country against the team, which didn't help matters. England travelled to the USA for a summer tournament and lost 2-0 to the hosts. **'Yanks 2 Planks 0'** ran the headline (the sub editors had run out of vegetables), before adding, 'You've gone and dung it again, Taylor.'

The campaign gained ferocity the next day as the *Sun* printed a page with a picture of Taylor's turnip head in a noose, with the headline **'The Boston Dangler**...Taylor is hanging on...you can finish him off'.

They were running a postal-vote referendum as to whether he should stay or go. Readers had to cut out a bit of paper reading 'I......... want Graham Taylor sacked as England manager. Signed........' England were left with the slimmest of chances to qualify, needing to beat San Marino by seven clear goals and hope for a Polish win over Holland. As it was, neither eventuality happened. Taylor resigned and the *Sun* wrapped up the campaign with the headline **'That's Your Allotment'**.

That was our lot of media viciousness against England for the time being – since those Taylor days there hasn't been an England disaster to speak of again. And as there has been a bit of a sea change in the way the tabloids have reported football since, I wonder if things will ever be quite so hysterical again. Newspapers have realised football's value to the public – rarely a week goes by without a front-page soccer story in the tabloids or the broadsheets – and have started to dwell less and less on the negative aspects of the game.

Instead they have made the footballers into stars. The top players from the more fashionable football clubs and the England team are being given the sort of attention usually reserved for pop stars, actors and royalty. It started with Paul Gascoigne, who endeared himself to the public with his tears in 1990 and has been hounded by the press ever since, having led the sort of lifestyle to make the story run and run. Other players to have become front-page stars are David Beckham (love affair), Paul Merson (drugs and gambling), Matt le Tissier (sex) and Ryan Giggs (haircut). Glenn Hoddle's split with his wife days after England qualified for the 1998 World Cup was considered to be the number-one news item that day. Any bit of trivia is enough, it seems. And the odder the better. Why the fact that Ian Wright stuck his buttocks through a Highbury window should be the front-page story of Britain's biggest-selling paper two days later perplexed me a little at first. Then I realised that it was quite a simple decision for the editor of the *Sun* to make. He realised that as far as his ten-million-odd readership was concerned, it was quite simply the most interesting piece of world news that had happened. Much better copy than abusive gestures at the Chelsea crowd.

Broadsheets too are starting to realise how important football news is to their readers. According to *Observer* reader polls the sports section is usually voted the second most popular section in the newspaper (behind the news section), and occasionally the most popular.

'We're living in pretty boring times for news,' says Alan Hubbard, the sports editor of the world's oldest Sunday paper, whom I interviewed in his large open-plan office on a miserable drizzly morning in December 1997. 'There are no major wars; politics have become very drab (all the parties are the bloody same), so sport in general and football in particular has taken on more importance in people's lives. People want to debate it and read about it. Since 1992 we have had to cater for that and produce more and more coverage.'

Hubbard, who looks like you'd imagine a sports editor to look, sees the start of the Premiership in 1992 as being the impetus for the increase in coverage football enjoys in his and other papers. 'We used to cover three or four matches every week, with a round-up,' he says. 'Now we cover every Premiership match, some of the more relevant Nationwide ones and have an increased number of accompanying features. We also preview that day's big match on Sky – we feel we have to even if it's Derby versus Bolton which you'd think nobody could give a shit about. In fact they do – there are more and more people who don't ever go to matches but just watch it on the TV who want to discuss it and read about it. Murdoch and co. at Sky have made the whole thing seem more important to people's lives, and they want to read about that on a Sunday morning. It's a sort of nouveau readership we have picked up.'

With a wave of his hand Hubbard rejects my supposition that there might have been a dumbing-down in the style of writing in the broadsheets to cater for the 'nouveau fan' who has, perhaps, a less broad knowledge of the game than a more traditional reader. 'There has been no specific instruction for writers to write up or down to a market,' he says. 'We are simply looking for quality writing laced with humour. Though as football has become more popular journalists have had to become more rounded to describe the game. We are no longer living in a world where people are interested in who scored the goals and what the manager said afterwards. Writers need to be aware of a number of other facets of the game: marketing, fiscal, legal, etc. In fact football journalists need to be much more aware of the world around them than any other speciality journalists.'

He does admit, however, that sports reports and features are getting a broader base of readership. 'We are aware from letters we receive and surveys that we are getting a larger number of women reading about football, and that the chattering classes, or the tattling classes if you like, have taken football up as a subject worthy of debate. The sport has changed over the years. The stereotypical English player and manager has seen foreign players who are more articulate than him come in and has been forced to change his act a bit. The result is that the whole sport has become a lot more spicy. It's become a lot more...sexy. That's it. It's become a lot more sexy.'

- 42 -
Football is the New Rock and Roll

Football was hip in the 1960s, when the Chelsea lads were part of the King's Road scene, players wore their hair pop-star long and George Best was nicknamed the 'Fifth Beatle'. By the time the 1970s were over, however, Chelsea were in the second division, most players had perms and Best was an ex-con alcoholic. Football had got a bit naff.

In the early-to-mid 1980s I was at college and there were many new things that were fit objects for obsession: cheap booze, girls with their own bedrooms, accessible drugs, cheap booze, politics, money problems, cheap booze. And, of course, the course.

I'm not saying I kicked football right into touch. But it became very difficult to juggle everything else *and* be able to keep up with football and rock music at the same time. And as music was a cool thing to talk about and spend time on, football rather lost the battle. A lot of people admitted to being a football fan, but those who went overboard were rather sad, anoraky figures. Watching football was OK, but talking about it was a bit naff. Rock and roll was the new rock and roll.

An important sign of football's naffness was that rock stars didn't sing or even talk much about it. Off-beat bands like Serious Drinking and Half Man Half Biscuit would sing off-beat songs about football, and Billy Bragg wrote the great lines:

How can you lie back and think of England
When you don't know who was in the team

John Peel kept flying Liverpool's flag on his late-night radio show, and the Undertones, who gloried in their own naffness, wrote a song about

Subbuteo; but most stars felt it was wise to keep any love of the sport in the cupboard with the skeletons.

Nowadays football has reached a height of coolness. Footballers are seen as ideal partners by bright young media stars and singers, people wear club shirts to fashionable nightclubs and, importantly, pop stars are starting not only to admit to liking football, but to sing about it too.

Oasis are such big Manchester City fans that they looked into doing a shirt sponsorship deal with the club; an album compilation geared to Euro 96 entitled *The Beautiful Game* attracted bands of the calibre of Black Grape, Primal Scream, The Shamen, Blur, Pulp and Supergrass, who all wrote special football-related songs; the Stone Roses got into trouble for wearing football shirts on stage; the Super Furry Animals released a single called 'This Man Don't Give a Fuck' with a picture of former Cardiff and Reading bad-boy Robin Friday on the sleeve. And, of course, the new national football anthem, 'Three Lions', which was a massive chart hit, was written by the Lightning Seeds, a band more familiar previously with *NME* readers than *Top of the Pops* viewers. The song is a perfect example, with its lyrics about Bobbies Moore and Charlton, of how the current football-loving trend is tied up with a retro love of all things 1960s and 1970s.

Football's 'hip replacement' has been widely attributed to Nick Hornby's book *Fever Pitch*, which also takes the reader back into those halcyon days of shinpadless players with meaty sideburns. Surely, however, the public's reception of the book and all its spin-offs (when's the video game coming out?) was made possible by earlier events in a recording studio rather than later ones in a writer's study. Nobody would have read the book if they hadn't thought it was the cool thing to do. A quick look into the music archives shows it was a song rather than a book that started the new football age rolling down the snowy mountain.

- 43 -
From Gracie Fields to the Lightning Seeds – Footie in the Charts

To set my argument in context it's important to look at the language of football when it's set to music; a short history of football in the recording studio. To take me through this bizarre world I consulted one of its most qualified experts, Jim Phelan, head of Exotica Records and half the team responsible for the popular Bend It! series of football-related pop songs. In our hour-and-a-half interview I never got to sit down – there simply wasn't room to in his little basement office, the epicentre of the football music world, which was overflowing with records, books and piles of paper relating to the subject.

Jim took me back to 1931 when Gracie Fields recorded the first football song that he has managed to locate, a tribute to Oldham called 'Pass! Shoot! Goal!', with the unforgettable lines:

In hobnail boots, they do or die
More of them die than do
Their football shirts are black and red
Their faces black and blue
(chorus)
The poor referee is kicked by three or four
Right between his whistle and the half-time score
Squeaking, shrieking, with all their heart and soul

You'll hear their angel voices shouting 'pass-shoot-goal!'

Strangely Gracie was a Rochdale lass and this was a song about Oldham Athletic, but Jim rates it a classic and, having heard it on *Bend It 91* many times since, I have to agree with him.

There wasn't much more for football fans to sing along to before or during the war 'apart,' says Jim, 'from a giveaway from the *Daily Herald* called "I Do Like to See a Game of Football" by Sydney Kite and his Orchestra which took the mickey out of radio football commentators for dividing the pitch into numbered squares, like a giant game of battleships.' But in the 1950s more footie records started making the soundlists – especially from calypso bands. The 'Exotic Football Calypso' by Edmund Ros and his Orchestra came out in 1953, followed by the excellent 'Man United Calypso' by Edric Connor which is still sometimes sung on the Stretford End terraces. *Record Collector* magazine reckons this to be the moment that 'marked the real beginning of football's association with pop music'. Here's an example of the choice lyrics:

The team that gets me excited
Manchester United
A bunch of bouncing Busby Babes
They deserve to be knighted

The 1960s was the decade when football and pop music really hit it off together – but their relationship spawned some bizarre offspring. The decade started fantastically for Tottenham Hotspur, who became the first club this century to win the double in 1960-61, and the occasion gave a group calling themselves the Totnamites the chance to release the brilliant 'Tip Top Tottenham Hotspur', one of Phelan's favourite numbers which he describes as 'Pearl and Dean meets soap commercial'.

Tip top Tottenham Hotspur
The greatest team of the year
Tip top Tottenham Hotspur
Raise your glass and give them a cheer

Hooray for the double and let's live it up
One drink for the league and another for the cup

But the decade also saw the start of the 'football stars as pop singers' era which started with Welsh striker John Charles, the 'Gentle Giant', who was as duff in front of the microphone as he was brilliant in the opposition penalty box, singing '16 Tons' coupled with 'Love In Portofino'. Charles was from Wales and he spent some time in Italy, so he knew a thing or two about crooning. He just didn't really know how to do it, ending up sounding, as *Record Collector* put it, 'like Sacha Distel with a beer gut'.

Things got a little better when the World Cup made its way to these shores, with established artists paying tribute: Lonnie Donegan brought us 'World Cup Willie', Joe Loss brought out 'The World Cup March' and Victor Sylvester and his Orchestra brought us 'The World Cup Waltz'. But they soon got a lot worse again, especially with the release of the 1967 'Spurs Go Marching In' EP, which had Spurs first-teamers singing old favourites: Terry Venables with 'Bye Bye Blackbird', Cyril Knowles and Alan Mullery singing 'Maybe it's Because I'm a Londoner' and Jimmy Greaves singing a strikingly daft rendition of 'Strollin''.

Things were to get worse. Just before the World Cup finals in 1970 the England squad recorded a song called 'Back Home'. Hurst, Moore, Charlton and co. had done much to restore the credibility of English football; in three minutes flat they destroyed any that the football-meets-music genre had built up. The song, a catchy singalong which spawned many imitators of the ' 'Ere we go, 'ere we go' variety, 'elbowed its way' to the top of the charts in April 1970. It didn't do the sport's image much good amongst the trendy youngsters of the time. 'Back then,' says Phelan, '*Top of the Pops* was still hip: there was always the possibility of a Hendrix performance or a live Who set. So the appearance of the entire England squad, decked out in morning suits and miming along to "Back Home, they'll be thinking of us, in every game we play" was a decidedly uncool sight. The concept of taking footballers who couldn't sing into a studio to make a record was born.'

The mood was set for a whole load of trash to be released which was to give football pop songs a bad name they have been trying to recover from ever since. 'Back Home' was a portent of exactly how tacky and awful the decade would become and football records didn't escape the general low quality that abounded at the time. In fact football was very much a shop window for the daftness of the era with the players' haircuts mirroring the style vacuum which prevailed.

From the beginning of the decade it became fashionable for every team who reached the Cup final to release a song commemorating the fact. In 1971 we had 'Good Old Arsenal', 1972 saw 'Leeds United' and 'Arsenal We're on Your Side', Sunderland's 1973 success came despite their song 'Sunderland We're on Our Way', 1974 saw Liverpool's 'Let's Go All the Way to Wembley'.

'Since then,' says Jim Phelan, 'every team – at national or domestic level – to reach a final has produced a record. With the exception of New Order's "World in Motion" or Skinner and Baddiel's recent "Football's Coming Home" they've all been pretty awful.'

Awful, yes, but some of them, it must be admitted, have got a great deal of 'so awful they're great' credibility, especially those with professional bands getting involved. Who could forget the Scotland squad's brave boast in 1978, which fell so flat on its face when they left their microphones behind to take to the field to play the likes of Peru and Iran in Argentina?

We're on the march wi' Ally's Army
We're all going to the Argentine
And we'll really shake 'em up
When we win the World Cup
'Cos Scotland are the greatest football team

Or the 1982 hit 'Ossie's Dream'? Not the Spurs fans, who still sing it at White Hart Lane.

Ossie's gone to Wembley
His knees have gone all trembley
Come on you Spurs
Come on you Spurs
Spurs are on their way to Wembley

Tottenham's going to do it again
They can't stop 'em
The boys from Tottenham
The boys from White Hart Lane

The 1970s saw football-terrace chanting and culture reach its height and this had an effect on the pop business. The Bay City Rollers, with their scarves around their wrists, used a football-style chant (to the tune 'Nick Nack Paddywhack'): 'B.A.Y., B.A.Y., B.A.Y. C.I.T.Y. with an R.O. double "L".E.R.S, Bay City Rollers are the best.' Sorry to remind you about that one. Gary Glitter, too, used football-style chanting in his songs, such as 'The Leader', and 'D'You Wanna Be in My Gang' which regularly made their way to the top of the charts.

The 1980s weren't much better. One of Liverpool's most embarrassing moments in their recent history was their 1-0 defeat by Wimbledon in 1988. It wasn't half as embarrassing, however, as the record they brought out before the final, possibly the most cringeworthy football song ever made – the infamous 'Anfield Rap', written by the club's Australian midfielder Craig Johnston and including a rap by John Barnes. Johnston has recently stated, 'I'd like to say on record that it's one of the worst songs I've ever heard and I cringe every time I hear it,' before applauding BBC viewers for their good taste in voting it the worst football pop record of all time.

If whole teams were embarrassing themselves on a regular basis, spare a thought now for those players, and even managers, who decided to go it alone.

Perhaps the worst example of this was Kevin Keegan who, in 1979, decided to start a pop career and released the song 'Head Over Heels in Love', which shot to number thirty-one in the charts, and was quite a big hit all over Europe. I was fifteen and football-obsessed, but I knew it was naff. I remember stacks of copies in the 10p bin at Woolworths. Desperate to make the top thirty Keegan followed this semi-disaster up with 'It Ain't Easy'. It wasn't. The record didn't make the top 100 and the permed one decided to concentrate on his football.

If their singing careers had taken off we might have missed the glittering managerial careers of such greats as Franz Beckenbauer, Johan

Cruyff, Jack Charlton and Terry Venables ('I've Got You Under My Skin'). Thankfully few of them charted.

It was current England manager Glenn Hoddle, however, who together with Chris Waddle recorded the defining moment in tacky football songs. 'Diamond Lights' reached number twelve in the charts in 1987 and earned the pair a *Top of the Pops* appearance. It wasn't long before they were both playing in France for the shame of it all.

As we've seen, John Barnes was responsible in 1988 for one of the worst episodes in the sorry history of footie music with his solo in 'The Anfield Rap'. Like a man who's lost the ball and is desperate to win it back he went all out to redeem himself two years later, doing another rap solo on the official 1990 World Cup song 'World in Motion'. Not only did he win the ball back, he chased up the pitch with it, ran past five defenders, and scored at the other end. The song was a hit – it reached number one – and crucially it was hip, too, written by trendy dance band New Order.

New Order were at the time one of the most well-respected bands in the country, having re-invented themselves as a dance band after the death of their former lead singer Ian Curtis, the main influence behind the seminal urban bass-driven angst-ridden sounds of their previous incarnation Joy Division. They were a wise choice; they decided to treat the commission as an artistic challenge, instead of making a traditional singalong. Previous football records had usually been at least five years behind the musical times, produced by people for people who didn't have their finger on the contemporary pulse; the 'World Cup Waltz' and several calypsos in the 1960s; folk songs in the 1970s, psychedelia and heavy metal in the 1980s. 'World in Motion' was right on the button: it was bought by people who wanted to dance to it more than football fans looking for a memento. As England prepared to play in the Italian tournament many young people were suddenly seeing the team in a new light, and were much more open to watching the tournament.

There was another factor, too. The BBC chose as their theme music the opera aria *Nessun Dorma* sung by Pavarotti. Again it was an inspired and ground-breaking choice. Not only did it help to make opera more popular with the masses, it also made football more stomachable to the middle-classes. English football started the World

Cup as an unfashionable largely laddish sport: by the end, after Lineker's goals, Gazza's tears, Pearce and Waddle's penalty misses, half the nation was obsessed.

The long-term effects of this shift in the public's view of football can be seen throughout the English game nowadays. It's not, as many people say, that the game has been hijacked by the gentry. The working-classes are still just as interested as they always were. It is that the game has been opened up to a broader range of people, and is being viewed on different levels. It's being considered intellectually and aesthetically as it never has been before. It's being used as a medium of artistic expression.

- 44 -
Football and Art

Here's where we rub our goatee beards and ask ourselves 'so what is art?' Here's a definition which sounds reasonable: 'A creation, of some aesthetic quality, that may be seen as being metaphorical, and which provokes critical discussion.'

Let's imagine the pitch as a canvas with the manager as a painter. His meticulous tactical preparations represent his idea. He might be following a traditional school of thought (4-4-2), or be startlingly original (1-2-3-4). His different paints are his players, who he carefully chooses and instructs before the game in which part of the canvas he wants them to go. During the game he makes his brushstrokes – instructing different players to do different things as the game goes on, occasionally adding new elements.

The people watching are sometimes moved to gasp with the beauty of the affair and afterwards expert critics write about the performance at length, often comparing the game to something else – a war maybe, or a piece of theatre. Afterwards the spectators talk heatedly about the value of what they have just seen.

OK, so I'm talking bollocks. At the end of the day football appeals far too much to the baser instincts to be considered art. But the game throws up certain moments of surprising skill and invention – a back-heel by Cantona, or a dribble by Maradona – which are of such sublime beauty that the question that started this section off is at least brought to mind. But if football isn't art itself, it's found itself in a position where, more and more, it's becoming a subject that artists are exploring.

In 1995 I found myself involved in a brief affair with a football-hating theatre producer. We went to the cinema – our main cultural common ground – so much that we got bored of it and one Saturday night we were desperate to do something different. She asked me if I wanted to go to the theatre.

Now don't get me wrong, I enjoy going to the theatre every now and then. But let's just say that it's a bit of a lie when I list it amongst my interests. And it wasn't my idea of a great Saturday night out. So I was reading through the theatre options in *Time Out* without much enthusiasm when a perfect solution revealed itself. The theatrical version of *Fever Pitch* was playing at the Unicorn.

It was a funny sort of audience. There were some Arsenal fans joining in with the songs at the front and some serious-looking theatre-types behind us. In the end we were both half-pleased with the result, like we'd seen a good 0-0 draw. It was a one-man play and the monologue wasn't intriguing enough to break the necessary monotony this entails. I know she didn't get all the football references, and I'm sure I missed some important theatrical nuances. I didn't tell her I'd seen more drama in a windy day at the Goldstone Ground, but I was tempted to.

It was rare to find such a beautiful compromise (I spotted a couple of other couples whom I was sure fell in the same bracket as us); it's not often that the worlds of theatre and football meet. In fact only one other example springs to mind. After Italia 90 *An Evening with Gary Lineker* was a hit; I didn't catch it at the theatre, but I saw the screen version and I enjoyed its black satirical humour.

The fact that both productions were put on in the 1990s shows how seriously the middle-classes take the game these days. As we've seen, theatrical references to the game in Medieval and Jacobean plays used it as an image of roughness and coarseness. We're in a period at the moment where artists of one kind or another are more likely to like football openly and therefore more likely to use it as a theme, stimulus or even subject for their work, knowing that their audience is more likely than ever before to know what they're going on about.

In the past football and art have rarely met, and when they have the results have usually been low-quality representations of the game. Any exceptions, such as Lowry's 'Going to the Match', have put the game in a rough or working-class context. Nowadays, however, it seems, some of this country's most creative minds are using the sport as a means of expressing themselves.

A case in point is Mark Wallingford, one of our most successful young artists, who was recently the runner-up in the Turner Prize with a football-related photograph. The photo captures some fans walking up Wembley Way, carrying a Union Jack with 'Mark Wallingford' written across it. A fan in the forefront of the picture, who has seen the camera, is raising his arms, which gives it its vibrancy.

Around Euro 96 there were a number of art exhibitions centred round the theme of football. Whilst in Manchester in the summer of 1996 I stumbled across one. On view were such items as several pairs of red stilettos with studs on them, some hand-drawn football stickers and a series of photos of Sunday League footballers wearing AC or Inter Milan shirts. The exhibition wasn't an earth-shattering experience that redefined my view of the world or the sport, but it killed a pleasant half hour.

Similarly the World Cup in 1994 was the stimulus for a group of young British artists in New York to show their appreciation of the game with an exhibition called Gol! with respected artists such as Roderick Buchanan – who had previously made a big splash by painting a goal-line on the floor of the Lisson Gallery – contributing a picture of Packy Bonner wearing a bib.

In April 1997 Manchester City Art Gallery proved that its name was an accident of fate and not a contrived statement of support by unveiling their latest acquisition – a portrait by Michael Browne of Eric Cantona as a Christ-like figure with other United players as disciples round his feet. Based on Piero della Francesca's *Resurrection of Christ* the painting was dismissed as being kitsch by most critics and criticised by the local Christian community as being blasphemous but further proved the high prestige of the sport in the world of art.

Photography has long been a staple component of football reporting. Some of the better examples of the genre, which avoid the sort of 'goalmouth scramble' clichés we are used to seeing in the newspapers, are starting to be looked at in a more studied manner. Stuart Clarke has recently had a highly successful tour with his 'Homes of Football', a study of the major changes in football stadiums recently forced by the Taylor report. In his home town of Carlisle the exhibition drew more visitors than a recent exhibition of the paintings of Lowry.

Football is becoming a common theme for sculpture, too. War heroes used to be the most common theme for statues in town centres.

Now we have changed our general attitude to how we view war (witness the hullaballoo surrounding the 'Bomber' Harris statue) and so we are starting to honour, instead, our footballing heroes after their death. They're just as heroic and much less controversial. Jackie Milburn has long graced the shopping centre in Newcastle, and a £50,000 bronze figure of Billy Wright, complete with baggy shorts and lace-and-cases ball, now proudly stands outside Molineux in Wolverhampton.

- 45 -
Escaping to Victory – Celluloid Soccer

It's quite fair to say that films which try to capture the drama of football on the pitch per se are largely bad and films that loosely base themselves in or around the world of football are largely better. Football at its best is highly dramatic and any attempt to dramatise it is rather missing the point.

'One of the problems in the past,' says Nick Hornby about films about football, 'has been that producers have had to choose between actors who can't play football or footballers who can't act.' In 1997 Hornby helped to produce a very rare animal indeed: a good football film. *Fever Pitch* translated itself much better on to the big screen than it did on to the stage – and it didn't need to move into the stadium to get its point across. 'Because *Fever Pitch* is about fans, and there isn't very much actual action, we have circumvented that problem,' continues Hornby. 'The film is about the people. Romance is the vehicle which carries the themes of the book and translates them from the page on to the screen.'

Hornby and the rest of the *Fever Pitch* team have learnt their lessons from quite a long history of footie films, which have only really worked when the sport has been a backdrop rather than the main flesh of the film.

The first known football film was made way back in 1911, and is one of few movies of the period to have been preserved. *Harry the Footballer* was a typical Edwardian melodrama about a star player kidnapped by the opposition, who are foiled by his wily girlfriend just in time for him to get into his kit and score the winning goal. It runs for eleven minutes and the plot has been re-used in countless comic strip cartoons.

The first full-length film (at eighty-seven minutes just three short of the full ninety) was the 1926 drama *Ball of Fortune*, based on the eponymous novel, which starred the great Welshman Billy Meredith playing himself – Cantona, eat your heart out. Another one worth a mention in pre-war dispatches is *The Arsenal Stadium Mystery*, featuring Leslie Banks as Slade of the Yard sleuthing around Highbury back in 1939. He's trying to sort out who it was who did in one of the Gunners' star players in a charity match against the Trojans. The film provides cameo roles for the whole Arsenal team of the time (who had just won the League championship) and quite a sizable part for manager George Allison. At the time football and the cinema were the two main working-class leisure activities so a project combining the two was a sure-fire success – and the film still does the mid-afternoon-slot rounds.

The first major post-war film to feature football (albeit loosely) was 1970's *The Italian Job*, which sees Michael Caine *et al* charging round Turin in Mini cars posing as football fans there for the international match against Italy, but really attempting a daring bullion heist. The film was set in a period when this country was feeling good about itself – this was post-World Cup 66 and pre-Three Day Week – and when, partially thanks to football, we were starting to cull our heroes (think Georgie Best, think Michael Caine) from the working-classes. England won the match, by the way, and the thieves got out of the city with the cash, even though the moany one was only supposed to blow the bloody doors off. In the same year *Kes*, the gritty Northern kitchen-sinker by Ken Loach, included an extremely funny vignette with Brian Glover as a games master rather biasedly refereeing a kickaround, pretending to be Bobby Charlton.

Another case in point is Bill Forsyth's charming *Gregory's Girl*, made in 1982, which sees gawky teenager John Gordon Sinclair ousted from the school team and replaced by the gorgeous Dee Hepburn. That's about as far as the football goes – the rest of the film is a witty love story. Sinclair doesn't bear any hard feelings – or rather he does – as he falls completely for the girl. It's an innocuous and very funny look at teenage life which didn't draw any influence at all from 1981's *Escape to Victory*, a film of few artistic pretentions which offers the best example of a film depicting footballers who couldn't act and actors who couldn't play football. Michael Caine and Sylvester Stallone are in the Hollywood corner, FIFA is represented by Pele, Ossie Ardiles, Bobby Moore, John Wark, Frank Thijssen and, oddly enough, Mike Summerbee. The film is a remake of an old Hungarian movie *The Last Goal*, and depicts a group of Allied POWs playing a German team and planning to escape at half-time. When they are being soundly beaten after forty-five minutes, after some terrible fouling by the Germans and some even worse refereeing, they face a tough dilemma; do they abandon their escape attempts in order to give the Jerries the second-half pasting they deserve or do they go ahead with the escape with the taste of defeat in their mouths? Well, what do you think they do? An escape isn't an escape if you're losing 4-0. Stallone, by the way, wasn't too happy at the physical demands of the game. He broke a finger and hurt both his knees, leaving the film set 'like a walking blood clot'. As POW films go it's not a patch on *The Great Escape*; as football matches go it wouldn't look out of place in the Dr Marten's League. However, it remains a cult classic for being so kitschly awful it's a joy to watch.

Two major football-related films were made in 1996 and together they serve to prove the point that films can often get away with being based around football but can rarely get away with actually being *about* football. *The Van*, the third film from Roddie Doyle's Barrytown Trilogy, is a poignant look at the lives of ordinary people trying to make a living out of a chip van business around the time of the Italia 90 World Cup. Although my favourite bit of the film is when it shows the action shot of David O'Leary hitting the ball into the Romanian net to put Jack Charlton's boys into the quarters, the rest of the film is appealing enough and evokes what I have been told many times was a remarkable couple of months in the Republic of Ireland. *When Saturday Comes*, on the other hand, is a template for what *not* to do in a football film, and was largely slated by the football magazines and the cinema critics alike. The filmies were well aware that the film was a collection of clichés cobbled together from the 1960s kitchen-sink dramas, while the football press was more than a little worried about the accuracy of the football content. Sean Bean comes on as a debutant substitute in Sheffield United's FA Cup semi final against Manchester United. When the Blades get a penalty in the last minute to give them the chance of winning the match, guess who takes it! It's almost as absurd as Gareth Southgate taking a spot-kick in the Euro 96 semi final.

It all set the scene for *Fever Pitch*, really, a film which set out to prove that the game wasn't just about when Saturday came, but when Sunday, Monday, Tuesday, Wednesday and Friday came, too. (I'm leaving Thursday free for sundry other activities.)

- 46 -
Nobby Stiles' Top Jaw – Football Literature

Thumping a volley into the net after shaking off your marker is pretty far removed from thinking up a good original metaphor, so maybe it's not surprising that, as a rule of thumb, footballers don't make good writers and writers don't make good footballers. Of course there are some exceptions. Sir Arthur Conan Doyle used to turn out occasionally for Portsmouth. Albert Camus and Vladimir Nabokov were goalkeepers of some repute. Former Charlton player Garry Nelson has 'written' a couple of creditable books about the life of a journeyman footballer and Eamonn Dunphy has brought out the fine *Only a Game*. But that's about it.

What is surprising is that there hasn't been much top-class literature about the sport by *anybody*. 'There have been as many good books about football as there are teeth in Nobby Stiles' top jaw,' wrote Michael Palin in a review of Nick Hornby's *Fever Pitch*, and as usual he's both funny and right.

Association football literature is almost as old as association football itself. Two years after the FA's inaugural meeting in Covent Garden in 1863 the first book on the subject was published. Called *Beeton's Football* and written by Frederick Wood, it was a much-needed description of the game and how it was played. Charles Alcock followed it up with a number of annuals and the important (if a little stuffy) *Football Our Winter Game*, which had a similar purpose.

However, when football stopped being an amateur gentleman's game and started being played and watched more by the working-classes (as early as the 1870s) less importance was attributed to it by publishers; there was precious little good literature written on the subject in the early-to-mid part of the 20th century. The best-selling football books were the cheap and nasty Aldine football novels published in the 1920s with titles like *Goal!*, *Through to the Final!*, *Larsington's Crack Shot*, *Dan of the Rovers*, *Dr Jim, Full-back*, *Dick Daring Scores Again* and *Hissed off the Field*, which were the precursors of the Roy-of-the-Rovers-type strip cartoons.

In fact it wasn't until football became hip in the 1960s, especially as Cup finals and other important matches started being broadcast on national television, that the middle-classes started taking an interest again, and a few more quality books started coming out. *The Soccer Syndrome*, by John Moynihan, is a colourful series of anecdotes from a journalist who both regularly watched football and played it, albeit at a Sunday park level.

The Football Man, written in 1968 by the *Observer* football correspondent Arthur Hopcraft, is rather more opinionated but has moments of incisiveness, and some brilliantly written passages bring the 1960s game to life and double up as valuable sociological references to boot. The book is structured around a series of essays giving Hopcraft's opinion on various elements of the game: the player, the manager, the director, the fan. Here he is on ticket distribution for the 1966 World Cup final, in a passage that shows firstly that Hopcraft was a real fan himself, and secondly that he knew what being a fan was all about – something which, of course, a certain Nick Hornby was to take a lot further some years on:

> *I watched this game not from the press box but from a seat in the stands and was impressed well before the game began by the unusual nature of some of the crowd around me. They were not football followers. They kept asking each other about the identity of the English players. Wasn't one of those Manchester players supposed to be pretty good? That very tall chap had a brother in the side, hadn't he? They were there in their rugby club blazers, and with their Home Counties accents and obsolete prejudices, to see the successors of the Battle of Britain pilots whack the Hun*

again. Some of them wept a bit at the end, and they sang Land of Hope and Glory with a solemn fervour I have known elsewhere only at Conservative Party rallies. I suspect that if they had found themselves sitting amongst a crowd of real, live football fans they might have been amazed by the degree of treacherous support available to Jerry. Some football fans prefer even German footballers to plump-living countrymen exercising the privilege of money to bag a place at an event thousands more would have given their right arms to see – and understand.

Both of these two books, written by football journalists, did a lot to get under the skin of the game, but their subject range was so broad – football itself – they ended up being rather over-stretched. Hunter Davies's *The Glory Game*, published in 1972, limited its subject matter and thus told us a good deal more. Davies, a young journalist, managed to persuade Tottenham Hotspur to allow him fly-on-the-wall access to their dressing room and training sessions for the whole of season 1971-72. (Imagine that happening nowadays!) It was the first time the public had been given such access to the day-to-day running of a club and did much to demystify the whole business of football. It was a huge success, and, twenty-six years later, is still in print.

Unfortunately the 1970s saw the eruption of football hooliganism, which had been bubbling for some time, and served to damage the reputation of the game and alienate many potential middle-class fans. English clubs became dominant in Europe, but paradoxically the nation became weak at international level and failed to qualify for the World Cups of 1974 and 1978, which further alienated floating supporters. The 1980s was a very lean time for football in general, and football literature in particular. The fanzine explosion saw football fans give themselves a vehicle for their writing but book publishers were scared to touch the subject, unless it was to give the go-ahead to tame ghost-written footballers' biographies.

However, the 1990 World Cup saw a sea change in the middle-classes' perception of football and the results in the publishing world were almost immediately apparent. In fact the 1990 World Cup was the subject of the first brilliant football book of the 1990s – Pete Davies's

All Played Out. Davies managed to get close access to the England camp and also to capture the atmosphere amongst the fans in Italy. While, as the title suggests, the theme of the book was the rotten nature of a sport that is very close to the writer's heart, Davies proved that the game could be discussed in intellectual terms and its commercial success made hitherto unconvinced publishers much more open to commissioning books on the game.

Of course the 1990s has since seen an explosion of football literature, not least Nick Hornby's *Fever Pitch*, the best-selling book ever about the sport. Hornby's work, an autobiographical account written around his obsessional support for Arsenal was not, as many people have rather shallowly suggested, single-handedly responsible for football making the cut in dinner-party conversations. Neither was it responsible for the injection of money into the game that led to the influx of exotic foreigners and the rise in prestige of the English game. Or entirely responsible for the reincarnation of 'new lad' from the jittery near-corpse of 'new man'. *Fever Pitch* fever has rather overestimated the importance of the work. But the fact that too much has been claimed of the book shouldn't diminish from its importance to modern football; it was certainly a strong catalyst which helped push along fundamental changes in attitude that had already started taking place.

I have recently re-read *Fever Pitch* and had forgotten (put off by all the hype) quite what a moving, funny and above all honest account it is. However, whilst the book has undoubtedly influenced publishers into being willing to risk publishing more books on the sport, it hasn't necessarily increased the output of good, well-written books. I approached Hornby to gauge his opinions on the importance of his book, but he very pleasantly refused me. So I went to Simon Kuper instead. Kuper, the author of a very good book about football and politics, *Football Against the Enemy*, had just seen the first edition of *Perfect Pitch*, in effect football's version of Granta, of which he was the editor, launched to some acclaim.

Kuper was well aware of the book's value. 'It linked football with the rest of life,' he says. 'It said "Being a fan is a major part of this man's emotional life." And it is a major part of lots of people's.'

Whilst he admits the book has had a positive effect on publishers' concepts of football as a subject for literature he isn't so happy about the resulting literature that has been published. 'Publishers always thought sports fans won't buy books because they're thick, which is false because a lot of these publishers themselves were sports fans. They would buy cricket books but they wouldn't buy football books. That was the taboo, which people were afraid to touch, because if you brought out a big football book, paid a lot of money for it and it flopped – people would say, "I told you so." So Nick Hornby's book told them that you *could* do this. The problem is *Fever Pitch* has spawned a lot of football books but I don't think it's spawned particularly good ones. Can you name me any classic football books that have come out since?'

I rather sycophantically (but perfectly truthfully) mentioned his own, which he thanked me for, before telling me that it was commissioned before *Fever Pitch* was published. Then I floundered around a little before admitting he was right.

'It's odd, isn't it?' he says. 'A survey last week showed that 18 million people in England and Wales, one in three, are football fans. Presumably this means that one in three writers are also football fans. (It's nothing to do with demographic breakdown because this survey also showed that if you're an A/B, ie, the higher social classes, you're just as likely to be a football fan as if you're a D/E, the lower social classes.) People like Martin Amis and Salman Rushdie are football fans. So why haven't these people written things about football?'

Before I could attempt an answer he launched into the reason. 'One obstacle in football is that you can't write about the game itself, that's always very boring. And Nick Hornby has written about being a fan so perfectly, what are you going to add? The only other area left is the players themselves, what they're really like, but only perhaps 100 people in the country have any access to them and most of them can't write good descriptive prose.'

As I shook hands with Kuper, who was rushing off to another meeting, I remembered one of the things he had said earlier, and felt rather sorry for him, juggling as he does a job as a financial journalist with the *FT* with the editorship of a biannual anthology of new football writing. He spends much of his precious spare time sifting through reams of unsolicited would-be contributions, many of them by attempted Nick Hornby write-alikes. 'One of the consequences of the Hornby bandwagon is that it gives unimaginative people a set of jokes and a language to express their views; it all becomes as clichéd as it was fifteen years ago,' he moans. 'That's a danger. I'd like to add this to the football literature debate; if you're dull and boring and you've got nothing to say, you've got this whole new vocabulary given to you by Hornby.'

If the book of great football books is pretty slim, we can take consolation in the fact that the entire *Rothmans Yearbook* collection (the sport's version of *Wisden*) would sag the sturdiest of shelves. There are reference books about almost any facet of football that you care to imagine. One book gives you match reports from all the post-war England matches. Another lists every result there has ever been in the FA Cup competition. Another gives you the score, team, referee and crowd of every international match featuring a European team since the war. Whatever you want, it seems, you can get it. As one of the directors of a football-writing agency I make it my business to try to buy up as many football reference books as I can. Last week a bookshelf full of them collapsed, injuring one of our employees. Honest. Well, it didn't actually injure him, but one of the books fell quite near his head.

The best of the football reference books is *Rothmans*, which I look forward to every year, I'm that sad. 1998-99 is the thirtieth year it has been published and if you have got the whole collection you've got just about everything you need to know about British football and a good deal more, besides.

It tells you all the vital statistics about all the British league clubs, as well as their full league record for the season before. It tells you all the results from all the British Isles international matches in history. It gives you a detailed day-to-day diary of the previous season. It gives you playing career details of every player in the league. It gives you details of all the transfers and transfer fees of the previous season. It gives you a list of all the managers every club has had. It gives you a lot more too. If you don't run a sports-writing business the best place to keep it would be right by the toilet. Constipation would be a boon.

Here are a few facts I gleaned from the 1996-97 edition (the first to hand):

Despite the fact that it was a Yorkshire derby, Barnsley's 7,150 crowd against Sheffield United on 8 September 1995 was nearly 4,000 down on their previous home game against Birmingham. Barnsley lost that game 5-0 to drop from third to seventh in the table.

While winning 3-2 at Torquay on 1 January 1996, Colchester United scored fifteen seconds after the kick-off and again fifteen seconds from the end of the game.

Port Vale's league double over neighbours Stoke City in 1995-96 was their first in over seventy years.

Struggling Torquay used forty-two first-team players in season 1995-96.

The Division Three play off final between Darlington and Plymouth Argyle on 25 May 1996 saw 43,431 fans at Wembley Stadium, 9,000 more than turned up to see England play Hungary in their last match at home before Euro 96.

Only three players named Murphy have ever played for the Republic of Ireland.

If you found those facts interesting you will understand what I mean when I claim that reference books are the most valid form of football literature. While there is room for analysis and putting football in a social perspective the most creative people in football are the players themselves while they are on the pitch. We are left with the spectacle, and, if that is our wont, sifting through the facts afterwards.

- 47 -
They Think It's All Over... – The Language of Commentators

I might be exaggerating a bit when I say that the best-known quote from a living Englishman is, 'There are some people on the pitch. They think it's all over...It is now' uttered by TV commentator Kenneth Wolstenholme in the last seconds of the 1966 World Cup final. Or then again I might not.

Because of all the replays – and the use of the words in the opening series of the eponymous TV quizshow – it has become virtually impossible for fans to think of the moment when Geoff Hurst hit England's fourth World Championship-clinching goal against West Germany without the accompaniment of Wolstenholme's words. Sadly football commentary is rarely so memorable. It's difficult to think of many other great moments in the game when the exact words of the commentator spring to mind. But have you ever tried watching a game on the box with the sound completely down? You might as well watch *Top of the Pops* without the volume.

We have seen in this book that language and football go hand in hand. To play football you have to learn quite a complicated system of communication. One of the main attractions of going to the stadium is to participate in the crowd's response to the game. TV being TV, however, the viewer's involvement in the communication process when you watch a game becomes almost entirely passive. However much you swear, shake your fist at the referee and ask your companion if they'd like a cup of tea, the commentators do most of the talking.

Nowadays the vast majority of football fans watch more games on TV than at the stadium. For most people most of the time, and for many people all the time, commentary is an intrinsic part of the experience of watching the game. Commentators are the most listened to figures in football. For many, their language *is* the language of football.

I met Ken Wolstenholme, who was effectively the first regular football commentator in the world, in a pizzeria in Ewell, Middlesex. I'd rung him up and asked him if he'd talk to me about his art, fixing the date and time several days before. When he sat down, punctual to the minute, he had a strange smile on his face. 'I didn't explain this to you on the phone,' he said, 'but my wife died yesterday.' Of course I didn't know what to say. I mumbled my condolences, wondered if he really wanted to go ahead with the interview, and asked him if he was OK.

I still don't really know why he hadn't cancelled the interview, but it made me realise what a consummate professional he was, with an old-style sense of duty and decorum, and that my generation had produced few of his type. His style of commentating, and the way that he became a commentator, comes from a different age, on a different wavelength to my own.

After a good deal of persistence and couple of lucky breaks had landed the young Lancastrian a job in radio at the BBC, he wrote to the Head of Outside Broadcasts asking for a position commentating on football. Four men were interviewed. 'I must have been the only Northener there because they chose me to commentate for the Northern region,' he remembers, 'with Jimmy Jewell, the former referee who had given a last-minute penalty in the 1938 FA Cup final. Poor old Jimmy had a massive heart attack one Sunday when he was having a bath and he died. That left them with me, that's how I got into television.

'I will never forget the two pieces of advice I was given in those early days by the Head of Outside Broadcasts, a huge man called SJ De Lotbiniere, as to which level I was to pitch my commentary. "Firstly, just remember," he said, "that on television people can see, as opposed to on radio. Secondly, always be aware that your listeners form a pyramid. Think of the people at the top as the people who play the game. Now if you only get them as an audience, you don't have an audience. Just below that you get the people who administrate the game, but add those to the top and you still don't have much of an audience. Then you have the followers of the game of football. Even they don't constitute an audience. Farther down you get people who love sport and watch it on television. Even with them you're not there. Then right at the bottom there are the people who just watch television, whatever's on. When you've got them you've got an audience. That's the people you're aiming at."'

In the early days of sports TV there weren't many people to aim at at all. The first televised football in 1936 (a match between Arsenal and Everton at Highbury) was only shown to visitors to the Radiolympia exhibition of the BBC's forthcoming broadcasts. The first Cup final to go on air, between Sunderland and Preston North End the following year, got an estimated audience of 10,000, one-tenth of the number of people who went to the stadium. Even when *Match of the Day* started in 1964 it was broadcast on BBC2 and only attracted 60,000 viewers.

The style Ken developed, heeding the words of his boss, was a back-seat one, which was informative and left a lot of room to let the pictures do the talking. 'The best bit of TV commentary I've ever heard was by the golf commentator Henry Longhurst, which I quoted to give the young John Motson some advice,' he says. 'Golfer Doug Sanders needed an easy pot to win the British Open. "Doug Sanders of the United States. Needs this for the Championship," said Longhurst. Then you saw Sanders getting his stance ready and he moved forward and pushed away what he's since admitted was an imaginary piece of grass. He'd obviously got the twitch and Longhurst, seeing this, said, "Oh dear." Sanders putted and the ball went wide. When I told Motson this story I asked him what he thought Longhurst said next. He didn't know. The truth is, he didn't say anything! What was there to say? He couldn't say "he missed it" could he? Millions had seen him miss it. That was real television commentary because the picture told the story.'

Wolstenholme stayed at the BBC until 1971, by which time the young David Coleman had arrived on the scene and shifted TV commentary into the modern age. He had talked the country through many great moments of football – including England's 1953 defeat to

Hungary. Real Madrid's 1960 7-3 demolition of Eintracht Frankfurt and Celtic's 1967 European Cup win over Inter Milan, but his plummy tones and old-fashioned style didn't fit into the sexy 1970s. Still, he'd left his mark, and as I write is still doing voiceovers for Channel 4's *Football Italia*.

I consciously didn't ask him about his most famous quote, hoping that he'd come to it himself. After an hour or so he did – along with the stream of his consciousness at the time. 'I saw some people get on the pitch and I said, "there are some people on the pitch," and I had a stopwatch and thought "any second now the referee's got to blow". He put his whistle in his mouth, and I made the excuse for the fans that they thought it was all over, and while I said that Geoff Hurst hit it, and it was obvious that it was the end, and I'm proud of the fact that I said "it is now" before the ball went into the net. Because I knew that if Geoff had missed it still would have been over because there's twenty or so yards behind the goal and by the time they got it back to the goalie the referee would have whistled anyway.'

Perhaps Wolstenholme wouldn't have been so famous if Geoff Hurst had hit it over the bar and his third goal had been the clinching moment of the game. That, remember, was the controversial one that hit the underside of the bar and landed over, as we like to believe, or on, as the Germans still claim, the goal-line. Here's what he said, 'Yes! Yes! No! No! The linesman says no! The linesman says no! It's a goal! It's a goal! Oh and the Germans go mad at the referee.' They wouldn't have named a TV series after that.

The 1966 World Cup saw the BBC experiment with the 'summariser', the expert sitting alongside the commentator to give a professional view of the game, which is often wrongly seen as being a modern development in commentating. The man in question was former Arsenal full-back Walley Barnes, who had joined the channel in 1956. Although Wolstenholme doesn't remember Barnes' role as being very important, 'I think he only spoke three times, he wasn't very talkative', if you listen out for him he is highly informative on a number of occasions about nuances of the game that only a player would see, such as the timing of a striker's jump or the necessity for defenders to maximise the keeper's uncertainty of the slippery ball by trying the odd long shot.

The next World Cup was Wolstenholme's last – his accent was obviously too BBC for the BBC, who were becoming aware that using personalities could help them sell their product. ITV were already starting to push this: in Mexico in 1970 they introduced the first 'panel of experts' in a studio in London, who analysed the game at halftime and after the final whistle. The panel comprised Malcolm Allison, Derek Dougan, Pat Crerand and Bob McNab. McNab, a relatively quiet man, was given a bell halfway through the tournament so he could make himself heard. The panel was hosted by Brian Moore and Jimmy Hill.

The BBC's answer was David Coleman. Coleman didn't let the pictures do the talking. Instead he never let up his constant chatter, telling you information about the players, the game, the fans, the weather, whatever came into his head. At the time it was quite controversial – Clive James said 'a colmantator is someone who tells you something you don't want to know, a commentator is someone who tells you something you do', but it was effective. Coleman, with his breathless style of speaking in short bursts, had the ability to make the traffic jam outside the stadium seem interesting. He became the first personality broadcaster in an age when the 'personality' was a growing cult.

The new style adopted by Coleman, who became such a well-known figure that the Beeb used his name in their midweek sports show *Sportsnight with Coleman*, was taking things too far too quickly. As television started broadcasting more and more football the need grew for more commentators and a new generation started emerging, who are still around today. Barry Davies, John Motson and Martin Tyler all had their different styles, the diversity of which helped push on their art a little further. In 1974, on the morning Martin Tyler was about to do his first live commentary he received a note from his friend John Motson, who'd got a little experience in the field under his belt. 'Talk little,' it read, 'but say a lot.' Motson was suggesting that Tyler should adhere more to the old style of football commentating than the new.

The new breed of commentators had one thing in common – a meticulous eye for detail and the willingness to spend long hours researching the matches they were about to cover. Football commentating was becoming more competitive and the better prepared you were the more likely you were to succeed. Davies landed his first job by gazumping his rivals whilst reporting on a section of a schoolboy match for his interview. He had been to the schools and learnt a little bit about the background of each player, information he used in his commentary, treating them as if they were professionals.

One of the enduring pub debates about football is whether Davies or Motson is the better commentator. Like most pub debates it can go on for ever because both men have their own qualities, both are highly professional and which one you prefer is a matter of taste. In 1977 both were given top live games to commentate on for the BBC: on 21 May Motson covered the FA Cup final between Manchester United and Liverpool and made his name with the rehearsed comment 'how apt that a player named Buchan should climb the 39 steps to collect the FA Cup'. Counting the steps that led to the Royal Box wasn't the only research Motson had done; he littered his commentary with statistics, asserting himself as a 'facts and figures man'.

Four days later Davies was in the gantry covering Liverpool's first European Cup final against Borussia Moenchengladbach. His performance was much more old-school. He spoke with calm authority, not trying to win the audience over with his enthusiasm and, above all, letting the pictures do the talking. When Ray Kennedy lined up a shot, he announced, 'Here's Kennedy...' then fell silent as the ball went over the bar. There was also a balance, a rhythm, an almost poetic element to some of his comments. He usually reserved his best for the goals. When McDermott scored Liverpool's first he announced, in quickening tone and increasing volume, 'That's nice...that's McDermott...and that's a goal!'

Nevertheless it was the more populist Motson who became the BBC's main man for big live matches, which increased in number after 1983 when the Football League permitted live broadcasts of their matches as long as they weren't at the same time as their other fixtures, bringing to life the Sunday afternoon (and Friday evening) game. A look at his performance in the 1988 FA Cup final shows a lot about his style. The most noticeable thing he brought to football commentary was his bombardment of the audience with trivia. He had countless little anecdotes about players which he brought out at opportune moments. Wimbledon striker John Fashanu greets the referee: 'John Fashanu always makes a point of shaking hands with the ref'; goalkeeper David Beasant comes into shot for the first time: 'a man who can see Wembley Stadium from his bedroom'; the camera flashes to manager Bobby Gould, sitting in the dug-out: 'Bobby Gould, who sat on that bench in 1975 as a substitute for West Ham against Fulham but never came on, which was one of the disappointments of his career'; Eric Young appears, wearing his brown headband: 'to protect scar tissue'.

Motson wasn't alone in the gantry (isn't that a great word?); alongside him was former professional Jimmy Hill who added his more tactically aware points of view when there was a break in the action. Motson had the knack of labelling the tactics Hill was analysing in a memorable way. 'This is what they call Route 1 football down Wimbledon way.' Hill acted too as a sounding board for Motson's strange jokes. Here's his one about the two guys from Liverpool wearing headbands to protect head injuries sustained before the game. 'I don't think the boxing analogy is too bad, today, Jimmy, with so many cuts around. It really looks as though Gillespie and Spackman have been in a ten-rounder.'

Motson is a Northerner but sometimes it's difficult to detect as his register is an odd mix of plummy BBC – 'that's precisely the sort of challenge that Wimbledon have been, shall we say, reputed to produce' – and colloquialism – he generally uses ref instead of referee. Occasionally he would use the player's full christian name, rather than the normal short form, like a schoolmaster suddenly becoming strict in order to demonstrate his authority: 'Vincent Jones to take the throw.'

At the end of the game, which underdogs Wimbledon surprisingly won 1-0, Motson again showed his ability to come out with memorable sum-up lines. 'And the Crazy Gang have beaten the Culture Club.' This nickname for Wimbledon has stuck so much that the club has the words 'Crazy Gang' embroidered into their shirts, clearly showing the power commentators have over shaping the language of football.

I interviewed Motson in 1996 for *XL* magazine, and he told me about the increased pressures of commentating in the modern world. 'When you cut out all the other peripheral things about commentating, you can actually boil it down to the fact that if you don't know the players upside down, backwards, inside out, then you're never going to give your brain the freedom to develop in any other way. If you're always wondering who's got the ball, then you'll never catch up.'

Motson goes to great lengths to get to know what players who are new to him look like. He is often to be seen at training sessions, and, he told me, if he has to commentate on a foreign team which he doesn't know, he will often sit in their hotel lobby before the game, observing them. Researching a match, he says, is a two-day job. 'If I'm doing a match on a Saturday I'm working on it from a Thursday lunchtime, either watching videos or ringing people up, or checking on names and pronunciations or going and seeing somebody training or assembling my notes, or whatever.'

The pronunciation of names, especially foreign ones, by commentators is an interesting phenomenon. ITV's Brian Moore is famously bad at them. What chance has a man, who for a whole season called Paul Scholes 'Paul Sholes', got with the likes of Hogni i Jakobstovvu, Slawomir Wojciechowski or Panoyotis Tsalouhidis? Motson, on the other hand, is quite meticulous with his name-pronunciation. 'You practise them on the way to the match, you practise them in the car, you practise them the night before, you check them with the player concerned when you can before the kick off.' You can just imagine him in the bath, chanting 'Jaroslaw Gierjekiewicz, Jaroslaw Gierjekiewicz, Jaroslaw Gierjekiewicz' like a mantra. He's right to be careful, mind, because there are numerous critics waiting to pounce on any mistakes he makes. Many football fans are sticklers for pronunciation. We are living in a world where Don Howe gets crucified for saying 'Gullit' with a hard 'g' instead of 'Hullit' in the Dutch way, whilst the whole art establishment has got away for years with saying the semi-Anglicised version of Van Gogh instead of 'Van Hogh'.

Motson in the flesh was an open sort of guy, with a hard, slightly impatient edge to him which you can just detect in his voice if you listen out for it. He told me everything I wanted to know, but cut up slightly rough when I asked him what I was dying to ask him. Didn't his wife get annoyed with him for watching football all the time? And he wouldn't be drawn out of the box on the subject of his sheepskin coat. 'I wear it because it's cold. That's the end of the story.'

The increased use of the colour commentator, a former or current professional who sits alongside the commentator to explain the technical and tactical aspects of the game, has been the biggest change in football commentary since that Wimbledon-Liverpool final. Nowadays a football commentary wouldn't be a football commentary without the likes of Ron Atkinson, Andy Gray and Kevin Keegan chipping in.

Martin Tyler recalls the first time colour commentators were used by ITV, in 1982 in the Spanish World Cup. 'I remember working with Ron Atkinson,' he says. 'We used to do pronunciation sessions before the game. It was important that we were consistent with the way we said the foreign names. He would choose the venue, it was usually by the pool.'

In the early days, as we have seen, the summariser would wait for a quiet moment and deliver a short summary of the technical aspects of the game he felt were relevant. Nowadays there is rarely a quiet moment, and some of the commentator-summariser relationships are becoming rather like double acts. It's the Mottie and Trev Show. Welcome to Andy and Martin's Funhouse. Put your hands together for Big Ron and Mooro.

The fact that two people are speaking rather than one almost entirely puts paid to the 'letting the football do the talking' aspect of football commentary. But letting the pundit do the talking is sometimes just as entertaining. Ron Atkinson, who as I have mentioned before rarely tries to dilute his training ground language to make concessions to the viewer, has become a favourite amongst fans, especially as he does little to hide his outrage when the team he wants to win is doing badly. 'Inzaghi's a mile offside!' he yelled in the first minute of the Manchester United-Juventus Champions League game in 1997, which United won 3-2 after going 1-0 down after twenty-four seconds. Watching the replay he said, 'The ball took a hell of a time to go into the net.' Then, after the restart, 'You almost have to look up at the scoreboard to make sure the damn thing's been given.'

Brian Moore alongside him, having learnt the proper pronunciation of 'Scholes', demonstrates that his own inimitable personal style hasn't lost any of its value. Moore, who has been ITV's mainman since the early 1970s, eschews Motson's facts and figures, apologising whenever he gives any. 'Sorry to bang on about statistics but they [Juventus] only lost five times in fifty-three games last season.' His strength is to do a radio-style commentary (Moore started on the radio and did the 1966 World Cup final for the BBC) describing the action but manipulating word and sentence stress to add to the sense of drama. This is particularly relevant to adjectives: 'Beckham's swinging these *good* free kicks in', 'Giggs put that *soaring* cross in'. Moore's voice suddenly gets all guttural for the italicised adjectives. He gets terribly worried when Juventus are close to United's goal, preceding his descriptions of their shots with 'ooooh'. And whenever anything surprising happens his catchphrase unwittingly pops out, 'My goodness'. It was terribly sad when ITV lost their top-flight football in the mid 1990s and this great elder statesman of the football world was reduced to commentating at Brentford. Long may they keep the Champions League.

Sky's main commentary team are Martin Tyler and Andy Gray who form such a strong partnership that the channel used them both to commentate on the Italy-England match which eventually saw England qualify for the 1998 World Cup, despite the fact that Gray is a Scot. He was a Sassenach for the night though, at one point using the pronoun 'we' for England and saying, in the ninety-fifth minute of the game, 'there can't be much time left. Come on ref, blow your whistle.' Gray provides much more to the partnership than just technical know-how – which Tyler is quite proficient at giving anyway. I'd describe his raw emotional responses as unfettered if cool, calm Tyler wasn't there to anchor him down. 'He gets stuck in, that Chiesa, doesn't he?' he said of the Italian striker in the same match, whilst later adding, after Wright had hit the post for England in the last seconds, 'that would have been the cherry on the icing on the cake, wouldn't it?' Tyler, bless him, simply replied, 'It would'. Tyler demonstrated at the end of the game, which finished 0-0, that he was quite a dab hand at the 'honest-I-didn't-prepare-it-earlier' summing up statement, too. 'Rome signposts the road to France for Glenn Hoddle and his men,' he gushed, in the sort of tone that tells you the ads are coming up. 'They've reached Olympian heights in the Olympic Stadium.'

In the short telephone interview he gave, Tyler told me some very interesting information. The first was an anecdote he used to illustrate an important point about imparting trivia. 'Former Liverpool defender Gary Gillespie told me in a quiet moment one day that he delivered one of his own children,' he said. 'I was bursting to convey this to the world, but I could never find an apt moment. Trivia is important but it has to be applied at the right moment or it sounds abrupt. Three years passed and I was commentating on a game between Scotland and Poland. Gillespie was facing his own goalkeeper, Andy Goram, and, trying to pass it back to him, panicked and lobbed it instead over his head and into the net. "Would you believe," I said, or words to that effect, "that a man who even once delivered one of his four children could lose his head at such a moment." '

He also neatly summarised the job requirements of a commentator. 'My job hasn't changed in the twenty-three years I've been doing it. It's to identify players; interpret the game (with the help of my co-commentator); research the match and impart the relative information and statistics. None of these criteria will ever change. The only thing that changes is the style of the commentator, which depends very much on the personality of the commentator in question. We're not actors, we are just being ourselves.'

A man who has done more to get people talking about football commentating than anybody since David Coleman is Jonathan Pearce, the Capital Gold radio commentator who Channel 5 use for their occasional TV broadcasts. Pearce has got up a lot of establishment noses with his breathless excitable pun-heavy commentary, despite heavily diluting his radio style. He is anathema to Kenneth Wolstenholme, the man who likes silence, who says of him, 'Jonathan Pearce is the antithesis of everything a television commentator has to be.' But in his way he is a pioneer, 'a fan with a microphone' as he calls himself, and a poetic touch, to boot. He started his TV career, commentating on the vital England-Poland World Cup match with the words 'Come on you England' and, during games, is constantly aware of the crowd and the part they can play in the game. 'The crowd's attempt to inject some atmosphere into the Bridge and pace into the game by singing "One Man Went To Mow" didn't really work,' he said in November 1997's Chelsea-Tromso game in the European Cup Winners' Cup. He also tends to eschew the sort of clichés that other commentators rely on, inventing new ways to describe the game. 'He came out there like the sub goalkeeper who nobody wanted, who stood up but never dived,' he said of the Tromso keeper, and, of Zola's crossing ability 'he arcs them in with pace and wit'.

Pearce was too busy to be interviewed for this book, so I'll have to nick a quote from an interview he did in 1997 for *Total Football* magazine, which was in reply to the reporter's question 'what would Pearce say if he was commentating on a last-minute World-Cup-final-winning goal by Alan Shearer?' 'Would I come up with a Wolstenholme "They think it's all over...it is now" immortal line?' he mused. 'In my case I don't think I would. I'd probably be so ecstatic I'd just say, "Shearer, Shearer, have my children." '

...It Is Now! The Conclusion

I used to do a lot of hitch-hiking around England in my twenties when my restless need to travel was far greater than the budget I could dedicate to it. I loved the whole process – the making of a sign, the element of risk that you wouldn't arrive, the utter snowballing misery of a three-hour wait in a shitty place suddenly and completely transformed into joy as a car pulled in and revealed he would take you to, or at least towards, your destination. Sometimes, if you were on a long journey and you had struck it particularly lucky, you were in the car with a complete stranger for three or four hours – usually someone who had picked you up in order to make *his* trip a little more interesting (it was rarely her for obvious reasons). The pressure to perform, as it were, was quite heavy.

These trips could become nightmares, especially with Glaswegian lorry drivers whom I had difficulty in understanding. The third 'pardon?' is about your limit: after that you just have to nod and agree, or shake your head and disagree and hope you'd read at least the gist of the question right.

I had a method to lead up to the million-dollar moment on long rides. Having got through all the details of where I was going and where he could drop me off I'd ask the driver where he was from. 'Bristol', he'd say, or 'Scunthorpe' or 'Derby' or 'Stoke'.

Let's imagine he said Bristol. I was ready to spring. 'City or Rovers?' I'd ask, and the quality of the next few hours would be decided by the look on his face, and his reply.

My heart would drop at 'I'm not really a football man myself', and I envisaged three hours of possibly difficult conversation about the state of the Liberal Party and how my grandfather used to grow leeks, too.

'Fucking hate City, I'm a Rovers fan,' was pure joy. I knew then that I could use the language of football as it was surely intended to be used – to break the ice and then bond with a fellow human being.

For an hour we'd have a rolling football conversation that could drift any way. The Brazil side of 1970. How Peter Ward had lost a yard of pace after his knee injury and was never quite the same player afterwards. How it was important to support an English team in Europe even though you might hate them when they were playing domestically. How important it was to be able to scream at the referee until your lungs hurt because it relieved much of the pressure inside you that had been building up during the week. Then we'd drift out of it. We'd be able to talk about the state of the Liberal Party and how my Grandfather used to grow leeks, too, and get something out of it because we'd be able to laugh together because we'd ascertained early on that we both thought that Phil Thompson's 1978 bubble perm was ridiculous.

For me all the stuff that I've been researching and writing about for the last six months and all the stuff you've been reading for the last 251 pages is, on one level, pretty irrelevant to the real language of football. The real language of football is that which the fans use when they're talking to each other on their way to work, while they're working or down the pub afterwards. It can range in depth and subtlety from giving news – 'I hear that Gerry Francis has gone, then' – to having discussions – 'You're wrong, Waddle was a much better England player than Barnes' – to using football as a metaphor for life or a tool for understanding human nature better.

On the other hand, what you've just read isn't at all irrelevant to the real language of football, because the real language of football needs constant fuel to feed its hungry flames and even if you think what you've just read is just a pile of facts thrown together I bet you didn't know some of them, and I bet, at some point, you will use some of them in a football conversation. I bet that I have added to your football vocabulary. That I have made your personal language of football that little bit richer.

Hold on, I could swear I saw some people on the pitch.

Index